BOGOTÁ

ANDREW DIER

Contents

Clockwise from top left: *mochilas*; La Candelaria neighborhood in Bogotá; town of Girón; Bogotá's Ciclovía.

DISCOVER

Bogotá

Colombians from every corner of the country come to its sprawling capital seeking opportunity and freedom. It's no surprise that it's the country's cultural capital as well. Something is always going on: a festival, a concert, a gallery opening. Bogotanos' reputation for being gloomy and cerebral is unfair. The *alegría* after dark is proof.

When the city becomes too intense, *páramos*, cloud forests, and lakes beckon. Parque Nacional Natural Chingaza, Parque Natural Chicaque, and Laguna de Guatavita are all only an hour away. A little farther are Boyacá and Santanderes, rich in history, natural beauty, and outdoor activities.

Forward looking and hopeful, Bogotá has laid out its welcome mat: *¡Bienvenidos!*

Clockwise from top left: flying kites at the Biblioteca Virgilio Barco; graffiti tour; the Presidential Guard; street artist; night view of Avenida Séptima.

Explore Bogotá

Planning Your Trip

When to Go

Because Colombia straddles the equator, the temperatures and length of days are nearly constant year-round. There are, however, distinct dry and rainy seasons. Throughout most of the country, the months of **December through February** and **July through August** are considered ***verano*** **(dry season).** ***Invierno*** **(rainy season)** is usually between **April and May** and again between **September and November.**

Colombia's **high tourist seasons** run from **mid-December through mid-January.** However, Bogotá becomes a ghost town at this time, when residents flock to the Caribbean coast. This can also be true during **Easter week (Semana Santa),** and, to a lesser extent, school vacations from **June to August.**

Passports and Visas

Travelers to Colombia who intend to visit as tourists for a period of under 90 days will need only to present a **valid passport** upon entry in the country. You may be asked to show **proof of a return ticket.** Tell the immigration officer if you intend to stay up to 90 days, otherwise they will probably give you a stamp permitting a stay of 60 days. Language schools and universities will be able to assist those who may require a yearlong **student visa.**

Vaccinations

There are **no obligatory vaccination requirements** for visiting Colombia. However, if you are traveling onward to countries such as Brazil, Ecuador, or Peru, you may have to provide proof of the vaccine upon entry to those countries.

The Centers for Disease Control and Prevention (CDC) recommends that travelers have **hepatitis A** and **typhoid** vaccinations. **Hepatitis B, rabies,** and **yellow fever** vaccinations are recommended for some travelers. If you plan to visit the Amazon region, **antimalarial drugs** may be recommended.

Transportation

Most travelers arrive by plane at the modern **Aeropuerto Internacional El Dorado** in Bogotá. There are numerous **daily nonstop flights** into Bogotá from the eastern seaboard of the United States, as well as from Houston, Dallas, Los Angeles, and Toronto. **Intra-country flights** are easy, safe, economical, frequent, and quick. **Private buses** and **taxis** are ubiquitous in the city, but the best way to sight-see is **on foot.**

The Best of Bogotá

Day 1

Fly into **Bogotá.** Set in the Andes at an elevation of 2,625 meters (8,612 feet), the Colombian capital city can be especially cool and the sun particularly potent. Dress in layers and take along sunscreen and an umbrella. In the late afternoon, wander the historic **Candelaria** district and marvel at the treasures of the **Museo del Oro.** Stay at the **Casa Platypus** downtown or **Cité** in the north.

Day 2

Visit the **Quinta de Bolívar,** Simón Bolívar's old country home. Don't miss the **Cerro de Monserrate,** a pilgrimage site with unsurpassed views of the metropolis. Hike up, then take a ride on the gondola or tram back down.

Learn about Colombia's past from the time of the Muiscas to its shaky years as an independent nation in the city's excellent museums, like the extensive art galleries of the **Manzana Cultural** and the mesmerizing **Museo del Oro.**

Day 3

Take a bus or hire a car for the 3.5-hour trip to the low-key pueblo of **Villa de Leyva,** one of Colombia's best-preserved colonial towns, in the department of Boyacá.

Enjoy the unique atmosphere in Villa de Leyva by walking its stone streets. Check out the woolen *ruanas* (ponchos) at **Alieth Tejido Artesanal,** and if you have time, visit the **Convento del Santo Ecce Homo** in the surrounding desert.

Stay at **Renacer,** a friendly hostel, or splurge at the **Hotel Plaza Mayor,** where the views of the plaza can't be beat.

Museo del Oro

Bogotá's Ciclovía

Day 4

Visit the **Santuario Flora y Fauna Iguaque** just outside of town and hike to the mist-shrouded **Laguna Iguaque** for some morning exhilaration. Relax in Villa de Leyva for the evening.

Day 5

Return to Bogotá. If it's a weekend day, go to the top of the **Torre Colpatria** for an incredible 360-degree view of the massive city. If it's a Sunday, enjoy the city's **Ciclovía** by renting a bike and joining the thousands of Bogotanos hitting the streets in this weekly ritual.

Walk along the pedestrianized Carrera 7, spending some time at the fantastic museums of the **Manzana Cultural,** including the **Museo Botero.** Catch a concert in the Florentine **Teatro Colón** or hear the **Orquesta Filarmónica de Bogotá** play at the Universidad Nacional campus.

Bogotá

Look for ★ to find recommended sights, activities, dining, and lodging.

Highlights

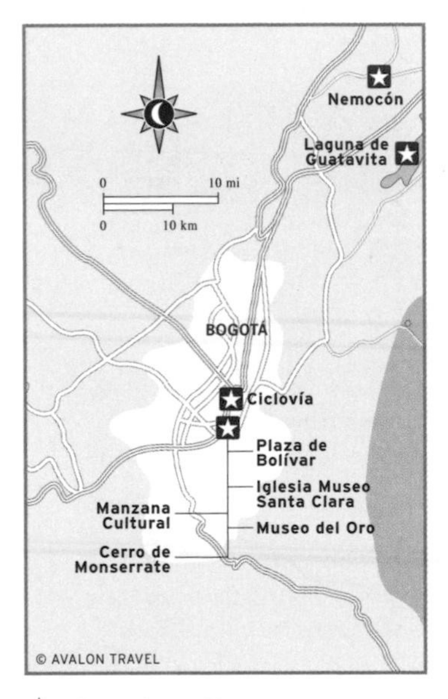

★ **Plaza de Bolívar:** Colombia's most important and most photographed plaza is named for Simón Bolívar, the man who gave the country independence (page 17).

★ **Iglesia Museo Santa Clara:** This colonial-era church, an example of Mudejar architecture, is often host to edgy art exhibits (page 20).

★ **Manzana Cultural:** Colombia's tumultuous history has given rise to some noteworthy creative expression that is on display in the art museums of the city's cultural block (page 23).

★ **Museo del Oro:** Anthropology, history, and art combine in this extraordinary presentation of pre-Columbian gold artifacts (page 27).

★ **Cerro de Monserrate:** The views from atop this hill are incredible both by day and by night (page 28).

★ **Ciclovía:** When a city can get a quarter of its population to get out and ride a bike on a Sunday, you know it's doing something right (page 43).

★ **Nemocón:** The plaza and streets of this little-visited salt-mining town are full of charm (page 68).

★ **Laguna de Guatavita:** This sacred lake is the source of the El Dorado myth (page 69).

A few years ago, visitors would arrive at the El Dorado airport and spend two days maximum in this busy Andean metropolis. Now people are staying awhile, and it's easy to see why.

There is the Museo del Oro, of course, undoubtedly one of the best museums in Latin America. There are precious few reminders of the Muisca settlement of Bacatá in this vast concrete jungle of today, but this museum is a stellar tribute to a people who all but disappeared within decades of the Spanish conquest.

Then there is the living museum that is the historic district, La Candelaria. Every street block has its unique story to tell: the flower vase that changed history, the loyal companion who saved the Liberator's neck, the generosity of a famous painter. Colonial churches surprise with their quiet, steadfast beauty, and grandiose buildings along Avenida Jiménez stand as testament to the aspirations of the "Athens of South America." Red buses, glitzy shopping areas, and stunning libraries set in manicured parks are proof that Bogotá can, with a little investment and good government, overcome the formidable challenges of its recent past.

HISTORY

As early as AD 300, the Muisca people settled along the Cordillera Oriental (Eastern Mountain Range) of the Andes Mountains, forming a loose confederation. Bacatá (now Bogotá) was the seat of the Zipa, head of the southern confederation. The Muiscas had an agricultural economy but also extracted salt and emeralds, wove fine textiles, and actively traded for cotton, shells, and gold with other indigenous peoples. The names of many

Previous: Monserrate as seen from the Quinta de Bolívar; Biblioteca Virgilio Barco.

of their settlements—Chía, Suba, Engativá—survive, though no physical traces remain.

Lured by tales of riches, three European armies converged on Muisca territory in 1538. An army headed by Spanish conquistador Gonzalo Jiménez de Quesada arrived from Santa Marta. Another army, headed by Spaniard Sebastián de Belalcázar, approached from the south. A third army, led by German expeditionary Nikolaus Federmann, followed a route from present-day Venezuela.

By the time Federmann and Belalcázar arrived, Jiménez de Quesada had plundered the Muisca lands. In August 1538 Jiménez de Quesada founded a settlement that he named Santa Fe de Bogotá del Nuevo Reino de Granada de las Indias del Mar, and by the late 17th century the town was home to roughly 15,000 people. European diseases had almost completely wiped out the Muisca population by that time, and marriages between Muiscas and the Spanish formed the *mestizo* base of the city.

The city was the seat of the first provisional government established after Colombia's declaration of independence in 1810. In 1819, the name of the city was changed to Bogotá, and it became capital of the newly formed Gran Colombia. The city was not connected by railroad to the outside world until the end of the 19th century—and then only to Girardot, a port on the Río Magdalena.

The early decades of the 20th century were a period of growth and prosperity. The postwar period was a time of rapid, haphazard development that saw the establishment of many new industries. Much of the growth was unplanned, and sprawling slums developed, especially in the south of the city.

By the 1990s, Bogotá had become synonymous with poverty, crime, and urban sprawl. A series of mayors, including Enrique Peñalosa and Antanas Mockus, transformed the city with large projects such as the TransMilenio rapid bus system and by investing heavily in education and basic services. In 2015, the city reelected Peñalosa on his promises of a metro, expanded public services, and greater security.

Despite all its challenges Bogotá continues to be the economic, cultural, and educational powerhouse of Colombia. The city is a magnet for people from all over the country and, in recent years, even from abroad.

PLANNING YOUR TIME

At the minimum, give Bogotá two days. In that short time span, you can cover La Candelaria, head up to Monserrate, discover the Museo del Oro, and enjoy some good meals in the Zona T, Zona G, or the Macarena.

With about five days you can explore neighborhoods like the Macarena, check out the botanical gardens, or make a day trip to the Parque Natural Chicaque or to Laguna de Guatavita. If you're here over a Sunday, you'll absolutely have to head out to the Ciclovía.

If you are staying in Colombia for 10 days, you can try a city-country combo by adding Villa de Leyva or exploring further afield in Boyacá and Santander.

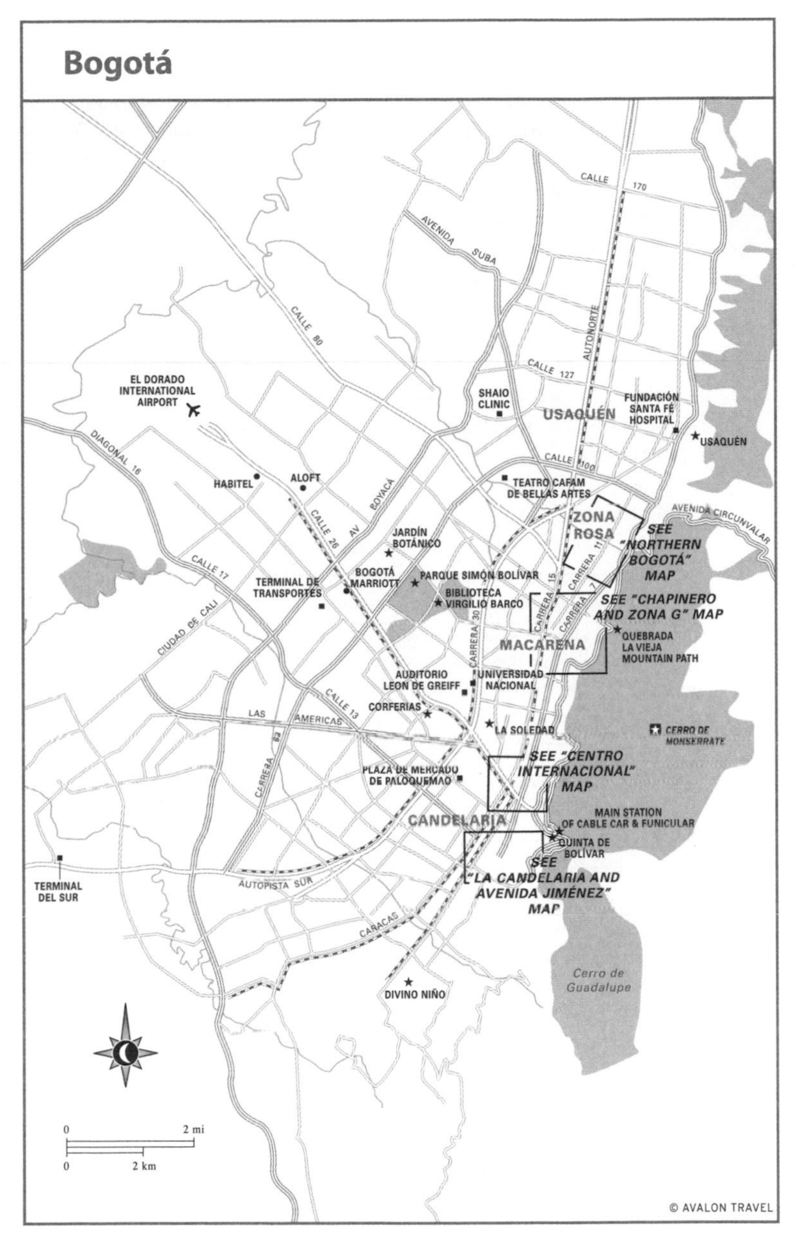

Many museums are closed on either Monday or Tuesday. The Museo del Oro is closed Mondays and the art museums of the Manzana Cultural are closed Tuesdays. During the end-of-year holidays and Holy Week (Semana Santa), Bogotá becomes a ghost town as locals head for the countryside, the coast, or abroad. There is very little traffic at those times, but many restaurants are closed and nightspots are empty, especially around Christmas. Bogotá is a particularly dull place to be on New Year's Eve. Semana Santa is perhaps less lonely and can be a good time to visit, especially when the biennial theater festival is on. On long weekends, many Bogotanos skip town; those from the provinces come for a visit.

SAFETY

Bogotá is much safer than it once was. The best advice is to, as Colombians would say, *"no dar papaya."* Literally, that translates to "don't give any papayas." Don't hand someone the opportunity to take advantage of you.

While strolling in La Candelaria, keep a watchful eye on cameras and other gadgets. Better yet, leave valuables—including passports—locked away in the hotel safe if possible. Private security guards and police now regularly patrol La Candelaria at night, although it may feel a little spooky after 10pm or 11pm.

Traveling by the city's SITP buses is safe and comfortable. The red TransMilenio buses can get crowded, so be aware of pickpockets. Private buses and *colectivos* are less safe and drivers can be reckless.

Bogotá has had a serious problem with taxi crime, commonly known as *paseo milonario.* But recent technological advances have nearly eliminated these crimes. Tappsi and EasyTaxi are popular and free smartphone apps in which you can request a cab, find out the name of the driver, and have your trip tracked by a friend. Alternatively, you can use ride-sharing apps like Uber. Avoid hailing cabs off the street, particularly when you are alone, when it is late at night, and when you are near nightclubs and upscale dining areas.

If you are heading out for a night on the town, do not accept drinks from strangers. Leave credit/debit cards, your passport, and expensive cell phones at home.

During an emergency, call 123 from any phone.

ORIENTATION

Sprawling Bogotá covers some 1,776 square kilometers (686 square miles), filling a large part of the *altiplano* (high plateau), or savannah. Much of your time will likely be spent along the corridor that is **Carrera 7** or **Avenida 7** (called the **Séptima**). The Séptima extends, parallel to the eastern mountains, from the Plaza de Bolívar in La Candelaria north through the Centro Internacional and Chapinero, and then to Usaquén and beyond.

Bogotá street addresses are generally easy to figure out. *Calles* (streets) run east-west (perpendicular to the mountains), while *carreras* go north-south (parallel to the mountains). For example, the Museo del Oro address is Calle 16 No. 5-41. This means it is on Calle 16, 41 meters from Carrera 5. The Centro Andino shopping mall is at Carrera 11 No. 82-71, or on Carrera 11, 71 meters from Calle 82. The higher the number of the *calle*, the farther north you are. Similarly, the higher the number of the *carrera*, the farther west you go.

The city planners also created *avenidas* (avenues), *diagonales*, and *transversales*. Both *diagonales* and *transversales* are streets on the diagonal. To add to the fun, some *calles* are also called *avenida calles*, because they are major thoroughfares, and likewise there are some called *avenida carrera*. Avenida Calle 26 is also known as Avenida El Dorado. Carrera 30 is also known as Avenida Quito or NQS. There are some streets that are called *bis*, as in Calle 70A *bis* or Carrera 13 *bis*. It's like an extra half street. Finally, addresses in the south of Bogotá have *sur* (south) in their address. The address for the 20 de Julio shrine is Calle 27 Sur No. 5A-27.

La Candelaria

La Candelaria is the oldest part of town, dating to the 16th century. With the Plaza de Bolívar at its heart, it is a neighborhood full of historic buildings, interesting museums, and hostels. This area, combined with Avenida Jiménez and Centro Internacional, is generally considered Bogotá's downtown or Centro. La Candelaria is bounded by Carrera 10 on the west, Calle 7 to the south, Carrera 1 to the east, and Avenida Jiménez to the north.

Avenida Jiménez

The northern border of La Candelaria, Avenida Jiménez is also known as the Eje Ambiental. This pedestrian street that is shared with a TransMilenio line winds from Carrera 10 eastward to Carrera 3, where it morphs into Carrera 2A. In addition to being the home of the Museo del Oro, colonial churches, the Quinta de Bolívar, and the Cerro de Monserrate, the area is also known for its grand early-20th-century architecture.

Centro Internacional

North of La Candelaria, the Centro Internacional is home to the Museo de Arte Moderno de Bogotá and the Museo Nacional, as well as the bullfighting ring and the iconic Torres del Parque complex. This neighborhood straddles the Séptima (Cra. 7) and spans from Avenida El Dorado (Cl. 26) north to Calle 36.

Just above this is the quirky neighborhood of **Macarena**, full of art galleries and cozy restaurants.

Chapinero

Most people consider Chapinero to extend from around Calle 45 to about Calle 72, although officially it continues north to Calle 100. Its western boundary is Avenida Carrera 14 (also known as Avenida Caracas), and its eastern boundary pushes up against the mountains.

The neighborhood's eastern half (east of the Séptima) is known as the **Chapinero Alto** and is mostly residential. To the west of the Séptima is a gritty commerce center that is also considered a hub of gay nightlife. There are no major sights in Chapinero.

Northern Bogotá

Northern Bogotá does not have many tourist sights, but it offers myriad options for dining, shopping, and nightlife. This neighborhood has its southern border at Calle 68 and houses pockets of activity in the **Zona G** (between Clls. 69-70 east of the Séptima to Cra. 5), the **Zona Rosa** (between Clls. 81-85 and Cras. 11-15), and the **Parque de la 93 area** (between Clls. 91-94 and Cras. 11-15).

In the Zona Rosa, Calle 82 and Carrera 13 form a T—hence the moniker **Zona T**—and are pedestrian streets lined with restaurants and thumping watering holes.

East of the Séptima between Calles 120 and 125 is **Usaquén,** a once traditional pueblo that has been enveloped by Bogotá. Usaquén is known for its Sunday flea market and restaurants.

Western Bogotá

Western Bogotá (west of Av. Cra. 14) includes the Parque Simón Bolívar, along with the Jardín Botánico and the Biblioteca Virgilio Barco.

Farther west, Avenida Carrera 30 intersects with Avenida El Dorado (Calle 26), which connects the El Dorado airport with downtown. In addition to its TransMilenio line, this nicely designed thoroughfare is lined with hotels, shopping centers, and the fortress-like U.S. Embassy.

Sights

Everything you need to see in Bogotá is downtown, from La Candelaria to the Centro Internacional. Most museums have at least limited English explanations, and some have English-language tours.

LA CANDELARIA

La Candelaria is a living museum. It is a reminder of Spanish power and ambition in the New World; a tribute to the yearning for freedom embodied by Colombia's founding fathers; and a reflection on the tenacity of the independent Colombian republic to persevere in the face of adversity. La Candelaria is a bustling place and has been for centuries. These days, university students, government bureaucrats, tourists, and old-timers who have lived in the area for decades pass each other along the narrow streets and frequent the same cafés.

You could spend a couple of days admiring the colonial churches and exploring the many museums in the area, but if you don't have that much time, three or four hours will give you a good sense of the area and its significance. All of the sights in La Candelaria are easily and best visited on foot. Areas above the Chorro de Quevedo (toward the eastern mountains), as well as some parts to the west, bordering Avenida Caracas, can be a little sketchy and should be avoided.

★ Plaza de Bolívar

Every respectable Colombian city has a Plaza de Bolívar, but none have quite the history of this one. Between Carreras 7-8 and Calles 10-11, the **Plaza de Bolívar** is the natural starting point for any tour of La Candelaria. Originally known as the Plaza Mayor, the plaza has had several reincarnations during its history. In colonial times, it was where the Friday market took place. It was also the setting for executions, including that of independence heroine Policarpa Salavarrieta. Following the death of Simón Bolívar in 1846, Congress renamed the plaza in his honor. A diminutive statue of the Liberator, the first of many Bolívar statues in the world, stands in the middle of the plaza. Today it's the location of demonstrations, inauguration ceremonies for the Bogotá mayor, and concerts.

CATEDRAL PRIMADA AND CAPILLA EL SAGRARIO

The neoclassical facade of the **Catedral Primada** (9am-4:30pm daily) dominates the plaza. Built in 1807, the cathedral was designed by Capuchin architect Fray Domingo de Petrés. The tombs of Gonzalo Jiménez de Quesada, founder of Bogotá, and independence figure Antonio Nariño are in a side chapel on the right. Next door to the cathedral is the **Capilla El Sagrario** (Cra. 7 No. 10-40, 8:30am-11:50am and 1pm-4pm Mon.-Fri., 8:30am-5pm Sun.). This chapel was built much earlier than the cathedral, in the 1600s. The interior is decorated with a Mudejar or Moorish-style vaulted wooden ceiling. Along the sides of the cross-shaped chapel are several large works depicting biblical scenes by Colombian baroque painter Gregorio Vásquez de Arce y Ceballos. A ceremony was held here to honor the army and Simón Bolívar following their decisive victory over the Spaniards at the Battle of Boyacá in 1819.

Plaza de Bolívar

La Candelaria and Avenida Jiménez

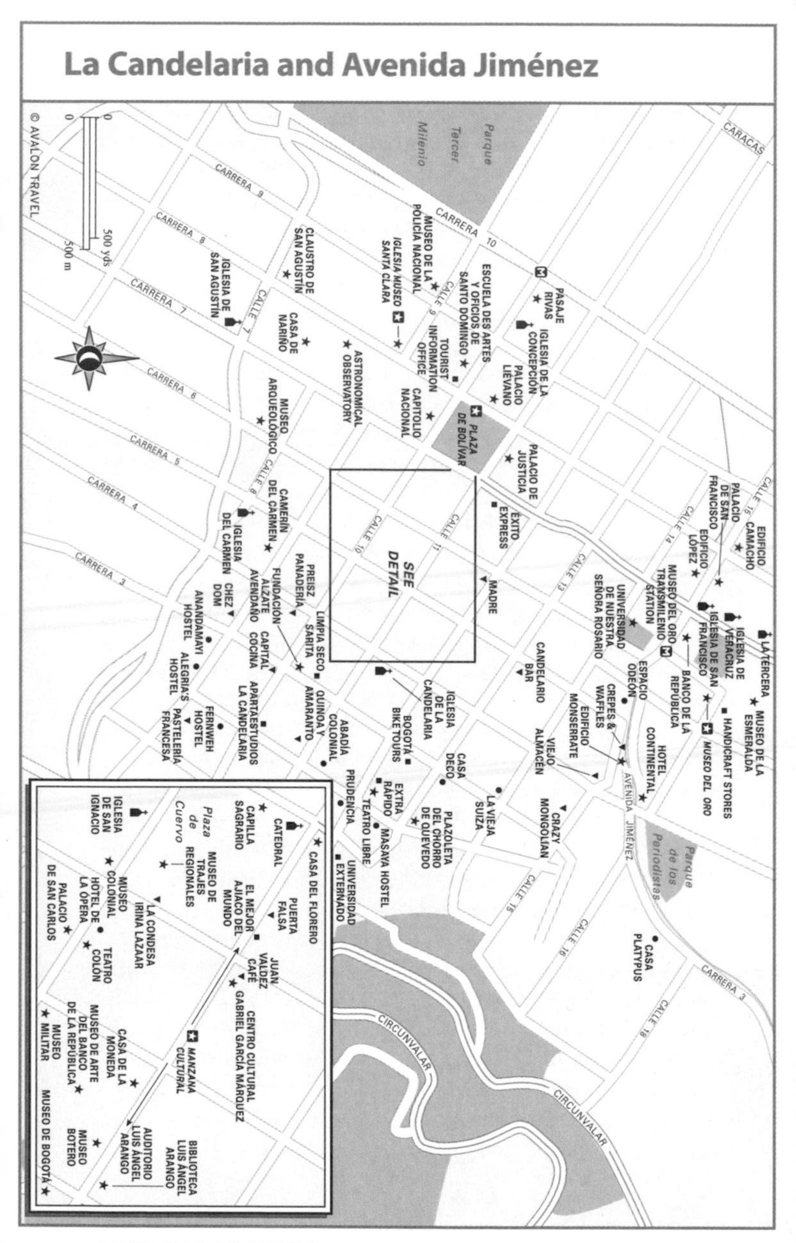

CASA DEL FLORERO

Across Calle 10 on the northeast corner of the plaza is the **Casa del Florero** (Cra. 7 No. 11-28, tel. 1/334-4150, 9am-5pm Tues.-Fri., 10am-4pm Sat.-Sun, COP$3,000), also known as the **Museo del 20 de Julio** or **Museo de la Independencia.** This small house used to be a general store run by a

Spaniard, José González-Llorente. The story goes that his refusal to lend a vase to a pair of Creoles sparked the ire of either incredibly sensitive or cunning locals, who launched a protest during the busy market day against Spanish rule. Historians today dispute much of the tale, but the shattered remains of that colorful vase are exhibited today in the museum. Maybe the most interesting exhibit in the museum is a room that shows the transformation of the Plaza de Bolívar over time, with raw footage of two of the most traumatic events in recent Colombian history: the Bogotazo riots following the assassination of Jorge Eliécer Gaitán in 1948 and the siege of the Palacio de Justicia following a takeover by the M-19 guerrilla group in 1985. There are some explanations in English. Tours are also available, usually in Spanish.

GOVERNMENT BUILDINGS

The newest building on the plaza, completed in 1991, is the **Palacio de Justicia** on the north side. Housing the Supreme Court and other high courts, this building replaced the previous structure, which was destroyed following the tragic events of 1985. (That building had replaced a previous justice building that was burned to the ground during the Bogotazo riots.) On November 6 of that year, M-19 guerrillas stormed the building, perhaps in cahoots with infamous drug kingpin Pablo Escobar, killing several justices and holding some 350 people in the building hostage. After an hours-long standoff, the military counterattacked, coordinating its assault from the Casa del Florero. The fight concluded the next day with the building engulfed in flames, the result of a military rocket. More than 100 people were killed, and controversy remains about the tragedy and the government's actions. Five years after the attack the M-19 demobilized, becoming a political movement. Today, it is telling that there is not even a plaque mentioning the tragedy. Nevertheless, clearly some wounds have healed: Former M-19 guerrilla Gustavo Petro was elected mayor in 2011, with his office (*alcaldía*) in the **Palacio Liéviano** on the west side of the plaza.

On the south side of the square is the neoclassical **Capitolio Nacional,** home of the bicameral Colombian Congress. Designed by architect Thomas Reed, the Capitolio took more than 70 years to build, finally being completed in 1926. Gargoyles keep watch atop the building behind the Ionic columns of the front. For about two months in 2009 the entire facade was covered with 1,300 massive ants, a project of Colombian artist Rafael Gómezbarros. The work was a commentary on forced displacement resulting from Colombia's armed conflict.

West of the Plaza

ESCUELA DE ARTES Y OFICIOS DE SANTO DOMINGO

One of the best trade schools in Latin America for woodworking, embroidery, silversmithing, and leatherworking is the **Escuela de Artes y Oficios de Santo Domingo** (Cl. 10 No. 8-73, tel. 1/282-0534, www.eaosd.org, 9am-5pm Mon.-Fri., free). Attracting artisans from around the world, this school receives support from the Fundación Mario Santo Domingo. Tours (9am, 10am, 11am, and 3pm Mon.-Fri.) are offered at four different times on weekdays; sign up by phone or email. Classes are open to anyone. The school is housed in two lovely colonial buildings from the 1600s that are connected by a courtyard. A store—which could be mistaken for a design museum—sells items made by students.

IGLESIA DE LA CONCEPCIÓN

The **Iglesia de la Concepción** (Cl.10 No. 9-50, 7am-5pm daily) was completed in 1595, making it the second-oldest church in the city. Along with a convent, it used to take up an entire block of old Santa Fe. The convent (which no longer exists) was built for the daughters and granddaughters of the conquistadors. The spectacular geometric designs on the ceiling and the polychromatic presbytery are among the most striking aspects of the church. If you pop in, you will see many faithful—most of humble means—in the pews, praying. This city block is called Calle del Divorcio. This refers to a nearby residence for separated or single women who were banished from their homes and not allowed into convents.

Farther down the street beyond the Iglesia de la Concepción is the historic labyrinthine artisans market known as the **Pasaje Rivas.**

MUSEO DE LA POLICÍA NACIONAL

The grandiose Palacio de la Policía, built in the early 20th century, was once the headquarters for the national police and today is home to the **Museo de la Policía Nacional** (Cl. 9 No. 9-27, tel. 1/233-5911, www.policia.gov.co, 9am-5pm Tues.-Fri., free). Tours are given by knowledgeable and friendly cadets who are fulfilling their one-year public service obligation. The museum does have its fair share of guns, but there are also exhibits on different technologies employed by police in pursuit of the bad guys, along with tributes to police dogs. If you go up to the rooftop, you can catch a unique perspective of the city. In the streets nearby are dozens of shops selling police and military uniforms.

★ IGLESIA MUSEO SANTA CLARA

It is easy to overlook the stone exterior of the **Iglesia Museo Santa Clara** (Cra. 8 No. 8-91, tel. 1/337-6262, www.museoiglesiasantaclara.gov.co, 9am-5pm Tues.-Fri., 10am-4pm Sat.-Sun., adults COP$3,000), but that would be a shame: This is one of the most beautiful sights in Bogotá. Once part of a convent for barefoot Franciscan nuns, known as Clarisas, the little church is an extraordinary example of Mudejar style in Santa Fe. The convent was completed in 1647; it originally housed 12 nuns who were descendants of conquistadors, along with 12 Creole maidens. Perhaps the most stunning design aspect can be admired by craning your neck and looking up: The single nave is beautifully illuminated by hundreds of golden floral motifs. The church is now strictly a museum, and it often hosts edgy contemporary art exhibitions. Admission is free on Sundays.

South of the Plaza

CASA DE NARIÑO

You can have your picture taken with members of the Presidential Guard (they don't mind) at the gates of the neoclassical **Casa de Nariño** (Cra. 8 No. 6-26, www.presidencia.gov.co), home to Colombia's presidents. As its name suggests, the presidential palace stands on the site of the birth house of Antonio Nariño, one of the early voices for independence in New Granada (the name given to the territory by the Spanish). In 1906 Nariño's house was razed to make way for the first presidential palace, which was designed by the same French architect who designed the Palacio Liévano on the Plaza de Bolívar. The palace has served as home for Colombian presidents off and on since 1886. Minutes after the 2002 inauguration of President Álvaro Uribe, the exterior of the palace was slightly damaged by missiles fired by FARC guerrillas. Several missiles landed on humble homes in slums nearby, killing 13.

Tours are given of the Casa de Nariño, but you must make a reservation several days in advance by filling out the form on their website. Even if you don't visit the interior of the palace, you can watch the changing of the Presidential Guard on Wednesdays and Fridays at 2:30pm and on Sundays at 3pm.

Also on the grounds of the Casa de Nariño is the oldest **astronomical observatory** in the New World. This was the initiative of famed botanist and scientist José Celestino Mutis. It was completed in 1803.

IGLESIA AND CLAUSTRO DE SAN AGUSTÍN

Facing the palace on the south side, the **Iglesia de San Agustín** (Cra. 7 No. 7-13, 9am-5pm Mon.-Sun.) was part of the first Augustinian monastery in the Spanish New World, completed in 1668. It is a three-nave temple, which distinguished it from other churches at the time. A 1785 earthquake destroyed the two towers (they rebuilt just one). In 1861, during liberal

Golden floral motifs adorn the nave at the Iglesia Museo Santa Clara.

reforms, the government took control of the church from the Augustinians. The next year the church was the scene of a presidential coup attempt during the Battle of San Agustín, as Conservatives attacked Liberals who were holed up in the church and adjacent monastery (which no longer stands). The church suffered damage yet again during the Bogotazo riots in 1948.

The **Claustro de San Agustín** (Cra. 8 No. 7-21, tel. 1/342-2340, 9am-5pm Mon.-Sat., 9am-4pm Sun., free) didn't serve long as a seminary, and in fact was used as a garrison in which Antonio Nariño was imprisoned. During the Bogotazo rampage, international delegates in town for the 9th Pan-American Conference sought shelter there from the mayhem on the streets. Today this beautiful cloister is run by the Universidad Nacional, which puts on temporary art exhibits and hosts educational activities.

MUSEO ARQUEOLÓGICO

The **Museo Arqueológico** (Cra. 6 No. 7-43, tel. 1/243-0465, www.musarq.org.co, 8:30am-5pm Mon.-Fri., 9am-4pm Sat., 10am-4pm Sun., COP$4,000) holds an extensive and nicely presented collection of ceramic work of pre-Columbian indigenous peoples. There is also a room containing colonial-era decorative arts, in acknowledgement of the history of this 17th-century home of a Spanish marquis. A small café adjoins the museum.

East of the Plaza

MUSEO COLONIAL

Well worth a visit, the **Museo Colonial** (Cra. 6 No. 9-77, tel. 1/341-6017, www.museocolonial.gov.co, 9am-5pm Tues.-Fri., 10am-4pm Sat.-Sun., COP$3,000) showcases a fine collection of art and religious artifacts from the colonial era, including the largest collection of works by Gregorio Vásquez de Arce y Ceballos. On the bottom floor is an exhibit that explores life in colonial times. The museum courtyard is quiet and green. Admission is free on Sundays.

This museum was historically part of the **Manzana Jesuítica,** a complex that included the adjacent **Colegio Mayor de San Bartolomé** (Colombia's oldest school, built in 1604) and the **Iglesia de San Ignacio,** from 1643.

TEATRO COLÓN

Modeled on the Teatro Santi Giovanni e Paolo in Venice, the **Teatro Colón** (Cl. 10 No. 5-32, tel. 1/284-7420, www.teatrocolon.gov.co) was designed by Pietro Cantini to commemorate the 400th anniversary of Christopher Columbus's 1492 landing in the New World. The theater was closed for several years during a massive overhaul. Today it sparkles. Tours (3pm Wed.-Thurs., noon and 3pm Sat., COP$5,000) are given, but the best way to experience the theater is by enjoying a performance.

PALACIO DE SAN CARLOS

Today housing the Ministry of Foreign Relations, the colonial-era **Palacio de San Carlos** (Cl. 10 No. 5-51, closed to the public) was the home of

Colombian presidents from 1825 until 1908. During the Bolívar dictatorship and the turbulent Gran Colombia period, Bolívar's companion Manuela Sáenz earned the nickname "Liberator of the Liberator" for helping him escape through a palace window—saving him from an 1828 assassination attempt. A plaque marking the exact spot draws the curiosity of passersby today.

MUSEUMS

The **Museo de Trajes Regionales** (Cl. 10 No. 6-18, tel. 1/341-0403, www.museodetrajesregionales.com, 9am-4pm Mon.-Fri., 9am-2pm Sat., COP$3,000) showcases traditional costumes from the different regions of Colombia but is best known for being the home of Manuela Sáenz, Simón Bolívar's companion. The museum is next door to the **Plaza de Cuervo,** a tropical patio in the middle of historic Bogotá. Behind the elegant palm trees is the house where Antonio Nariño is said to have translated the Declaration of the Rights of Man from French into Spanish in 1793. After making about 100 copies of it for distribution to rouse the masses, he panicked and began to frantically destroy them. (He would later be imprisoned by the Spanish authorities.)

The **Museo Militar** (Cl. 10 No. 4-92, tel. 1/281-3086, www.museo-militar.webnode.com.co, 9am-4pm Tues.-Fri., 10am-4pm Sat.-Sun., free, must present identification) is in a 17th-century house that was home to independence hero Capt. Antonio Ricaurte. Dozens of mannequins dressed in Colombian military uniforms keep visitors company as they amble the corridors of the museum. One room is dedicated to Colombia's participation in the Korean War, in which 4,300 Colombians fought, with 163 losing their lives. Colombia was the only country in Latin America to send troops in support of the United Nations/United States coalition. Two patios are filled with cannons, tanks, and fighter jets.

The **Museo de Bogotá** (Cra. 4 No. 10 18, tel. 1/352-1864, www.museodebogota.gov.co, 9am-6pm Tues.-Fri., 10am-5pm Sat.-Sun., free) has a permanent exhibition that examines the development of Bogotá through the years, and temporary shows have highlighted photography, historical figures in the city, and neighborhood profiles.

★ Manzana Cultural

The **Manzana Cultural** (Cl. 11 No. 4-41) of the Banco de la República is the most important "Cultural Block" in Colombia. It comprises the Biblioteca Luis Ángel Arango, the library's concert hall, the Museo Botero, the Museo de Arte, the Colección de Arte del Banco de la República, and the Casa de la Moneda.

BIBLIOTECA LUIS ÁNGEL ARANGO

The plain **Biblioteca Luis Ángel Arango** (Cl. 11 No. 4-14, tel. 1/343-1224, www.banrepcultural.org, 8am-8pm Mon.-Sat., 8am-4pm Sun.) is reportedly one of the busiest libraries in the world, with over 5,000 visitors each day. Part of the same complex and located behind the library, the **Casa Republicana** (8am-8pm Mon.-Sat., 8am-4pm Sun., free) often hosts temporary art exhibits. There is also a stunning chamber music concert hall in the large complex.

COLECCIÓN DE ARTE DEL BANCO DE LA REPÚBLICA

With 14 galleries highlighting Colombian art from the 17th century to present day, the **Colección de Arte del Banco de la República** (Cl. 11 No. 4-21, tel. 1/343-1316, www.banrepcultural.org, 9am-7pm Mon. and Wed.-Sat., 10am-5pm Sun., free) is an excellent opportunity to discover Colombian art. Look for the series of "dead nuns." It was customary to paint nuns twice in their lifetimes: once when they entered the convent and once more moments after passing away. The nuns from this series lived at the nearby convent of the Iglesia de la Concepción.

Another highlight is the spectacular—if a tad gaudy—*La Lechuga* monstrance (a monstrance is a receptacle to hold the Host). It's called *La Lechuga*, meaning lettuce, because of its 1,486 sparkling emeralds, but it is also adorned by hundreds of diamonds, rubies, amethysts, and pearls. The Spaniard who created this extraordinary piece charged the Jesuits the equivalent of a cool US$2 million when he finished it in 1707. Hidden away in a vault for over 200 years, it was acquired by the Banco de la República in 1987 for US$3.5 million.

Nineteenth-century landscapes, portraits by impressionist and Bogotá native Andrés Santa María, and works from an array of well-known Colombian artists from the 20th century (including Alejandro Obregón, Eduardo Ramírez, Guillermo Wiedemann, and Luis Caballero) are other museum highlights. Free guided tours in Spanish are offered several times a day.

MUSEO DE ARTE DEL BANCO DE LA REPÚBLICA

Behind the Colección de Arte, and housed in a brilliantly white boxlike construction, is the **Museo de Arte del Banco de la República** (Cl. 11 No. 4-21, tel. 1/343-1316, www.banrepcultural.org, 9am-7pm Mon. and Wed.-Sat., 10am-5pm Sun., free), which hosts temporary exhibits and has one floor dedicated to 20th-century Latin American and European art from the Banco de la República collection.

MUSEO BOTERO

In the **Museo Botero** (Cl. 11 No. 4-41, tel. 1/343-1316, www.banrepcultural.org, 9am-7pm Mon. and Wed.-Sat., 10am-5pm Sun., free) there are still lifes, portrayals of everyday life in Colombian pueblos, and social commentaries by one of the most well-known contemporary Colombian artists, Medellín-born Fernando Botero. In addition to paintings of corpulent Colombians, there are bronze and marble sculptures of chubby cats and bulgy birds. One side of the lovely colonial house, which surrounds a sublime courtyard, displays the artist's collection of European and American art, including works by Picasso and Dalí—all donated by the *maestro* so that Colombians of all backgrounds could enjoy them without paying a peso. Once the home of archbishops during the colonial era, the building was torched during the 1948 riots of the Bogotazo. It's been painstakingly restored. Guided tours are offered daily.

CASA DE LA MONEDA

Connected to the Museo Botero and the Colección de Arte by patios and a Botero gift shop, the **Casa de la Moneda** (Cl. 11 No. 4-93, tel. 1/343-1316, www.banrepcultural.org, 9am-7pm Mon. and Wed.-Sat., 10am-5pm Sun., free) was where the New World's first gold coins were produced starting in the early 17th century. The museum's **Colección Numismática** shows the history of the Nueva Granada mint.

CENTRO CULTURAL GABRIEL GARCÍA MÁRQUEZ

Designed by Rogelio Salmona, the **Centro Cultural Gabriel García Márquez** (Cl. 11 No. 5-60, tel. 1/283-2200, www.fce.com.co, 9am-7pm Mon.-Sat., 10:30am-5pm Sun., free) was a gift from the Mexican government in honor of the 1982 Nobel Prize winner for literature, Colombian Gabriel García Márquez. (The author lived in Mexico from the 1960s until his death in 2014.) On the main level, where you can enjoy a sunset view of the cathedral, is a bookstore with an ample selection of books on Colombia. Next to the Juan Valdez Café below is an exhibition space.

AVENIDA JIMÉNEZ

Avenida Jiménez used to be the Río San Francisco and the extreme northern boundary of Santa Fe. Most of the historic buildings on this street can only be enjoyed from the exterior. In 2000, in an effort to reinvent the historic Avenida Jiménez, architect Rogelio Salmona created the **Eje Ambiental** (Environmental Corridor), which extends from the Universidad

courtyard at the Casa de la Moneda

de los Andes campus to Avenida Caracas. Vehicular traffic is banned here except for the red buses of the TransMilenio. Ample pedestrian space has made this a pleasant place for a stroll.

A fantastic pedestrian zone extends along Carrera 7 from the Plaza de Bolívar to Calle 26. This busy commercial area is a fun way to check out the city's core and do a little shopping, sightseeing, and people-watching.

Historic Architecture

Impressive buildings line the entire length of Avenida Jiménez. Most of these gems were built in the early 20th century. To the west side of the Séptima (Cra. 7) are: the neoclassical **Palacio de San Francisco** (Av. Jiménez No. 7-56), prior home to the Cundinamarca departmental government; the **Edificio López** (Av. Jiménez No. 7-65), by the same construction firm that built the Chrysler Building in New York; and the modernist **Edificio Camacho,** farther down and on the right.

It was on the southwest corner of the Séptima and Avenida Jiménez that populist Liberal Party presidential candidate Jorge Eliécer Gaitán was assassinated on April 9, 1948, the event that sparked the tragic Bogotazo riots. Up to 3,000 were killed in the unrest. This precipitated the bloody period of La Violencia that quickly engulfed the entire country. At the present-day McDonald's, a plaque and flowers mark the spot where the tragedy took place. A young Gabriel García Márquez, then a law student at the Universidad Nacional, lived near the Palacio de San Francisco at that time, and with his building in flames, it's said that he and his brother rushed back inside—to save his typewriter.

On the eastern (mountain) side of the Séptima, notable buildings include the modernist **Banco de la República** (Cra. 7 No. 14-78); the **Universidad de Nuestra Señora del Rosario** (Cl. 12C No. 6-25), founded in 1653, which is housed in a colonial building that was originally a monastery; the **Edificio Monserrate** (Av. Jiménez No. 4-49), which was home to *El Espectador* newspaper; the fabulous restored **Hotel Continental** (Av. Jiménez No. 4-19), once the most exclusive hotel in town; the neoclassical **Academia Colombiana de Historia** (Cl. 10 No. 9-95); the 17th-century **Iglesia and Convento de las Aguas** (Cra. 2 No. 18A-58), where Artesanías de Colombia has a store; and finally (at the end of the Eje Ambiental), the campus of the **Universidad de Los Andes,** one of the top universities in Latin America, with several stunning new buildings. Los Andes has around 19,000 students.

Churches

Typical of most all colonial-era churches, the **Iglesia de San Francisco** (Cl. 16 No. 7-35, 6:30am-8pm Mon.-Fri., 6:30am-12:40pm and 4:30pm-8pm Sat.-Sun.) looks somber from the outside, but inside it's adorned with a fantastic golden altar, considered a masterwork of American baroque. This is the oldest of all the churches in the city, built by the Franciscans in 1557. The church is often full of working-class faithful. Adjacent to the

San Francisco is the **Iglesia de Veracruz** (Cl. 16 No. 7-19), which is where several independence figures, executed by the Spaniards, are laid to rest.

The third church in this row is called **Iglesia La Tercera** (Cl. 16 No. 7-35, 7am-6pm Mon.-Fri., 11am-1pm Sat.-Sun.), and it is one of the jewels of colonial churches in Bogotá. It was built in the late 18th century, about 50 years before Colombian independence. Architecturally, a highlight is its barrel-vaulted ceiling decorated with geometric designs and altarpieces made of cedar and walnut. Unlike other churches, the interior is not covered with gold leaf.

★ Museo del Oro

Some visitors come to Bogotá specifically to see the world-renowned **Museo del Oro** (Gold Museum, Cra. 6 No. 15-88, tel. 1/343-2233, www.banrepcultural.org/museo-del-oro, 9am-6pm Tues.-Sat., 10am-4pm Sun., COP$4,000). The museum tells the story of how—and why—the native peoples of Colombia created such incredibly detailed and surprisingly modern designs of gold jewelry and religious objects. What's on view is but a fraction of the museum's collection, which begin with its first acquisition in 1939.

What is astonishing about the collection is the sophistication of the work. It is almost all smelted, with Muisca and Sinú peoples employing a "lost wax" technique, with various metals being purposefully alloyed. Here, rather than large, hammered pieces as found in countries like Peru, you will see intricately crafted and designed jewelry.

One of the highlights is the golden raft created by local Muisca people. The raft portrays the ritual of El Dorado, "the Golden One." Another piece to look for is the collection's first acquisition, the Quimbaya Póporo. This was used during religious ceremonies. The unforgettable Offering Room is filled with golden treasures. English explanations are excellent throughout the museum (so is the audio tour). Just beyond the gift shop is a restaurant that specializes in Colombian and Mediterranean cuisine. Saturday is a good day to visit the museum, as there may be fewer school groups visiting. On Sunday, admission is free. There are guided tours (11am, 3pm, and 4pm) daily, some of which are in English

Museo de la Esmeralda

On the 23rd floor of the Avianca building is the **Museo de la Esmeralda** (Cl. 16 No. 6-66, tel. 1/482-7890, www.museodelaesmeralda.com.co, 10am-6pm Mon.-Sat., COP$5,000). The museum has an impressive re-creation of an emerald mine and several examples of different emeralds from Colombia and elsewhere. Guides, fluent in Spanish and English, will make sure you know that the best emeralds do—without a doubt—come from Colombia, primarily from the Muzo mines in the Boyacá department. Although there is little pressure to do so, you can purchase all different classes of emeralds, and the facility's jewelers can transform the emeralds you choose into rings or earrings within a day. Even if you are not interested in purchasing an emerald it is fun to check out the gems under a magnifying glass, as you learn why some emeralds are much more precious than others. The museum also has a small store on the main floor of the building that sometimes has coupons for discounted museum entry. Security at the Avianca building is stringent, and you will need to bring a photocopy of your passport and produce the telephone number of your hotel for entry.

Quinta de Bolívar

The **Quinta de Bolívar** (Cl. 21 No. 4A-30, tel. 1/336-6410/19, www.quintadebolivar.gov.co, 9am-5pm Tues.-Fri., 10am-4pm Sat.-Sun., COP$3,000, free Sun.) is a lovely country estate that was presented by Francisco de Paula Santander, vice president of the República de Gran Colombia, as a gift to Simón Bolívar in 1820. Bolívar stayed there during his brief and sporadic visits to Bogotá, a city he did not like. He spent approximately 432 nights here, give or take. Built in 1800, the estate is a beautiful example of a late colonial-era house. It's furnished with period pieces and set in a beautiful garden under cypress and walnut trees. It is just a five-minute walk uphill from the Quinta to Monserrate.

★ Cerro de Monserrate

It's worth the ride or hike to the top of **Cerro de Monserrate** (Cra. 2 Este No. 21-48, tel. 1/284-5700, www.cerromonserrate.com, 6:30am-midnight Mon.-Sat., 6:30am-6:30pm Sun.) for memorable views of the city by day or night. There are two different ways to reach the peak, one easier than the other. For the easy way, take either the **funicular tramway** (6:30am-11:45pm Tues.-Fri., 6:30am-4pm Sat., 6:30am-6:30pm Sun., round-trip COP$19,000) or the **gondola** (6:30am-midnight Mon., noon-midnight Tues.-Sat., 10am-4:30pm Sun., round-trip COP$19,000). It's cheaper on Sundays, so expect long lines.

The second option involves hiking to the top. Due to large crowds on weekends and holidays, this is a good plan for a weekday morning. The path is open 5am-4pm Wednesday-Monday. There is no charge to make the somewhat challenging ascent on foot. Moving at a brisk clip, the walk will take less than 45 minutes.

In the past there have been reports of bandits lingering in the woods along the path, but the security situation has vastly improved. Police cadets are stationed at three or four points along the trail until 4pm, and when there are no police there are plenty of other hikers or vendors selling refreshments.

If you feel as if you have done your exercise for the day once you achieve the peak, you can purchase a one-way ticket at the top to ride either the funicular tramway or the gondola back down.

For some, the white chapel at the top, the **Santuario de Monserrate,** is the goal of this hike. It is not architecturally notable, and it has been destroyed and rebuilt several times since the 1600s, but it is the highest church around, at about 3,152 meters (10,341 feet) above sea level. Inside, a

17th-century sculpture of the Fallen Christ of Monserrate attracts religious pilgrims. Some climb the hill on their knees during Holy Week, believing that the Fallen Christ grants miracles to those who do so.

There are two pricey restaurants on the top of the mountain—a romantic setting for marriage proposals and a favorite spot for locals to bring visitors. These are French-Colombian **Restaurante Casa San Isidro** (tel. 1/281-9270, www.restaurantecasasanisidro.com, noon-midnight Mon.-Sat., COP$40,000) and **Restaurante Casa Santa Clara** (tel. 1/745-4628, www.restaurantecasasantaclara.com, noon-5pm Tues.-Fri., noon-4pm Sat.-Sun., COP$25,000), which specializes in Colombian fare.

To the south of Monserrate rises the **Cerro de Guadalupe,** topped by a large statue of the Virgin. It can only be accessed by road and was, until recently, unsafe to visit. If you would like to visit (the views are about the same as from Monserrate), take a microbus on Sunday from the intersection of Calle 6 and Avenida Caracas. As you enter the ticket office at the base of Monserrate, you may see an old photograph of a tightrope walker crossing the 890 meters (2,900 feet) from Monserrate to Guadalupe blindfolded. This stunt was performed by Canadian daredevil Harry Warner in 1895.

CENTRO INTERNACIONAL

Museo de Arte Moderno de Bogotá

Across from the Parque de la Independencia on Avenida 26 is the **Museo de Arte Moderno de Bogotá** (Museum of Modern Art of Bogotá, Cl. 24 No. 6-00, tel. 1/286-0466, www.mambogota.com, 10am-6pm Tues.-Sat., noon-4:30pm Sun., COP$5,000). It often puts on interesting exhibitions highlighting Colombian and Latin American artists. Nicknamed MAMBO, it is a creation of architect Rogelio Salmona.

Torre Colpatria Observation Deck

The **Torre Colpatria Observation Deck** (Cra. 7 No. 24-89, tel. 1/283-6665, 6pm-9pm Fri., 8am-8pm Sat., 8am-5pm Sun., COP$5,000) offers unparalleled 360-degree views of Bogotá. The vista of the city from this 50-story tower is arguably superior to that of the Cerro de Monserrate. At night the tower goes into disco mode, displaying colorful lights.

Parque de la Independencia

The **Parque de la Independencia,** long a favorite for young lovers and those seeking a pleasant stroll under the towering eucalyptus and wax palm trees, was created in 1910 in celebration of Colombia's 100-year anniversary of independence from Spain. The **Quiosco de la Luz** houses a tourist information center (Punto de Información Turística, or PIT). Adjacent to the Parque de la Independencia is the green corridor of the **Parque del Bicentenario,** a long-delayed urban revitalization project that opened in 2016.

Within the park is a planetarium, the **Planetario de Bogotá** (Cl. 26B No. 5-93, tel. 1/281-4150, www.planetariodebogota.gov.co, 10am-5pm

Tues.-Sun., COP$5,000). Next to that is the **Plaza de Toros de Santamaría.** The neo-Mudejar brick arena was built in the 1930s by a Spanish architect and was modeled after bullfighting rings in Madrid. Bullfighting is a controversial topic in Bogotá, and its future is uncertain. But the bullring is photogenic, especially from atop the Torre Colpatria.

About 100 steps up from the bullfighting ring and planetarium are the iconic **Torres del Parque.** These three brick apartment buildings, rising parallel to the eastern mountains, were designed in the 1960s by Rogelio Salmona, the most accomplished architect from Bogotá during the late 20th century. French-born Salmona studied with Le Corbusier and was awarded the Alvar Aalto Prize in 2003 for his lifetime achievements. Public space takes up almost three-fourths of the area in the tower complex, and its art galleries, cafés, and bodegas are nice places to linger on a rainy day.

Museo Nacional

The **Museo Nacional** (Cra. 7 No. 28-66, tel. 1/381-6470, www.museonacional.gov.co, 10am-6pm Tues.-Sat., 10am-5pm Sun., free) was designed by English architect Thomas Reed (who also designed the Capitolio Nacional) in the late 1800s to serve as the penitentiary for Cundinamarca, which was at that time one of nine states of the United States of Colombia. The prison was a cross-shaped panopticon, with a central tower from which guards could monitor prisoners housed in the three wings. It was in the late 1940s that the prison was converted into a museum. The permanent collection examines the history of Colombia from pre-Columbian cultures to the 20th century. On the top floor is a nice introduction to late 20th-century Colombian art. The museum often holds temporary exhibits on the ground floor. There are usually at least minimal English descriptions throughout. Art books and handicrafts are sold at the museum shop. A Juan Valdez Café brews coffee in the inviting interior courtyard and sculpture garden.

The Torres del Parque were designed by Rogelio Salmona.

Parque Nacional

A center of activity on the weekends, the **Parque Nacional** (between Cras. 5-7 and Clls. 35-39) is the largest park in downtown Bogotá and the second oldest in the city. The park is set between a lovely English Tudor-style neighborhood called La Merced and, to the north, the Universidad Javeriana, which was founded by the Jesuits. On Sundays and holidays when there is Ciclovía, free aerobics classes draw huge crowds in the park. On the northwest corner of the park is a whimsical sculpture by Enrique Grau called *Rita 5:30*.

Cementerio Central

The most important cemetery in Colombia is the **Cementerio Central** (Cra. 20 No. 24-80, tel. 1/269-3141, 9am-4pm daily), where prominent political, cultural, and business figures rest. Before its construction in 1830, distinguished persons were buried in churches following Spanish tradition. Francisco de Paula Santander, who is known as Colombia's Thomas Jefferson; Gustavo Rojas Pinilla, a military dictator from the 1950s; Luis Carlos Galán, a Liberal Party candidate killed under orders of Pablo

Escobar; Carlos Pizarro, assassinated head of a rebel group; and Leo Kopp, the German founder of the Bavaria brewery, are all buried here.

There is a part of the cemetery where thousands of victims from the Bogotazo riots from April 1948 are buried, many of them chillingly listed as "N. N." ("no name"). Women sell cut flowers outside of the cemetery gates and graffiti provides bursts of color. Keep your wits about you when walking through the farther expanses of the cemetery, as security guards may not be nearby to ward off pickpockets. This is a popular spot on weekends, but is emptier on week days.

Immediately west of the cemetery is a remarkable art installation called ***Auras Anonimas*** by Colombian artist Beatriz González. This abandoned columbarium (a structure used to house ashes) is covered with around 9,000 primitive black-and-white paintings of people carrying away the dead. It is a powerful reflection on the human toll of the armed conflict in Colombia.

A memorial to victims of violence of the armed conflict is adjacent to the Cementerio Central. The **Centro de Memoria, Paz y Reconciliación** (Cra. 19B No. 24-86, tel. 1/381-3030, www.centromemoria.gov.co, 11am-1pm and 2pm-4pm Mon., 8am-10am, 11am-1pm, and 2pm-4pm Tues.-Fri., free) is one of the first memorials of its kind in Colombia. It is an educational space, where schoolchildren come to hear firsthand accounts from victims of the conflict.

NORTHERN BOGOTÁ

Parque de la 93

The **Parque de la 93** (between Cras. 11A-13 and Clls. 93A-B) is a manicured park with a playground surrounded by restaurants. Workers from the area stroll the park on their lunch hour. On soccer game days, big screens are set up for fans to watch the match.

Usaquén

Once upon a time, charming **Usaquén** was its own distinct pueblo. Now at the fringes of sprawling Bogotá, Usaquén has somehow retained some colonial charm. It has become a dining and drinking hot spot with many restaurants and bars around the main square. On Sundays the neighborhood comes alive during its popular **flea market** (Cra. 5 at Cl. 119B).

WESTERN BOGOTÁ

The sights of Western Bogotá can be reached by SITP buses Z7 and 59B.

Parque Simón Bolívar

When it was built in the late 1960s, **Parque Simón Bolívar** (between Clls. 53-63 and Cras. 48-68, 6am-6pm daily) was in the countryside. Now, it's the middle of the city. The park is an excellent place for watching Bogotanos at play, especially on the weekends. Numerous festivals and concerts take place here. There are more than 16 kilometers (10 miles) of trails in the park.

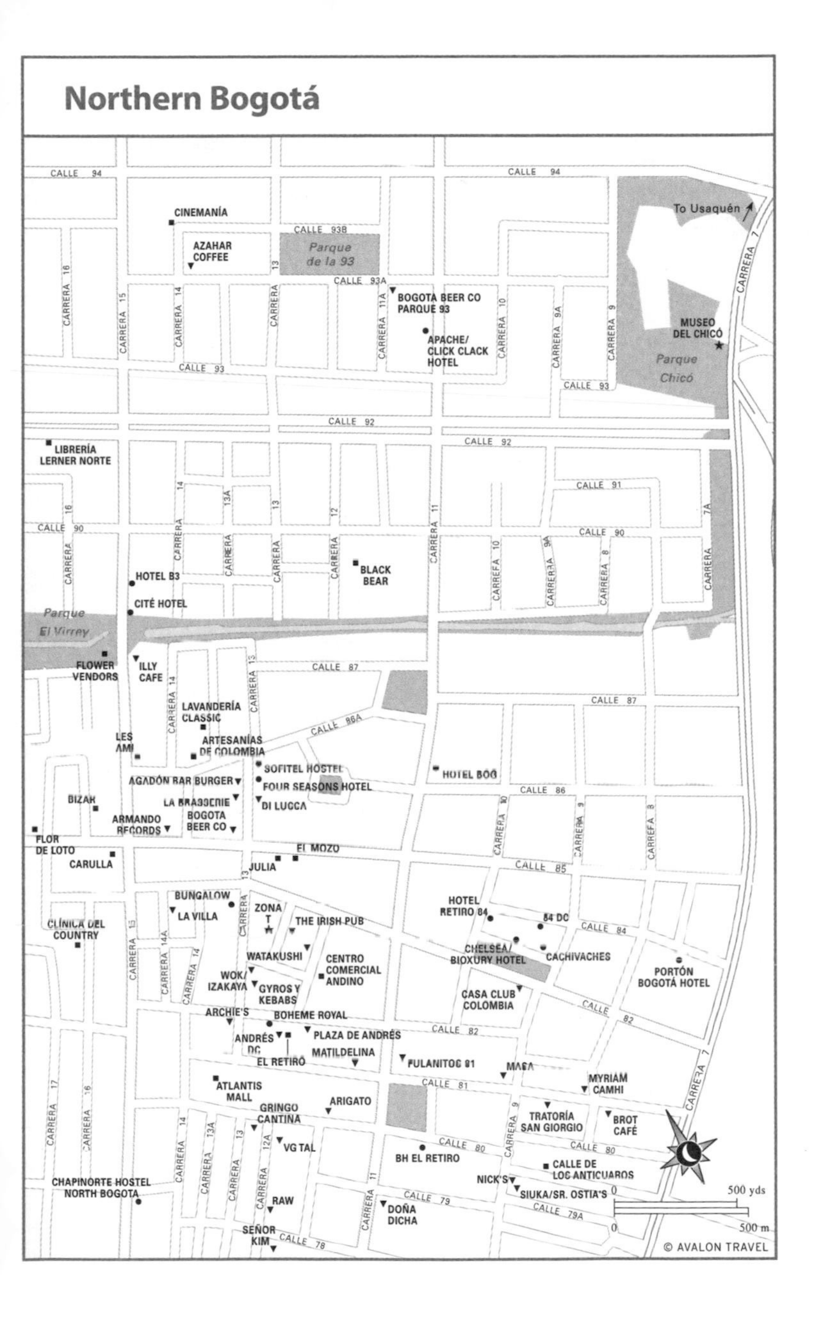

Northern Bogotá
CALLE 94
CINEMANÍA
AZAHAR COFFEE
CALLE 93B
Parque de la 93
CALLE 93A
BOGOTA BEER CO PARQUE 93
APACHE/ CLICK CLACK HOTEL
To Usaquén
MUSEO DEL CHICÓ
Parque Chicó
CALLE 93
CALLE 92
LIBRERÍA LERNER NORTE
CALLE 91
CALLE 90
BLACK BEAR
HOTEL B3
CITÉ HOTEL
Parque El Virrey
FLOWER VENDORS
ILLY CAFE
CALLE 87
LAVANDERÍA CLASSIC
CALLE 86A
ARTESANÍAS DE COLOMBIA
LES AMI
SOFITEL HOSTEL
FOUR SEASONS HOTEL
HOTEL BOG
AGADÓN BAR BURGER
LA BRASSERIE
DI LUCCA
CALLE 86
BIZAH
ARMANDO RECORDS
BOGOTA BEER CO
FLOR DE LOTO
CARULLA
EL MOZO
JULIA
CALLE 85
BUNGALOW
LA VILLA
ZONA T
THE IRISH PUB
HOTEL RETIRO 84
84 DC
CALLE 84
CLÍNICA DEL COUNTRY
WATAKUSHI
CENTRO COMERCIAL ANDINO
CHELSEA/ BIOXURY HOTEL
CACHIVACHES
PORTÓN BOGOTÁ HOTEL
WOK/ IZAKAYA
GYROS Y KEBABS
CASA CLUB COLOMBIA
ARCHIE'S
BOHEME ROYAL
CALLE 82
ANDRÉS DC
PLAZA DE ANDRÉS
EL RETIRO
MATILDELINA
FULANITOS 81
MASA
MYRIAM CAMHI
ATLANTIS MALL
CALLE 81
ARIGATO
GRINGO CANTINA
TRATORÍA SAN GIORGIO
BROT CAFÉ
VG TAL
CALLE 80
BH EL RETIRO
CALLE DE LOS ANTICUAROS
CHAPINORTE HOSTEL NORTH BOGOTA
NICK'S
SIUKA/SR. OSTIA'S
RAW
CALLE 79
CALLE 79A
DOÑA DICHA
SEÑOR KIM
CALLE 78
CARRERA 7
CARRERA 7A
CARRERA 8
CARRERA 9
CARRERA 9A
CARRERA 10
CARRERA 11
CARRERA 11A
CARRERA 12
CARRERA 12A
CARRERA 13
CARRERA 13A
CARRERA 14
CARRERA 14A
CARRERA 15
CARRERA 16
CARRERA 17
0 500 yds
0 500 m
© AVALON TRAVEL

In August, traditionally the windiest month, thousands of families try their luck at catching a breeze with their colorful kites.

Biblioteca Virgilio Barco

With the downtown skyline and mountains providing a picturesque background, the **Biblioteca Virgilio Barco** (Av. Cra. 60 No. 57-60, tel. 1/379-3520, www.biblored.gov.co, 2pm-8pm Mon., 8am-8pm Tues.-Sat., 9:30am-5:30pm Sun.), designed by architect Rogelio Salmona, is one of four fantastic library-parks in the city created by Mayor Enrique Peñalosa. The purpose of these mega libraries is to provide citizens access to books, Internet, and cultural/educational opportunities in a peaceful environment. Green spaces like this are few and far between in lower-income neighborhoods. A bike path encircles the park and is popular with young inline skaters and joggers. The well-maintained grounds are a playground for both the young and the old—and their dogs.

Jardín Botánico

Colombia is one of the most biodiverse countries on the planet, and the **Jardín Botánico** (Botanical Garden, Av. Cl. 63 No. 68-95, tel. 1/437-7060, www.jbb.gov.co, 8am-5pm Mon.-Fri., 9am-5pm Sat.-Sun., COP$2,700) does an excellent job of highlighting that diversity. It won't be hard to find the Colombian national tree, the iconic wax palm. And inside the greenhouse, be on the lookout for the official Bogotá orchid. The gardens take visitors on a tour of the many different climate regions in the country—from the *páramos* (highland moors) to cloud forests to tropical jungles. Feel free to stray from the paths and get closer to the plants.

Entertainment and Events

Bogotá is the cultural capital of Colombia. All regions of Colombia are represented in the musical traditions here. Merengue, salsa, *cumbia* (traditional Caribbean music), *vallenato* (love ballads accompanied by accordion): You name it, you can hear it.

NIGHTLIFE

Bogotá has a bar, club, or party for every taste. Popular nightspots are scattered along the Carrera 7 corridor. To get the latest on nightlife, and find out about parties, check out Vive In (www.vive.in) and the magazine *GO* (www.goguiadelocio.com.co), as well as each club's Facebook page.

The largest concentration of nightlife is in Northern Bogotá. There are over 100 gay and lesbian bars and clubs in the city; the Plaza de Lourdes (Cra. 13 and Av. Cl. 63) in Chapinero is a good place to start, as it has a group of gay bars surrounding it.

Expect to pay COP$10,000-30,000 cover at clubs, unless there's a big-name DJ or band, when covers are higher. Covers can include a *consumible* (complimentary drink). Pay for drinks with small bills or exact change, as some wayward bar staff may attempt to keep the change, especially from visitors. Tips are not generally expected at bars.

All electronic music clubs are gay friendly and become even more so as the night wears on. Clubs stay open until 3am generally, with some operating until daylight. After-parties exist, but these can be sketchy affairs.

La Candelaria

Candelario Bar (Cra. 5 No. 12B-14, tel. 1/342-3742, 9pm-3am Fri.-Sat.) gets rowdy, with a student crowd singing and drinking to reggaetón and Latin beats.

Cuban Jazz Café (Cra. 7A No. 12C-36, tel. 1/341-3714, www.cubanjazzcafe.com, 5pm-3am Wed.-Sat.) is a hot spot for mojitos and *son* music. Check out **Viejo Almacén** (Cl. 15 No. 4-30, 6pm-2am Tues.-Sun.), a tango bar named after the famous nightspot of the same name in Buenos Aires.

Avenida Jiménez

Quiebra Canto (Cra. 5 No. 17-76, tel. 1/243-1630, 6:30pm-3am Wed.-Sat., cover COP$10,000) is a classic haunt where jazz, funk, and salsa are often the order of the night. Wednesdays are especially popular at this two-floor joint.

Centro Internacional

In the Macarena, cool **Baum** (Cl. 33 No. 6-24, cell tel. 316/494-3799, 10pm-5am Fri.-Sat., COP$35,000) packs in an enthusiastic crowd of locals and visitors who lose themselves to the beats of top international DJs.

Late-night dancing goes underground at **Vlak** (Cra. 6 No. 26B-61, cell tel. 321/439-7610, COP$25,00), a basement club near the bullfighting ring.

Chapinero

The salsa is hot at **El Titicó** (Cl. 64 No. 13-35, cell tel. 310/696-2240, www.eltitico.com.co, 8pm-3am Fri.-Sat.), a live music and dancing venue in an edgy area of Chapinero.

Video Club (Cl. 64 No. 13-09, www.videoclub.com.co, COP$25,000) does electro-house music at its cool location in Chapinero. It's a good idea to wear a long-sleeved shirt, because most of the action is on the top-floor terrace. The club hosts special events marketed to gay clientele on Sundays.

Octava (Cra. 8 No. 63-41, www.cluboctava.com, 10pm-6am Fri.-Sat.) has an awesome sound system and sophisticated beats. The crowd is a little older than at most clubs.

A change of pace is on tap at **B&L Piano Pub** (Cra. 4A No. 66-03, cell tel. 322/351-8791, noon-3pm and 6pm-midnight Mon.-Wed., noon-midnight Thurs.-Sat.), where jazz and blues grab the spotlight. This hidden gem in an upper-crust area features live music most nights.

Theatrón (Cl. 58 No. 10-32, tel. 1/235-6879, www.theatrondepelicula.com, 9pm-5am Fri.-Sat., cover COP$30,000) is a giant disco catering to the gay crowd, with about 13 different spaces in its Chapinero location.

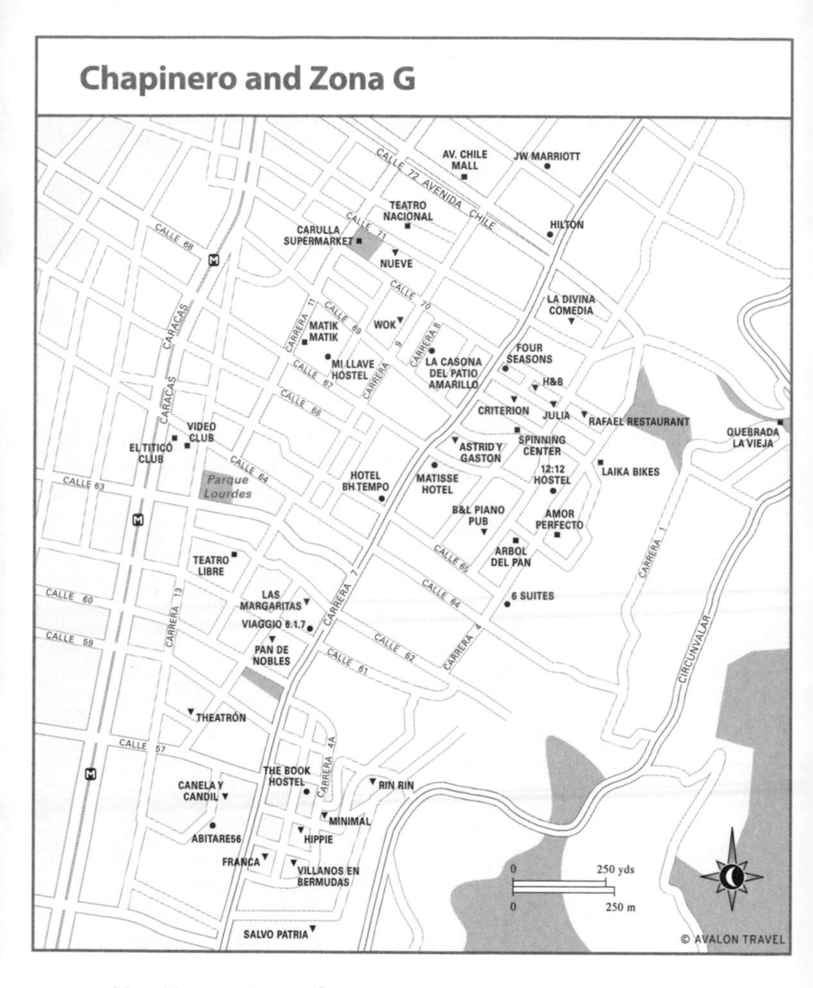

Northern Bogotá

Thanks to **Bogotá Beer Company** (www.bogotabeercompany.com), a successful chain of pubs with several locations throughout the city, sipping on a Candelaria artisan beer has become trendy in Bogotá. They also serve decent burgers. Try one of the northern locations: one on Calle 85 (Cl. 85 No. 13-06, tel. 1/742-9292, ext. 316), and one in the Parque de la 93 area (Cra. 11A No. 93A-94, tel. 1/742-9292, ext. 313).

Sit on the terrace and listen to rock music at always-packed **The Pub Bogotá** (Cra. 12A No. 83-48, tel. 1/691-8711, www.thepub.com.co, noon-close daily, no cover), where you're in a strategic position to watch people cruising the Zona T.

Chelsea Bar (Bioxury Hotel, Cl. 83 No. 9-48, 11th fl., cell tel. 310/325-7674, www.bioxury.com, Thurs.-Sat.) is a happening terrace bar near the Zona Rosa. In the center of the Zona Rosa is **Bungalow** (Cra. 13 No. 83-47, cell tel. 317/369-7889, 7pm-3am Thurs., 5pm-3am Fri.-Sat.), a chic terrace bar with DJs and cocktails. Also in the Zona Rosa, **Armando Records** (Cl. 85 No. 14-46, www.armandorecords.org, hours vary Tues.-Sat., cover COP$15,000) attracts a slightly grungy but cool crowd. The terrace is a fun (but sometimes cold) spot. Live bands and international DJs regularly play here.

La Villa (Cra. 14A No. 83-56, hours vary Tues.-Sat., cover COP$15,000) hosts the popular Gringo Tuesdays parties, but has all kinds of themed parties catering to locals and visitors alike.

Apache (Cra. 11 No. 93-77, tel. 1/635-1916, www.clickclackhotel.com, noon-2am Mon.-Sat.) is the place for music, burgers, and sports on television. It's atop the Click Clack Hotel in the Parque de la 93 area.

The **W Lounge** (Av. Cra. 9 No. 115-30, tel. 1/746-7111, www.wbogota.com, 8pm-1am daily) at the W Bogota Hotel is a swanky space dominated by a graffiti-style mural. On weeknights, the after-work crowd and W guests settle into the sofas here. DJs spin on weekend nights, where an occasional cover is charged.

On Wednesday nights, the place to go is **Cavú Club** (Cra. 15 No. 88-71, tel. 1/249-9987, www.cavuclub.com, 9pm-3am Wed., cover COP$20,000). Here the music played is a mix of pop genres and there is usually a performance by a drag queen.

THE ARTS

Cultural Centers

The **Fundación Gilberto Alzate Avendaño** (Cl. 10 No. 3-16, tel. 1/282-9491, www.fgaa.gov.co, 9am-5pm Mon.-Fri., free) in La Candelaria puts on theater and music performances featuring local talent and hosts art exhibits.

In the gorgeous neighborhood of La Merced, bordering the Parque Nacional, **Cine Tonalá** (Cra. 6 No. 35-37, tel. 1/285-9391, www.cinetonala.com, noon-11pm Sun. and Tues.-Thurs., noon-3am Fri.-Sat.) has a robust program of art films (with beer specials) and hosts cool parties.

Near Centro Internacional, **Casa Kilele Casa Cultural** (Cl. 28a No. 16A-31, tel. 1/487-7921 or cell tel. 320/858-4703) is the funky home of a wide range of parties, concerts, performances, workshops, and yoga classes.

A cool space on pedestrian Avenida Jiménez is **Espacio Odeón** (Cra. 5 No. 12C-73, www.espacioodeon.com, 10am-5pm Mon.-Fri.), where there is often an art installation on view.

Art Galleries

Bogotá is a magnet for artists from across Colombia. There are interesting galleries in neighborhoods across the city that are open to all, not just art buyers. **Artería** (www.periodicoarteria.com) offers fantastic free walking tours of different gallery districts in Bogotá.

In the Macarena, look for **Valenzuela Keller** (Cra. 5 No. 26B-26, tel. 1/661-1961, www.vkgaleria.com, 10am-1pm and 2pm-6pm Mon.-Fri.,

11am-4pm Sat.) and **Alonso Garcés** (Cra. 5A No. 26-92, tel. 1/337-5827, www.alonsogarcesgaleria.com, 10am-1pm and 2pm-6pm Mon.-Fri., 10am-2pm Sat.).

In the industrial area of San Felipe in western Bogotá are an astonishing number of galleries. Some of the best include experimental **Galería Beta** (Cl. 75A No. 20C-52, tel. 1/255-5902, www.galeriabeta.com, 10am-5pm Mon.-Fri., 2pm-5pm Sat.), **Galería SGR** (Cl. 74 No. 22-28, tel. 1/631-8027, www.sgr-art.com, 10am-6pm Mon.-Fri., noon-4pm Sat.), which highlights renowned contemporary Latin American artists, and nature-focused **Flora Ars + Natura** (Cl. 77 No. 20C-48, tel. 1/675-1425, www.arteflora.org, 2pm-6pm Mon.-Fri., 10am-1pm Sat. by appt.).

Classical Music and Opera

You may not think of classical music when you think Bogotá, or South America for that matter, but the city is home to two excellent orchestras and an opera, and hosts talented performers year-round. As is the case for most concerts and events in Bogotá, purchasing tickets in advance from Tu Boleta (tel. 1/593-6300, www.tuboleta.com) is the most convenient option.

The excellent **Orquesta Filarmónica de Bogotá** (www.filarmonica-bogota.gov.co) performs often on the Universidad Nacional campus at the **Auditorio Leon de Greiff** (Cra. 45 No. 26-85, www.divulgacion.unal.edu.co) and occasionally at other venues. The Auditorio León de Greiff is hard to miss: There is a huge stencil of iconic revolutionary Che Guevara on its exterior. There is often an international guest soloist at these concerts. Although tickets are available at the *taquillas* (ticket offices) at these theaters a few hours before performance time, it is recommended to purchase tickets, which are usually inexpensive (COP$20,000), in advance at a Tu Boleta outlet.

The **Sinfónica Nacional de Colombia** (www.sinfonica.com.co, tickets COP$60,000) often performs classical music at the spectacular **Teatro Mayor Julio Mario Santo Domingo** (Av. Cl. 170 No. 67-51, tel. 1/377-9840, www.teatromayor.com) in the western *localidad* of Suba.

At the **Sala de Conciertos Luis Ángel Arango** (Cl. 11 No. 4-14, tel. 1/381-2929, www.banrepcultural.org/musica, ticket office 1pm-8pm Mon.-Fri.) in La Candelaria, chamber music concerts featuring acclaimed international artists are regularly held in the company's spectacular modernist theater in the Biblioteca Luis Ángel Arango.

The **Ópera de Colombia** (tel. 1/608-8752 or 1/608-2860, www.operadecolombia.com), one of the few opera companies in South America, is highly regarded. They perform classic operas during their season, which usually extends from August to October. The **Teatro Jorge Eliécer Gaitán** (Cra. 7 No. 22-47, tel. 1/379-5750, ext. 213, www.teatrojorgeeliecer.gov.co) and the **Teatro Colón** (Cl. 10 No. 5-62, tel. 1/284-7420, www.teatrocolon.gov.co) are two classic venues that host opera performances, as well as other concerts and events.

Theater

The country's most prominent theater company, the **Teatro Nacional** (Cl. 71 No. 10-25, tel. 1/217-4577, www.teatronacional.com.co, tickets COP$70,000) has three different theaters in Bogotá, and regularly puts on comedic and dramatic productions. Their main theater, Teatro Nacional Fanny Mikey, is named in honor of beloved Argentinian actress Fanny Mikey, who moved to Bogotá and started its famed theater festival.

FESTIVALS AND EVENTS

Festival Iberoamericano de Teatro

Every even year during Holy Week, theater and dance take over the city during the **Festival Iberoamericano de Teatro** (www.festivaldeteatro.com.co). Attracting more than 100 prestigious international troupes and companies and over 170 representing Colombia, this festival is a living tribute to Fanny Mikey, an Argentinian actress who adopted Colombia as her home. She started the biennial affair in 1988. Known for her bright red hair and distinctive smile, she passed away in 2008. With over 800 performances in the span of two weeks, this is one of the largest such theater festivals in the world. The festival kicks off with a Saturday parade. There are always theater groups from English-speaking countries, and there are typically many circus and dance performances. To take a break from the show, you can always party at the **Carpa Cabaret** at night, where you can drink and dance alongside actors from across the globe. Besides performances in theaters, there is an impressive series of free performances in parks and plazas in neighborhoods across the city and workshops for acting students.

ArtBo

More than 50 art galleries representing 100 artists from the Americas converge on Bogotá each November during **ArtBo** (www.artboonline.com), known more formally as the **Feria Internacional de Arte de Bogotá,** one of the top contemporary art fairs in Latin America. It is held each year at the Corferias fairground (Cra. 40 No. 22C-67, www.corferias.com).

Feria de Artesanías

In December, and just in time for Christmas, the Corferias fairground (Cra. 40 No. 22C-67, www.corferias.com) is the setting for the fantastic—if overwhelming—**Feria de Artesanías** (www.expoartesanias.com). During two weeks, artisans come from across Colombia to showcase and sell their handicrafts. Many artisans, particularly indigenous peoples and Afro-Colombians from rural areas, have their trip to Bogotá sponsored by Artesanías de Colombia, the event's organizer. Most shoppers plan on multiple visits in order to see everything. The fair is also a great place for tasty Colombian snacks like *patacones* (fried plantains).

Gay Pride

Taking place during either the last weekend of June or first weekend of July and coinciding with a long weekend is Bogotá's **gay pride celebration.** The parade, called La Marcha, kicks off on a Sunday at noon from the Parque Nacional and makes its disorganized but festive way down the Séptima to the Plaza de Bolívar. Anyone can join in the parade. Bars and clubs host pride parties over the long weekend.

Music Festivals

Free music festivals take center stage at the Parque Simón Bolívar (between Clls. 53-63 and Cras. 48-68) during the latter half of the year. The most popular outdoor music festival is **Rock al Parque** (www.rockalparque.gov.co, July), the largest free outdoor rock festival in Latin America. Other festivals include **Gospel al Parque** (Aug.), **Hip Hop al Parque** (Oct.), **Salsa al Parque** (Nov.), and the Colombian music showcase of **Colombia al Parque** (Nov.).

International and Colombian jazz artists perform annually at the long-running **Festival Internacional de Jazz de Bogotá.** Most concerts are held at the **Teatro Libre** (Cl. 62 No. 9-65, tel. 1/217-1988) in Chapinero. The festival usually takes place in early September, with tickets available via Tu Boleta.

Shopping

LA CANDELARIA

The narrow streets of this main tourist neighborhood are lined with small shops specializing in Colombian *artesanías* (handicrafts), the quality of which ranges from trinkets to the refined.

For a fun stop while sightseeing, check out **Pasaje Rivas** (between Cras. 9-10 and Clls. 10-11), a bazaar that dates to the late 19th century. The passages are so narrow that it's impossible to not interact with carpenters selling furniture and women peddling hand-woven baskets and curios. For high-quality hand-carved utilitarian wood items and more, check out the shop of the **Escuela de Artes y Oficios Santo Domingo** (Cl. 10 No. 8-73), a well-regarded school for craftspeople.

AVENIDA JIMÉNEZ

Avenida Jiménez (Calle 13) is a pedestrian thoroughfare that also functions as the northern border of La Candelaria. It winds from Carrera 10 toward the mountains and Carrera 2. The surrounding city blocks are always bustling with shoppers and merchants peddling practically everything.

Surrounding the Plaza de San Victorino (Cras. 11-13 and Clls. 12-13) is the eponymous shopping area of **San Victorino,** known for its vibrant atmosphere and countless shops where locals head for deals on clothing and household goods.

To the north of Avenida Jiménez is a **used book market** (Cra 8A and Clls. 15-16), and on bustling Calle 19 are specialty shopping centers—including the multilevel **Centro Comercial Vía Libre** (Cl. 19 at Cra. 5), almost exclusively devoted to tattoo parlors. There are also some cafés that serve alcohol, providing liquid courage to the soon-to-be tattooed.

Colombia is one of the top emerald-producing countries in the world, and Bogotá is probably the best place in the country to pick up one of those gems. It would be wise to walk into jewelry stores armed with knowledge about gem quality and prices. To get that education, check out the **Museo Internacional de la Esmeralda** (Cl. 16 No. 6-66, tel. 1/286-4268, 10am-6pm Mon.-Sat.), then visit one of the many stores on the block of Carrera 6 between Calles 10 and 13.

Recommended places to peruse handicrafts include the dozens of small stalls in the **Galería de Artesanías Colombianas** (Cl. 16 between Cras. 5-7), across the street from the Museo del Oro, and the much finer (and more expensive) shop of **Artesanías de Colombia** (www.artesaniasdecolombia.com.co), which is managed by the same entity that hosts the amazing Feria de Artesanías every December. Hammocks, ceramics, woven goods, toys, and jewelry, all meticulously produced by skilled artisans from throughout the country, are sold at their shops. One location is on the grounds of the Iglesia Las Aguas (Cra. 2 No. 18A-58, tel. 1/284-3095, 9am-6pm Mon.-Fri.).

NORTHERN BOGOTÁ

The Zona Rosa, surrounded by upscale wealthy neighborhoods, is mostly known for its glitzy American-style shopping malls. These include the **Centro Comercial Andino** (Cra. 11 No. 82-71, tel. 1/621-3111, www.centroandino.com.co, 10am-8pm Mon.-Sat., noon-6pm Sun.), **El Retiro Centro**

hand-woven baskets for sale along Pasaje Rivas

Comercial (Cl. 81 No. 11-94, tel. 1/745-5545, www.elretirobogota.com, 10am-8pm Mon.-Sat., noon-6pm Sun.), and **Centro Comercial Atlantis Plaza** (Cl. 81 No. 13-05, tel. 1/606-6200, www.atlantisplaza.com, 8am-1am Mon.-Sat., 11am-1am Sun.). Here you will find dozens of Colombian and international clothing stores for all budgets and a smattering of other specialty shops (books, handicrafts, music, cosmetics, etc.).

Bogotá's high-end jewelers specialize in locally mined gold. In the Centro Comercial Andino are two of the city's best: **Liévano** (Cra. 11 No. 82-71, Local 157, tel. 1/616-8608, 10:45am-7:45pm Mon.-Sat.), which specializes in gold and emerald jewelry and high-end Swiss watches, and **Bauer** (Cra. 11 No. 82-71, tel. 1/478-5454, 11am-7pm Mon.-Sat.), which was founded by a German immigrant in 1893 and is popular for its wedding bands and other pieces of jewelry. **L.A. Cano** (Cra. 11 No. 82-51, shop 2-10, tel. 1/610-1175, 9am-8pm Mon.-Sat.) is known for its gold pre-Columbian motifs.

A short stroll from the Zona Rosa malls is a street dedicated almost exclusively to **antiques.** The **Calle de los Anticuarios** (Cl. 79A between Cras. 7-9) is lined by antique shops as well as some restaurants. **Cinco en Punto** (Cl. 79B No. 8-31, tel. 1/248-9798, 10am-6pm Mon.-Sat.) offers a range of curios, from vases to furniture. **Anticuario Novecento** (Cl. 79B No. 7-60, tel. 1/606-8616, www.anticuarionovecento.com, 10am-6:30pm Mon.-Sat.) has a wide collection that includes religious art from colonial Colombia along with Baccarat crystal from the 1930s. **Bolívar Old Prints** (Cl. 79B No. 7-46, tel. 1/695-5006, www.bolivaroldprints.com, 10:30am-6pm Mon.-Sat.) specializes in old maps from Latin America and is owned by a French expat.

The rich agricultural area of the savannah of Bogotá, on the outskirts of the city, is filled with flower farms. Flower markets in the city provide a glimpse of the country's floral diversity. About a 10-minute walk from the Zona Rosa in the **Parque El Virrey** (Cl. 86 at Cra. 15, daily) is a popular flower market of dozens of stalls. Near the market is a storefront of **Artesanías de Colombia** (Cl. 86A No. 13A-10, tel. 1/691-7149, www.artesaniasdecolombia.com.co, 10am-7pm Mon.-Sat., 11am-5pm Sun.).

Farther north in the colonial neighborhood of Usaquén is the **Mercado de las Pulgas Toldos de San Pelayo** (Cra. 7B No. 124-77, 8am-5pm Sun.), a large flea market held every Sunday. Here, you can expect to find handicrafts, antique furniture, artwork, and artisanal foods, among other items. Bargaining is acceptable and prices are reasonable.

BIKING

★ Ciclovía

At 7am every Sunday and on holidays, about 120 kilometers of Bogotá's roads are closed to vehicular traffic so that cyclists, joggers, dog walkers, skaters, and people-watchers can claim the streets. The **Ciclovía** started in the 1970s as a neighborhood initiative. Today it is an institution, and one of the few spaces in which people of all classes in Bogotá mix. On sunny days, over two million people have participated in the Ciclovía.

The event is most enjoyable on a bike, especially because you can cover a lot more of the city pedaling rather than walking. Two of the most popular routes are Avenida Séptima (Av. Cra. 7) and Carrera 15. It's an excellent way to see parts of the city that you might not have otherwise considered.

The Ciclovía is easy to figure out and do on your own. Helpful staff and volunteers are stationed along the entire route. Bike repair stations are located on all routes; they'll inflate flat tires for about COP$1,000.

The city's weather changes quickly, so pack a lightweight rain jacket and apply sunscreen. Vendors sell freshly squeezed orange juice along the way. Watch the time—at 2pm, the cars come roaring back.

Ciclopaseo de los Miércoles

On Wednesday nights, it's not uncommon to see more than a hundred cyclists of all ages and abilities taking a ride along the *ciclorutas* (bike paths) and streets of Bogotá. The **Ciclopaseo de los Miércoles** has been going strong for about seven years. The group typically meets at bike shops in Northern Bogotá. Find out about the next ride on their Facebook page. There is no charge to join the ride.

The Sunday Ciclovía is a Bogotá institution.

Bike Rentals

Some hostels and hotels have bicycles available to their guests for rent.

Bogotá Bike Tours (Cra. 3 No. 12-72, tel. 1/281-9924, www.bogotabiketours.com), run by the attentive American owner, Mike, is a popular agency based in La Candelaria.

An agency that works with many big hotels is **Bogotravel Tours** (tel. 1/ 282-6313, www.bogotraveltours.com). They have bikes for rent at the Hilton Hotel (Cra. 7 No. 72-41) and a downtown location (Cl. 16 No. 2-52). They also offer tours.

Laika Bikes (Cra. 4 No. 69-23, cell tel. 310/625-7170, www.laikabikes.com) is another bike store.

HIKING

Bogotá's city limits include a great expanse of rural areas. The mountains surrounding the city are just too inviting to not explore. There are more paths to conquer besides the one to the top of the **Cerro de Monserrate.**

Amigos de la Montaña (www.amigosdelamontana.org) is a group that maintains a couple of mountain trails in the Chapinero area. Most popular is the **Quebrada La Vieja** (Cl. 71 No. 1-45, 5am-9am Mon.-Sat., free), a path along a babbling brook up a mountain that leads to a statue of Mary. The return is by the same path, and it will take about two hours to make the round-trip. It is wildly popular with locals. To get to the beginning of the trail, take a cab. Or, if you're coming from Zona G on foot, walk east along the south side of Calle 72. Follow the sidewalk that parallels a stream until you reach the busy Circunvalar. Continue through the pedestrian tunnel, after which you'll find the entrance gate. No guide is needed for this hike.

Another group, **Camino Bogotano** (cell tel. 300/224-0289, www.caminobogotano.wordpress.com), regularly organizes hikes in the mountains around the city that you can join for COP$30,000. Reserve a spot on their website. Another organization, **Caminar Colombia** (tel. 1/366-3059, www.caminarcolombia.com, COP$45,000 incl. transportation), offers ecological walks, usually on Sunday. On the day of the hike, the group usually meets at 6:30am at the Los Héroes shopping center (Cra. 19A No. 78-85). The TransMilenio station there is called Los Héroes.

The city's environmental office organizes interesting guided **ecological walks** (tel. 1/377-8881, www.ambientebogota.gov.co/caminatas-ecologicas, free) throughout the city. It may take some time to sign up for the program and for a particular walk.

BIRD-WATCHING

Some serious bird-watching can be done right in the city, in and around the wetlands of the 200-acre **Parque La Florida** (Km. 2 Autopista Medellín, no phone, 7am-5pm daily, free) in western Bogotá. Two endemic species, the Bogotá rail and Apolinar's marsh-wren, are birds to keep an eye out for, but well over 100 species have been documented in the park.

Diana Balcázar, a wetlands bird expert and author of several books, offers interesting morning bird-watching excursions through **Birding Bogotá and Colombia** (cell tel. 310/249-5274, www.birdingbogotaand-colombia.com, hotel pickup included). Tours include a species checklist, breakfast and snacks, and an English-speaking guide.

TOURS

Walking Tours

The **Bogotá Tourism Office** (www.bogotaturismo.gov.co) offers a free two-hour walking tour of La Candelaria in Spanish (10am and 2pm daily) and in English (10am and 2pm Tues. and Thurs.). Tours start at the tourist information office on the southwest corner of the Plaza de Bolívar. To reserve your spot, stop by the office, call (tel. 1/555-7692), or email (informacionturistica@idt.gov.co) a day before you want to go.

One of the city's most popular tours is the **Graffiti Tour** (cell tel. 321/297-4075, www.bogotagraffiti.com, COP$20,000 requested donation). During about 1.5 hours, you'll take a walk through a world you might not have thought much about. Throughout La Candelaria and on the gritty downtown streets, there is some compelling street art to be seen. Tours are given in English by graffiti artists, who will offer their take on Colombian history and politics to boot. The tour's meeting point is usually at Parque de los Periodistas near Avenida Jiménez—but you'll be notified of the official spot upon making your reservation.

Bus Tours

If your time is limited and you're looking for an easy way to hit the main sights, consider a hop-on, hop-off bus tour. The green double-decker buses of **TurisBog** (El Retiro shopping mall, Entrance 3, tel. 1/467-4602, 9am-5:30pm Wed.-Sat., www.turisbog.com, adults COP$60,000) stop four times a day at each of the route's eight stops, including the Jardín Botánico, Parque de la 93, El Retiro mall, Cerro de Monserrate, the Museo Nacional, and La Candelaria. Included with your ticket is an audio guide and a map.

Bike Tours

If you'd like the camaraderie of a group of other visitors as you get to know the city and get in a little exercise, try one of the many excursions offered by **Bogotá Bike Tours** (Cra. 3 No. 12-72, tel. 1/281-9924, www.bogotabik-etours.com). The company offers bike tours around the city and many walking tours, such as an unusual graffiti tour.

Excursion Tours

Many hotels can arrange tours to attractions such as Zipaquirá and Laguna de Guatavita.

There are some extraordinary national natural parks (*parques nacional natural,* or PNN) quite close to Bogotá, making for excellent day hiking. Visits to these parks can be a bit difficult to organize without transportation or familiarity with the area. **Aventureros** (Cra. 15 No. 79-70, tel.

1/467-3837, www.aventureros.co) organizes mountain bike trips outside of Bogotá, for instance to the Desierto de Tatacoita near Nemocón. **Ecoglobal Expeditions** (tel. 1/579-3402, www.ecoglobalexpeditions.com) organizes excursions to destinations throughout Colombia, including the famous Caño Cristales and hikes in El Cocuy. They also can organize day trips to parks near Bogotá, such as the Parque Natural Nacional Sumapaz, containing the world's largest *páramo* (highland moor), and the PNN Chingaza. **Colombia Oculta** (tel. 1/630-3172, ext. 112, cell tel. 311/239-7809, www.colombiaoculta.org) is a similar organization, with similar destinations.

Food

The Bogotá dish par excellence is *ajiaco*. This is a hearty potato and chicken soup, seasoned with the herb *guascas*. On a dreary day, there's nothing better. Heated debate can arise about what else to include in the soup. A small piece of corn on the cob usually bobs in the soup, as does a dollop of cream, but capers and avocado slices are controversial additions.

Having just a tiny Asian population, Colombia doesn't have dazzling Asian cuisine, but you'll be pleasantly surprised at the variety in Bogotá.

Reservations are helpful on weekend evenings. Restaurant staff will be more than happy to order a cab for you by phone.

Tap water in Bogotá—*de la llave*—is perfectly safe and good tasting.

LA CANDELARIA

Colombian

The classic place for a huge tamale and a hot chocolate, the **Puerta Falsa** (Cl. 11 No. 6-50, tel. 1/286-5091, 7am-10pm Mon.-Fri., 8am-8pm Sat.-Sun., COP$18,000) claims to be one of the oldest operating restaurants in Bogotá, having opened in 1816. It gets crowded here.

★ **El Mejor Ajiaco del Mundo** (Cl. 11 No. 6-20, tel. 1/566-6948, 11am-7pm Mon.-Fri., noon-6pm Sat., COP$15,000) lives up to its name, which means "the best *ajiaco* in the world." The restaurant's large bowls of *ajiaco* stew are beloved by locals.

International

With exposed beams adding to an unpretentious atmosphere, **Capital Cocina y Café** (Cl. 10 No. 2-99, tel. 1/342-0426, noon-3pm and 6:30pm-9:30pm Mon.-Fri., 4pm-10pm Sat., COP$24,000) serves surprisingly sophisticated dishes at reasonable prices, offering Colombian cuisine as well as dishes like pork ribs and seafood salad. It is vegetarian friendly, and there is often a fish-of-the-day special.

Prudencia (Cra. 2 No. 11-34, tel. 1/394-1678, www.prudencia.net, noon-4pm Mon.-Fri., 12:30pm-5:30pm Sat., COP$28,000) boasts of serving *comida campesina* (country food) from around the world. It's rather elegant for La Candelaria, with an open kitchen and chandeliers. Daily specials depend on what's in season, and there are always vegetarian (and sometimes gluten-free) options. This spot is only open during the week.

Vegetarian

Using Andean ingredients, the tiny **Quinoa y Amaranto** (Cl. 11 No. 2-95, tel. 1/565-9982, 8am-4pm Mon., 8am-9pm Tues.-Fri., 8am-5pm Sat.) is a cozy downtown haven for vegetarians. With three-course lunches for around COP$16,000, it offers bang for your buck.

Pizza

Go find mother if you want pizza in La Candelaria—**Madre** (Cl. 12 No. 5-83, tel. 1/281-2332, www.madre.la, 8pm-2am Mon.-Sat., COP$29,000), that is. The *jamón serrano* pizza gets high marks, along with the gin ice cream. With its great drinks and live music on Friday nights, this spot is bringing cool back to La Candelaria.

Cajun

Cajun food is the thing at **La Condesa Irina Lazaar** (Cra. 6 No. 10-19, tel. 1/283-1573, lunch Mon.-Sat., COP$35,000). This tiny, American-run spot is easy to miss, but if you are in the mood for pork chops or crab cakes, this is the place. There are only six tables, so it's best to make reservations. If you can persuade him, the friendly owner might open the restaurant for you for dinner.

Cafés, Bakeries, and Quick Bites

Preisz Pastelería (Cra. 4 No. 9-66, tel. 1/481-8544, 8am-6pm Mon.-Fri., 10am-4pm Sun., COP$14,000) bakes their own bread, and is a cheerful and inexpensive spot for sandwiches and salads. They also serve yerba maté drinks and homemade *alfajores* (sandwich-style cookies with dulce de leche in the middle).

Set in a funky house with an interior patio and nooks for relaxing, ★ **Chez Dom** (Cl. 9 No. 3-11, tel. 1/342-8266, 10am-9:30pm Mon.-Sat., COP$15,000) is a French café that also serves healthy lunches. A small organic market adjoins this cute spot.

AVENIDA JIMÉNEZ AND CENTRO INTERNACIONAL

Colombian

For a hearty meal of *mamona* (grilled meat), run to **Asadero Capachos** (Cl. 18 No. 4-68, tel. 1/243-4607, www.asaderocapachos.com, 11:30am-3:30pm Tues.-Thurs., 11:30am-5pm Fri.-Sun.), an authentic *llanero* (cowboy) restaurant. For under COP$20,000 you get a healthy portion of tender, slow-grilled meat, fried yuca, and a *maduro* (fried plantain), which all goes down well with a beer. On weekends they have live music and dance performances. Vegetarians will have a difficult—but not impossible—time here.

Fish soups, shrimp cocktails, and *arepas de huevo* (corn cakes filled with egg) are some of the dishes on the menu at **Misia by Leo Espinosa** (Transversal 6 No. 27-50, tel. 1/795-4748, 9am-10pm Mon.-Sat., 9am-4pm Sun., COP$25,000). They do fantastic breakfasts and brunches, and you must try the loquat milkshake. Misia is near the Ibis Hotel and Museo Nacional.

Specializing in cuisine from the agricultural region of Boyacá, ★ **Doña Elvira** (Cra. 6 No. 29-08, www.restaurantedonaelvira.com, noon-4pm Mon.-Sat.) serves hearty soups, like *ajiaco*, and lots of potatoes, corn, and beans, as well as dishes like fried catfish. This restaurant has been in the same family since 1934.

Set in what appears to be a crumbling old house is one of the gems of downtown Bogotá. ★ **A Seis Manos** (Cl. 22 No. 8-60, tel. 1/282-8441, 11:30am-11:30pm Mon.-Sat., COP$24,000) has delicious lunches of Colombian-Mediterranean fusion with a lot of flair. At night it's a major cultural center, with DJs, performances, film screenings, and language exchanges. Visit their Facebook page to find upcoming events.

On a quiet street behind the Museo Nacional, ★ **Donostia** (Cl. 29 Bis No. 5-84, tel. 1/287-3943, noon-4pm Mon., noon-4pm and 7pm-11pm Tues.-Sat., COP$30,000) is a swanky place for tapas and wine. They serve Spanish-Colombian cuisine.

Mexican

In Parque Bavaria, **San Lorenzo** (Cra. 13 No. 28A-21, tel. 1/288-8731, 11am-4pm Mon.-Fri., COP$23,000), on the 4th floor of the old Bavaria brewery, packs in the banking crowd at lunch. This restaurant serves consistently good Mexican food. Sometimes mariachis will serenade diners.

International

In the Macarena neighborhood, it's all about Swedish-style meatballs at innovative **Köttbullar** (Cl. 26C No. 3-05, tel. 1/620-1632, www.kottbullar.co, noon-4:30pm Sun. and Tues., noon-10:30pm Wed.-Sat., COP$19,000), where the dish is served in a multitude of preparations and sauces. The meatballs go well with a locally brewed beer, and Köttbullar even serves some veggie variations on the meatball. This is a cool place.

Breakfast

Pastelería La Florida (Cra. 7 No. 21-46, tel. 1/341-0340, 6am-9pm daily, COP$16,000) is a local institution, a Colombian version of a greasy spoon. Breakfast is big here; options include tamales, eggs, waffles a la mode, and hot chocolate.

Cafés, Bakeries, and Quick Bites

Andante Ma Non Troppo (Cra. 5 No. 26C-57, tel. 1/284-4387, 8am-8pm Mon.-Sat., 8am-3pm Sun., COP$16,000) is a long-running café that serves breakfast, sandwiches, and salads in one of the most iconic buildings in Bogotá, the Torres del Parque. It's more atmospheric than memorable.

Crepes & Waffles (Av. Jiménez No. 4-55, tel. 1/676-7600, www.crepesywaffles.com.co, noon-8:30pm Mon.-Sat., noon-5pm Sun.) is a chain found all over Colombia. Fill up on a *crepe de sal* (savory crepe) for around COP$18,000, or order a mini-waffle with Nutella and vanilla ice cream. This location is in the easy-on-the-eyes Monserrate building on the Eje Ambiental.

CHAPINERO

Colombian

Las Margaritas (Cl. 62 No. 7-77, tel. 1/249-9468, noon-4pm Tues.-Fri., 8am-5pm Sat.-Sun., COP$15,000) has been around for over a century. Try the *puchero,* a meaty stew, on Thursday. The *ajiaco* (chicken and potato soup) is also good.

For the best of original coastal cuisine, try friendly **MiniMal** (Cra. 4A No. 57-52, tel. 1/347-5464, www.mini-mal.org, noon-3pm and 7pm-10pm Mon.-Wed., noon-3pm and 7pm-11pm Thurs., noon-11pm Fri.-Sat., COP$25,000). The stingray *cazuela* (stew) is one of the more exotic items on the menu. There's also a funky gift shop.

Latin American

In a cool setting of exposed brick walls and minimalist design is **Cantina y Punto** (Cl. 66 No. 4A-33, tel. 1/644-7766, noon-10pm Mon.-Sat., noon-6pm Sun., COP$32,000). Top menu items include duck mole, fried tuna, and thirst-quenching margaritas and other tequila drinks.

Classy **Astrid & Gastón** (Cra. 7 No. 67-64, tel. 1/211-1400, www.astridygastonbogota.com, noon-3pm and 7pm-11pm Mon.-Sat., COP$50,000), direct from Lima, and stylish **Rafael** (Cl. 70 No. 4-65, tel. 1/255-4138, 12:30pm-3pm and 7:30pm-11pm Mon.-Sat., COP$45,000) are rivals for the top Peruvian spot in town. At Astrid, try an only-in-Colombia *coca* pisco sour. **La Despensa de Rafael** (Cl. 70A No. 9-95, tel. 1/235-8878, www.rafaelosterling.pe, 12:30pm-3:30pm and 7:30pm-11pm Mon.-Sat., noon-4pm Sun., COP$38,000) is a Peruvian-fusion bistro in Quinta Camacho run by Rafael.

Arepas La Reina (Cra. 6 No. 57-15, tel. 1/605-1877, 10am-7pm Mon.-Sat.) serves arepas filled with black beans, grilled chicken, or beef with avocado and cheese, just like in Caracas, Venezuela. It's enough for lunch.

International

Salvo Patria (Cra. 54A No. 4-13, tel. 1/702-6367, www.salvopatria.com noon-11pm Mon.-Sat., COP$22,000) is inventive and trendy, serving both Colombian and international cuisine. There's a variety of interesting appetizers, sandwiches, meaty main courses, and vegetarian options. You'll be tempted to try a carafe of gin *lulada* (a drink made with the juice of a *lulo,* a tangy fruit). There's a daily lunch special.

Dishes at **Villanos en Bermudas** (Cl. 56 No. 5-21, tel. 1/211-1259, 7pm-11pm Tues.-Sat., COP$80,000) are works of art. This small-plates place is one of the city's most creative dining spots. Its chefs use fresh, local ingredients in the experimental tasting menu of eight small dishes. You'd never know judging by its ordinary exterior.

★ **Franca** (Cl. 56 No. 6-33, cell tel. 316/880-1627, noon-3pm and 6pm-9pm Mon.-Fri., noon-midnight Sat., noon-6pm Sun., COP$28,000) is a bistro in Chapinero Alto that has great burgers (and veggie burgers) and emanates neighborhood charm. On Sundays they have a barbecue that is also vegetarian friendly.

French

French restaurant **Criterión** (Cl. 69A No. 5-75, tel. 1/310-1377, noon-4pm and 7pm-11pm Mon.-Sat., 9am-1pm and 7pm-11pm Sun., COP$60,000) is the standard-bearer when it comes to haute cuisine in Bogotá. It is the creation of the Rausch brothers, who are among the top chefs in the city.

Tapas

The small, unassuming **Nueve** (Cl. 70A No. 10A-18, noon-4pm and 7pm-midnight Mon.-Sat., COP$42,000) is actually quite sophisticated, serving small plates. Coconut rice cakes with grilled prawns in a lemongrass sauce is a favorite here. Fantastic wines from across the globe are available by the glass.

Italian

Giuseppe Verdi (Cl. 58 No. 5-35, tel. 1/211-5508, noon-11pm Mon.-Sat., noon-9pm Sun., COP$20,000) has been around for over four decades, serving typical Italian dishes featuring house-made pasta. They have added a small terrace café for more informal meals or a glass of wine.

★ **Trattoría de la Plaza** (Cl. 66 No. 22-45, 2nd fl., tel. 1/211-1740, noon-5pm Sat.-Thurs., noon-10pm Fri., COP$48,000) is a sophisticated Italian restaurant that boasts superb presentation and a wide range of wines. Reservations are required at this elegant lunch place.

At **La Divina Comedia** (Cl. 71 No. 5-93, tel. 1/317-6987, noon-3:30pm and 7pm-11pm Mon.-Sat., COP$30,000), go for the divine *tortellata* (a mix of stuffed pastas).

Lebanese

Despite its location on the busy speedway of Carrera 5, intimate **Zátar** (Cra. 5 No. 69-15, tel. 1/317-8974, noon-3:30pm and 6pm-9pm Mon., noon-3:30pm and 6pm-10pm Tues.-Fri., noon-10pm Sat., COP$24,000) is one of the city's best places for Lebanese cuisine.

Asian

The pan-Asian chain **Wok** (Cra. 9 No. 69A-63, tel. 1/212-0167, www.wok.com.co, noon-11pm Mon.-Sat., noon-8pm Sun., COP$23,000) is hard to beat. Don't let the fact that it is a chain dissuade you: The menu is astoundingly extensive, inventive, and fresh. Hearty fish soups and curries based in coconut milk will warm you up, and there are numerous vegetarian dishes, such as a Vietnamese-inspired grilled tofu sandwich. The quality of their sushi is also good. Wok is an environmentally and socially responsible company, working with family farmers and fishers in small communities throughout Colombia. A second location is in the Museo Nacional (Cra. 6 Bis No. 29-07, tel. 1/287-3194) in Centro Internacional.

Vegetarian

Don't be turned off by the name: ★ **Hippie** (Cl. 56 No. 4A-15, tel. 1/675-7154, www.hippie.com.co, 11:30am-11pm Mon.-Fri, 9am-11pm Sat., 9am-5pm Sun., COP$24,000) serves delicious food, and even the most button-downed diners will feel at ease at this cute place in Chapinero Alto. Many menu items have organic ingredients, and there are many vegan and vegetarian dishes. They sell crystals and incense next door.

Burgers

Gordo (Cra. 4A No. 66-84, tel. 1/345-5769, noon-11pm daily, COP$22,000) excels at the basics of hamburgers and french fries. The fried pickles get high marks.

Breakfast and Brunch

Árbol de Pan (Cl. 66 Bis No. 4-63, tel. 1/481-7465, 8am-8pm Mon.-Sat.) is known for almond croissants, mimosas, and brunch.

NORTHERN BOGOTÁ

Colombian

At ★ **Fulanitos 81** (Cl. 81 No. 10-56, tel. 1/622-2175, lunch daily, COP$20,000) there is always a line at lunchtime, and for good reason: This is Cali cuisine at its best. Try the *chuletas de cerdo* (pork chops) or *sancocho* (soup), and have a refreshing *lulada* (a drink made with the juice of a *lulo*, a tart tropical fruit).

For a crash course in Colombian cuisine in an elegant atmosphere, visit **Casa Club Colombia** (Cl. 82 No. 9-11, tel. 1/744-9077, noon-midnight daily, COP$28,000). In a lovely house from the mid-20th century, where the fireplace is always lit, *bandeja paisa* (dish of beans, various meats, yuca, and potatoes) and favorites from all corners of the country are on the menu. This is a great brunch option on weekends.

It's always a celebration at **Andrés Carne de Res,** an obligatory stop for all visitors to Colombia. Music, costumed waiters, samples of Colombian food from across the country, drinks, and dancing is what it's all about here. The original location is **Andrés** (Cl. 3 No. 11A-56, tel. 1/863-7880, noon-3am Thurs.-Sat., noon-11pm Sun., COP$50,000) in the countryside of Chía, about 45 minutes from Bogotá. A more convenient location is **Andrés D.C.** (Cl. 82 No. 12-21, tel. 1/863-7880, noon-midnight Sun.-Wed., noon-3am Thurs.-Sat., COP$35,000), in town. Look for the windmills next to the El Retiro mall. **La Plaza de Andrés** (Cl. 82 No. 11-75, 8am-9pm Mon.-Thurs.,

10am-10pm Sat.-Sun., COP$25,000) is also in the mall. It offers the color and diversity of cuisine of the original, but without the raucous atmosphere. This location doesn't have table service, but it's still pretty fun.

Welcome to Bogotá's version of Santa Marta. **Gaira Cumbia Café** (Cra. 13 No. 96-11A, tel. 1/746-2696, www.gairacafe.com, 9am-10pm Mon.-Wed., 9am-2am Thurs., 9am-3am Fri.-Sat., 9am-6pm Sun., COP$25,000) specializes in good Caribbean cuisine that's popular with locals. Musician Guillermo Vives and his mom run the show here, and Guillo often performs. He is the brother of Carlos Vives, the multiple Grammy Award-winning *vallenato* singer. On weekend mornings there are special activities for children, while on weekend nights, reservations are essential, and there may be a cover for live music events. The line between dining and partying gets rather blurry as the night wears on.

Latin American

Delicious margaritas, a fun atmosphere, and tasty tacos are the order of the day or night at ★ **Gringo Cantina** (Cl. 80 No. 12A-29, tel. 1/622-2906, noon-11pm Mon.-Thurs., noon-1am Fri.-Sat., noon-6pm Sun., COP$32,000), a colorful spot that looks like it belongs on a laid-back beach in Mexico. It's popular with gringos and locals alike.

International

Harry Sasson (Cra. 9 No. 75-70, tel. 1/347-7155, noon-midnight Mon.-Sat., noon-5pm Sun., COP$35,000) is named for a celebrity Colombian chef. In a gorgeous house refitted with modern touches, this contemporary classic is a favorite among the city's power players. (You can tell by the serious-looking bodyguards waiting outside in their SUVs.) Try the chestnut prawns. And go for a Hendrick's gin and tonic—a favorite among this crowd.

In a fantastic setting bordering a park, **Black Bear** (Cra. 11A No. 89-06, tel. 1/644-7766, noon-11pm Mon.-Sat., noon-6pm Sun., COP$36,000)

Andrés Carne de Res

packs guests in around its boisterous bar, satisfying appetites with grilled octopus, hearty burgers, and smart cocktails.

European

Not even a sign can be seen at minimalist ★ **Klaas** (Cl. 77A No. 12-26, tel. 1/530-5074, noon-11pm Mon.-Sat., COP$45,000), a restaurant run by a Belgian chef. The weekly menu offers just a few three-course options. It's mostly French-inspired cuisine, and specialties often include *coq au vin* and salmon lasagna. There is always a vegetarian menu, and the wines are thoughtfully paired. In the evenings, look for the candlelit tables on this quiet street 10 minutes from the Centro Comercial Andino.

Italian

At unpretentious **Trattoría San Giorgio** (Cl. 81 No. 8-81, tel. 1/212-3962, noon-10:30pm Mon.-Sat., noon-6pm Sun., COP$22,000), Italian regulars are often found sipping wine and enjoying a multicourse meal.

DiLucca (Cra. 13 No. 85-32, tel. 1/257-4269, noon-midnight daily, COP$25,000) turns out consistently good pastas and pizzas, and also offers delivery. The atmosphere is rather lively inside.

Julia (Cl. 85 No. 12-81, tel. 1/530-2115, noon-10pm daily, COP$30,000) serves delicious thin-crust gourmet pizzas. This spot doesn't disappoint.

Asian

★ **Izakaya** (Cra. 13 No. 82-74, 3rd fl., tel. 1/622-5980, noon-10:30pm Mon.-Sat., noon-8:30 Sun., COP$30,000) is a fantastic Japanese restaurant in the Zona T. Here you feel like you're in Tokyo—except the friendly waitstaff speak Spanish. Izakaya serves small, beautifully presented dishes and sake.

Excellent service awaits at sleek **Watakushi** (Cra. 12 No. 83-17, tel. 1/744-9097, noon-3pm and 6pm-11pm Mon.-Thurs., noon-11pm Fri.-Sat., noon-5pm Sun., COP$35,000), one of the many restaurants operated by local restaurant wizard Leo Katz. Reservations are needed on weekends.

Don't let the lack of decor and plastic chairs at **Arigato** (Cl. 80 No. 11-28, tel. 1/248-0764, www.restaurantearigato.com, 11am-9pm Mon.-Sat., COP$25,000) turn you off. The food at this family-run Japanese restaurant is authentic. The fresh fish is flown in regularly from the Pacific coast.

★ **Señor Kim** (Cl. 78 No. 12-09, cell tel. 300/218-8175, noon-3pm and 5pm-8pm Mon.-Fri., 1pm-7pm Sat., COP$18,000) is a sweet Korean place run by a friendly Korean-Colombian couple. It's small but popular, and soups like *kimchi jjigae* and noodle dishes like *japchae* are fantastic.

Indian

There are few Indian restaurants in Bogotá, but of those, **Flor de Loto** (Cl. 85 No. 19A-24, tel. 1/383-7543, noon-3pm and 6pm-9pm Mon.-Sat., COP$24,000) is probably the best. The head chef is originally from the Punjab region of India, and this cash-only place feels authentic.

Burgers

Agadón Burger Bar (Cra. 13 No. 85-75, tel. 1/255-4138, noon-10pm Mon.-Sat., noon-6pm Sun., COP$20,000) will leave you satisfied. It's run by a pair of Israelis, and features portobello burgers on the menu. It's across from the Four Seasons.

Vegetarian and Vegan

★ **Raw** (Cra. 12A No. 78-54, cell tel. 304/335-9578, www.hoymesientoraw.com, 8:30am-8:30pm Mon.-Fri., 8:30pm-4pm Sat., COP$22,000) offers fresh and delectable vegan dishes. This delightful café has a daily three-course lunch special, a la carte menu items, and smoothies.

For a delicious vegetarian lunch (usually with a soup of the day, main course, juice, and dessert) or a veggie burger and fries, head to cheerful **VG Tal** (Cra. 12A No. 79-26, tel. 1/316-3538, 9am-7pm Mon.-Fri., 9am-5pm Sat., COP$20,000), on a quiet side street near the Atlantis Plaza shopping mall.

Cafés and Quick Bites

When it comes to *onces* (Colombian tea time), **Myriam Camhi** (Cl. 81 No. 8-08, tel. 1/345-1819, 7am-8pm daily, COP$18,000) takes the cake. The *napoleón de Arequipe* and chocolate flan satisfy a sweet tooth, but healthy breakfasts and lunches, including a decent salad bar, are also featured. Across the street is **Brot Café** (Cl. 81 No. 7-93, tel. 1/347-6916, 7:30am-7pm daily, COP$16,000), a neighborhood spot that does breakfasts, including large fresh fruit bowls and tasty chocolate baguettes. It's open for lunch, but is more popular late in the afternoon.

With benches set up outside, **Siuka** (Cl. 79A No. 8-82, tel. 1/248-3765, 9am-7pm Mon.-Sat., 11am-5pm Sun., COP$14,000) is a welcome midmorning or late-afternoon place to meet for brownies and a barley tea.

If you can find ★ **Les Amis Bizcochería** (Cra. 14 No. 86A-12, tel. 1/236-2124, 8:30am-7:30pm Mon.-Fri., 9am-6pm Sat.), you'll love it. This bakery-café makes delicious French and Colombian pastries and has a couple of tables for clients. It's on the 2nd floor of an ordinary-looking apartment building.

★ **Brown** (Calle 77A No. 12-26, tel. 1/248-0409, www.brownesunare-posteria.com, 11am-6pm Mon.-Fri., 11am-4pm Sat.) is intimate and cute as a button and has a light lunch menu (half a sandwich, soup, salad, and drink for COP$16,500) and scrumptious brownies. There are about four tables outside and a couple inside.

Build your own salad, or just stop by for pastry and dessert at **Masa** (Cl. 81 No. 9-12, tel. 1/466-1552, noon-9pm Mon., 7am-9pm Tues.-Fri., 8:30am-9pm Sat., 8:30am-5pm Sun., COP$23,000), a corner restaurant with pleasant open-air seating.

Accommodations

Many visitors choose to stay in the colonial center of La Candelaria, as there is a wealth of hostels along the neighborhood's narrow streets. This area is very quiet, so nighttime incidents of crime are not unheard of. Be cautious when out late at night in this area.

Increasing options are available in other parts of the city for travelers of all budgets and interests. Neighborhoods such as Chapinero Alto (the eastern side of the Séptima in Chapinero) and Zona G are home to cool restaurants and close to easy transportation options on Carrera 7 (the Séptima). For getting around, it's good to be close to that important artery. The same could be said for Avenida Calle 26 (Av. El Dorado), a major thoroughfare that has easy transportation links to the rest of the city.

Some of the best hotels in Bogotá are well-known international luxury brands. There are two superb **Four Seasons** hotels: the **Four Seasons Bogotá** (Cra. 13 No. 85–46) and the **Four Seasons Casa Medina** (Cra. 7 No. 69A-22) near Zona G. Comfort and attention at these cannot be beat. **Hilton** (Cra. 7 No. 72-41) and **JW Marriott** (Cl. 73 No. 8-60) are neighbors along the Séptima not far from Zona G. The **Marriott** (Av. Cl. 26 No. 69B-53), meanwhile, is located on Avenida Calle 26 toward the airport. The **W Bogotá** (Av. Cra. 9 No. 115-30), near Usaquén, is the headquarters of cool when it comes to hotels in Bogotá.

Weekend rates are often less expensive in hotels that cater to business travelers, and may drop even further on *puentes* (long weekends).

LA CANDELARIA

Travelers on a budget will find plentiful friendly options in La Candelaria close to all the important sights. It can feel a little desolate late at night, and there are occasional reports of crime, so be alert.

Under COP$70,000

★ **Fernweh Photography Hostel** (Cra. 2 No. 9-46, tel. 1/281-0218, www.fernwehostel.com, COP$37,000 dorm, COP$110,000 triple w/shared bath) is very cool and laid-back. Stunning photos of Colombia adorn the walls. There are peaceful common areas, including a relaxing backyard patio. A fluffy dog called Wolf protects the guests. Daylong photography workshops are offered for COP$300,000. The two dorm rooms have nine and four beds, and there are two private rooms.

At **Alegria's Hostel** (Cl. 9 No. 2-13, tel. 1/282-3168, cell tel. 313/419-1288, www.alegriashostel.com, COP$35,000 dorm, COP$65,000 d) there are ample common areas with hammocks, and some cozy private rooms with fireplaces. There's a big dorm room with 10 beds and a smaller one with 4 beds.

Set in an old house in La Candelaria overflowing with rustic charm, **Anandamayi Hostel and Hotel** (Cl. 9 No. 2-81, tel. 1/341-7208, cell tel. 315/215-5778, www.anandamayihostel.com, COP$40,000 dorm,

COP$140,000 d shared bath) has three interior patios bursting with plants, flowers, and the occasional hummingbird. The atmosphere is warm, despite the chilly nights. There is one large dorm room with 10 beds. The rest of the rooms are private, mostly with shared baths.

Masaya Intercultural (Cra. 2 No. 12-48, tel. 1/747-1848, www.masaya-experience.com, COP$36,000 dorm, COP$110,000 d) near LaSalle University offers different accommodation options depending on your budget or style, from luxurious private rooms to dorms. Guests and students congregate by the bar and restaurant area in front. The common areas, which include outdoor patios, can be social, so bring earplugs. The two dorms rooms have four and six beds and privacy curtains, and there are six private rooms. The staff has tons of information on activities to keep guests occupied.

COP$70,000-200,000

★ **Casa Platypus** (Cra. 3 No. 12F-28, tel. 1/281-1801, www.casaplatypusbogota.com, COP$47,000 dorm, COP$189,000 triple) is a comfortable, clean, and friendly guesthouse with 17 rooms. The rooftop terrace is an excellent place to unwind with a glass of wine after a day hitting the streets. Breakfast gets good marks. Platypus is run by Germán, who was one of the first people to set up a hostel in Bogotá, back when only the intrepid dared to visit. The dorm rooms (only four beds apiece) don't have bunks, which makes late-night arrivals less disruptive.

The **Abadía Colonial** (Cl. 11 No. 2-32, tel. 1/341-1884, www.abadiacolonial.com, COP$150,000 s, COP$200,000 d), an Italian-run midrange option with 12 rooms, is pleasantly quiet around the interior patio. The on-site restaurant specializes in Italian cuisine.

There are 18 rooms at ★ **Apartaestudios La Candelaria** (Cl. 10 No. 2-40, tel. 1/281-6923, www.apartaestudioscandelaria.com, COP$160,000 d), a good and spacious option for those wanting solitude.

COP$200,000-500,000

★ **Hotel de la Ópera** (Cl. 10 No. 5-72, tel. 1/336-2066, www.hotelopera.com.co, COP$350,000 d) still reigns as the luxury place to stay in La Candelaria. The hotel comprises two converted homes, one Republican style and one colonial. There are two restaurants, including a rooftop spot that has one of the best views downtown. The hotel also offers a spa. You can expect very professional service here.

Casa Deco (Cl. 12C No. 2-36 tel. 1/283-7032, www.hotelcasadeco.com, COP$192,000 d) is a nicely refurbished art deco building with 21 well-appointed and spacious, if somewhat chilly, rooms. The terrace is an excellent place for relaxing on a late afternoon.

CENTRO INTERNACIONAL

The TransMilenio line on the Séptima has played a major role in transforming this area into a walkable and well-situated place to stay while discovering the city. There are only a few accommodation options in this neighborhood. The area is perfectly safe during the day, but you'll want to avoid walking around late at night.

COP$70,000-200,000

In the heart of the Centro Internacional, few surprises are in store at ★ **Ibis Museo** (Transversal 6 No. 27-85, tel. 1/381-4666, www.ibishotel.com, COP$120,000), part of a French budget hotel chain. Across from the Museo Nacional, the hotel has 200 small but adequate rooms and a 24-hour restaurant (breakfast not included). Good restaurants like Leo Cocina are nearby, and it's close to all downtown attractions. Just avoid nighttime strolls in this area. This is a nice place to be on Ciclovía Sundays, although they don't provide bikes for guests.

CHAPINERO

Halfway between La Candelaria and the Zona Rosa is Chapinero, straddling either side of the Séptima. On the eastern side of the Séptima is **Chapinero Alto,** a tree-lined residential neighborhood where small, trendy restaurants are cropping up. Stay in this area if you're looking for quiet but still want to be close to the action—either end of town is just a short bus ride away. The western side of the Séptima is a bit grittier and is populated mostly by mom-and-pop shops. There's some activity here at night, as there is a group of gay bars around the Plaza de Lourdes (Cra. 13 and Av. Cl. 63).

Under COP$70,000

A relative newcomer to the area, having opened in 2014, **12:12** (Cl. 67 No. 4-16, tel. 1/467-2656, cell tel. 317/635-4047, www.1212hostels.com.co, COP$38,000 dorm, COP$138,000 d) earns praise from budget travelers who appreciate this hostel's cleanliness, comfort, and attention to details like privacy curtains for beds in the dorm rooms. Some of the dorm rooms are large, with 8-10 beds. It has a nice location near the Zona G restaurant area, and cool, cheery decor in the common areas. There are just two private rooms here.

Mi Llave Hostel (Cra. 10A No. 67-29, cell tel. 316/805-1661, www.millavehostels.com, COP$35,000 dorm, COP$130,000 d) opened in 2015, and has a cute patio in back and good coffee. It's in a great location close to the Zona G.

COP$70,000-200,000

The Viaggio chain has nine reasonably priced furnished apartment buildings in Bogotá. **Viaggio 6.1.7.** (Cl. 61 No. 7-18, tel. 1/744-9999, www.viaggio.com.co, COP$131,000 d) is a high-rise centrally located on the Séptima. Rooms have tiny kitchenettes, but breakfast is included in the price. You can rent rooms on a daily, weekly, or monthly basis.

Classical music fills the air at intimate **6 Suites** (Cra. 3B No. 64A-06, tel. 1/752-9484, cell tel. 315/851-1427, www.6suiteshotel.com, COP$139,000 d), which has exactly that number of rooms in a small house. Some packages include a dinner of Argentine cuisine. There is a Saturday vegetable and fruit market in a small park next to the house, as well as a round-the-clock police station.

On a quiet street but within easy walking distance to restaurants and public transportation, the **Casona del Patio** (Cra. 8 No. 69-24, tel. 1/212-8805, www.casonadelpatio.com, COP$127,000 d) is a comfortable and economical choice, especially for its high-end address. Many of the 24 rooms (several with two twin beds) have natural light and wooden floors.

Two small hotels in appealing English Tudor-style houses make the grade for those on a quest for charm. Near the trendy Chapinero Alto neighborhood, ★ **The Book Hotel** (Cra. 5 No. 57-79, tel. 1/745-9988, www.thebookhotel.co, COP$150,000 d) offers 27 comfortable rooms and a pleasant lobby filled with books.

With just 10 rooms, the **Matisse Hotel** (Cl. 67 No. 6-55, tel. 1/212-0177, cell tel. 300/463-5053, www.matissehotel.com, COP$150,000 d) is a five-minute walk to the Zona G and very close to the busy Séptima. Some rooms may not have windows—or ones that open.

WESTERN BOGOTÁ

There are several international chain hotels close to the airport along Avenida Calle 26 (Av. El Dorado). With a TransMilenio line on this broad, tree-lined thoroughfare, it's easy to hop on one of the red buses and spend the day visiting the major sights in La Candelaria. There are few points of interest in this neighborhood, but there is the **Gran Estación mall** (Av. El Dorado No. 62-47). Plus, along the Avenida and the TransMilenio line is a pleasant bike route and jogging path.

COP$70,000-200,000

In the old, tree-lined neighborhood of La Soledad is the 13-room, family-run **Hotel Parkway Bogotá** (Av. Cra. 24 No. 39B-32, tel. 1/288-5090, www.hotelparkway.com.co, COP$103,000 s, COP$146,000 d). It's ripe for a renovation, but it's friendly. Larger rooms are in the main house, up a retro spiral staircase, with smaller rooms surrounding a huge lawn in back. It's about 15 minutes to La Candelaria from here. Within walking distance are some cafés and cultural centers.

The ★ **Aloft Hotel** (Av. Cl. 26 No. 92-32, tel. 1/742-7070, www.starwoodhotels.com/aloft hotels, COP$169,999 d) is stylish and modern, offering an excellent breakfast buffet with a view, as well as a large lawn set against a backdrop of skyline and mountains. It's in an odd location in a business park, but it is within five minutes of the airports. There are 142 rooms in this property. It's about a five-minute walk to the Portal El Dorado TransMilenio station.

NORTHERN BOGOTÁ

Uptown is a good option if comfort trumps budget and you want to be close to loads of excellent restaurants.

Under COP$70,000

Within walking distance of restaurants and shopping is **Chapinorte Bogotá Guesthouse** (Cl. 79 No. 14-59, Apt. 402, tel. 1/256-2152, cell tel. 317/640-6716, www.chapinortehostelbogota.com, COP$64,000 s with shared bath). There are just a handful of private rooms, most of which have shared baths. There's a kitchen provided for guest use. The hotel is on a popular Sunday Ciclovía route (Carrera 15).

COP$70,000-200,000

On a quiet street in a wealthy neighborhood within easy walking distance to the Zona T, **Retiro 84 Apartasuites** (Cl. 84 No. 9-95, tel. 1/616-1501 www.retiro84.com, COP$173,000 d) has 16 rooms. It's comfortable and is reasonably priced for this high-rent part of town. This spot is popular with business travelers in town for longer stays.

Hotel Le Manoir (Cl. 105 No. 17A-82, tel. 1/213-3980, www.lemanoir-egina.com, COP$120,000 d) is a sound midrange hotel, located in a residential neighborhood between Usaquén and the Parque de la 93 area. There are 52 rooms here.

The ★ **NH Royal Metrotel** (Cl. 74 No. 13-27, tel. 1/657-8787, www.nh-hotels.co, COP$182,000 d) is massive. It has over 300 rooms, and thus is a popular choice for visiting tour groups. It has a similarly large terrace and a gym. It's located in a quiet area about a 10-minute walk to the Zona Rosa.

COP$200,000-500,000

BH (www.bhhoteles.com) is a Colombian chain of business hotels, with several locations throughout the city. **BH Retiro** (Cl. 80 No. 10-11, tel. 1/756-3177, COP$217,000 d) overlooks a busy and delightful park, and is a five-minute walk to the Centro Comercial Andino. There's not much in the way of services here, but it's clean and comfortable.

Cool ★ **84 DC** (Cl. 84 No. 9-67, tel. 1/487-0909, www.84dc.com.co, COP$248,000 d) blends in well in this upscale neighborhood, just blocks from the Zona T. It has 24 spacious, modern rooms, and the breakfast area downstairs has lots of natural light and a patio.

★ **B3** (Cra. 15 No. 88-36, tel. 1/593-4490, www.hotelesb3.com, COP$260,000 d) is one of the most striking hotels in town, thanks to its wonderful living plant wall. The lobby area is a lively place in the early evening, when guests munch on tapas and sip cocktails at the bar. Upstairs, rooms are minimalist and spacious. The hotel has a few bikes available for guests, and the Ciclovía passes directly in front on Sundays. Joggers can hit the paths of Parque El Virrey next door.

Although it's right next door to the revelry of Zona Rosa, you'd never know it in your quiet, comfortable room at the **NH Royal La Boheme** (Cl. 82 No. 12-35, tel. 1/644-7100, www.nh-hotels.co, COP$250,000 d).

At **B.O.G.** (Cra. 11 No. 86-74, tel. 1/639-9999, www.boghotel.com, COP$420,000 d), every detail has been thought out. The smart restaurant in the lobby, featuring Spanish touches, serves great lemonade. The rooftop pool is luxurious. A giant photograph of an emerald in the gym and spa area downstairs may inspire you to buy one.

Right on Parque El Virrey, the location of ★ **Cité** (Cra. 15 No. 88-10, tel. 1/646-7777, www.citehotel.com, COP$400,000 d) couldn't be better. The terrace of the hotel's restaurant, Le Bistro, is a popular place for Sunday brunch for both guests and nonguests alike. This 56-room hotel has a rooftop pool and bikes for guests to use during the Ciclovía, which passes by every Sunday and holiday.

The discreet **Hotel Portón Bogotá** (Cl. 84 No. 7-55, tel. 1/616-6611, www.hotelportonbogota.com.co, COP$400,000 d) prides itself on its tight security, making it a favorite of visiting diplomats. It has an elegant old-school feel, especially in the restaurant and lounge area, where they light the three fireplaces every evening at 7pm. It's on a quiet street within walking distance to the Zona T.

Information and Services

VISITOR INFORMATION

For information on all things Bogotá, go to a **Punto de Información Turística** (PIT). There is usually someone on staff who can speak English, provide you with a map, and answer questions. In La Candelaria there is a PIT on the southwest corner of the Plaza de Bolívar (tel. 1/283-7115, 8am-6pm Mon.-Sat., 8am-4pm Sun.). Other locations include the **Quiosco de la Luz** (Cra. 7 at Cl. 26, tel. 1/284-2664, 9am-5pm Mon.-Sat.) in the Parque de la Independencia, the international terminal of the airport (T1, no phone, 7am-10pm daily), and at two bus terminals: the Terminal de Transportes (Diag. 23 No. 69-60, Local 127, tel. 1/555-7692, 7am-7pm Mon.-Sat., 8am-4pm Sun.) and the Terminal del Sur (Autopista Sur, Local 67, tel. 1/555-7696, 7am-1pm daily).

TELEPHONES

The telephone code for Bogotá and many surrounding towns is 1. To call a cell phone from a landline, first dial 03 and then the 10-digit number. To do the reverse, call 03-1 (the 1 for Bogotá). When in the city, there is no need to dial 1 before a landline number.

Prepaid cell phones or SIM cards can be purchased at any Claro or Movistar store.

Emergency Numbers

The single emergency hotline is 123. Most operators don't speak English. You should provide the neighborhood you are in and a precise street number.

U.S. citizens who have health, safety, or legal emergencies can contact the **U.S. Embassy** at 1/275-2000.

NEWSPAPERS AND MAGAZINES

The ***City Paper*** is a free monthly newspaper in English with information on events, interesting profiles, and essays. It's distributed to hotels, restaurants, and cafés during the first two weeks of the month. Two other free papers, ***ADN*** and ***Metro,*** both in Spanish, are distributed on street corners in the mornings. ***Cartel Urbano*** and ***Artería*** are free publications covering cultural events. ***GO*** is a monthly publication on things going on in the city.

El Tiempo and ***El Espectador*** are the two main newspapers in town, and are good sources for information. ***Semana*** is considered the best news magazine, and is published weekly.

SPANISH-LANGUAGE COURSES

The Spanish spoken in Bogotá is considered neutral and clear, making the city an excellent place to study Spanish. The best schools are operated by the major universities in town and offer a variety of options, including one-on-one tutoring and larger classroom environments. The city's best schools include the **Universidad Externado** (Centro de Español para Extranjeros/CEPEX, Cra. 1A No. 12-53, tel. 1/282-6066, ext. 1221, www.uexternado.edu.co/cepex, 12-hour course COP$403,000) and the **Universidad Javeriana Centro Latinoamericano** (Transversal 4 No. 42-00 6th fl., tel. 1/320-8320, www.javeriana.edu.co). There are several Spanish-language schools in La Candelaria, like **Spanish World Institute** (Cra. 4A No. 56-56, www.spanishworldinstitute.com, tel. 1/248-3399, 20-hour course US$245) and **International House Bogotá** (Cl. 10 No. 4-09, tel. 1/336-4747, www.ihbogota.com, US$220/week).

MONEY

ATMs are everywhere throughout the city, and are the best option for getting Colombian pesos. Transaction fees vary. Some ATMs on the streets are closed at night. Be cautious when taking out money.

To change money, try **New York Money** at the Centro Andino mall (Centro Comercial Andino, Av. Cra. 11 No. 82-71, Local 3-48, tel. 1/616-8946, 9:30am-8:30pm daily), Atlantis Plaza (Centro Comercial Atlantis Plaza, Cl. 81 No. 13-05, Local 301-A, tel. 1/530-7432, 10:30am-8pm daily), or at the Granahorrar shopping center (Centro Comercial Avenida Chile, Cl. 72 No. 10-34, Local 320, tel. 1/212-2123, 10am-7pm daily). They are also open on holidays. You'll need to show your passport to change money.

VISAS AND OFFICIALDOM

To stay beyond the 60 or 90 days allowed to visitors from the United States, Canada, Australia, New Zealand, and most European countries, you will need to go to **Migración Colombia** (Cl. 100 No. 11B-27, tel. 1/595-4331, 8am-4pm Mon.-Fri.). It is best to go there a few days before your current visa expires.

HEALTH

Altitude

At 2,580 meters (8,465 feet), Bogotá is the third-highest capital city in the world (behind La Paz, Bolivia, and Quito, Ecuador). It is common to feel short of breath and fatigued during the first two days at the higher altitude. Other symptoms of altitude sickness include headache and nausea. Take it easy for those first few days in Bogotá and avoid caffeine and alcohol. If you are sensitive to high altitude, see a doctor before your trip for a prescription medication to mitigate the effects.

Sunburns are more common at higher elevations, as there's less atmosphere blocking out UV rays. Apply sunblock regularly, even when it's cloudy.

Hospitals, Clinics, and Pharmacies

Bogotá has excellent physicians and hospitals. Two of the best hospitals are the **Fundación Santa Fe** (Cl. 119 No. 7-75, www.fsfb.org.co, emergency tel. 1/629-0477, tel. 1/603-0303) and the **Clínica del Country** (Cra. 16 No. 82-57, tel. 1/530-1350, www.clinicadelcountry.com). For sexual and reproductive health matters, **Profamilia** (Cl. 34 No. 14-52, tel. 1/339-0900, www.profamilia.org.co), a member of the International Planned Parenthood Federation, offers clinical services. It is steps away from the Profamilia TransMilenio station on Calle Caracas.

Mom-and-pop pharmacies are all over the city and can be less stringent about requiring physical prescriptions. **Farmatodo** (tel. 1/743-2100, www.farmatodo.com.co) has around 30 locations in Bogotá; some are open 24 hours a day.

LAUNDRY

Wash-and-dry services that charge by the pound or kilo are plentiful in La Candelaria and Chapinero. This service is often called *lavandería*, as opposed to dry cleaning (*lavado en seco*). In La Candelaria two such services are **Limpia Seco Sarita** (Cra. 3 No. 10-69, tel. 1/233-9980) and **Extra-Rápido** (Cl. 12 No. 2-62, tel. 1/282-1002). In Chapinero there is **Lava Seco** (Cra. 9 No. 61-03, tel. 1/255-2582), another **Lava Seco** (Cl. 66 No. 8-20, tel. 1/249-7072), and **Lavandería San Ángel** (Cl. 69 No. 11A-47, tel. 1/255-8116).

A good dry cleaning service is **Classic** (Cra. 13A No. 86A-13, tel. 1/622-8759).

GETTING THERE

Air

Modern and user-friendly **Aeropuerto Internacional El Dorado** (BOG, Cl. 26 No. 103-09. tel. 1/266-2000, www.elnuevodorado.com) is the largest airport in the country. All international and most domestic flights now depart from T1, the main terminal. The following airlines serve domestic locations from T1: Avianca, LATAM, Satena, EasyFly, and Viva Colombia. There is a wealth of services in T1, including a Crepes & Waffles restaurant that's open 24 hours. There are money exchange offices and ATMs just outside of the customs area.

The smaller **Puente Aéreo,** or **T2,** is a secondary terminal used only by Avianca, and it serves smaller domestic destinations. It's less than half a kilometer from T1. All Avianca domestic flights depart from T2, except for flights to Barranquilla, Cartagena, Cali, Medellín, and Pereira. If you have a connection that requires a transfer between T1 and T2, there is a complimentary shuttle bus service provided. Airline staff (usually from Avianca) are available around the clock to assist those needing to transfer terminals.

AIRPORT TRANSPORTATION

Leaving the baggage claim and customs area, you will be approached—insistently—by taxi services, but these are not recommended. Instead, look for the official taxi queue outside the terminal. Metered taxis cost around COP$25,000-35,000 to most points in town.

SITP and TransMilenio bus service is also available, but it can be difficult to purchase a Tullave transit card at the airport. The **16-14 bus** is a free airport shuttle that takes passengers to the Portal El Dorado TransMilenio station, about half a mile from the airport, where Tullave cards can be purchased. From there, catch a red TransMilenio bus (COP$2,000) into the city, about a 30- to 45-minute ride. If you don't have a lot of luggage, this can be an inexpensive way to get into town.

Bus

Bogotá has three bus terminals: the **Terminal del Sur,** the **Portal del Norte,** and the main bus station, the **Terminal de Transportes** in Salitre.

TERMINAL DE TRANSPORTES

The **Terminal de Transportes** (Diagonal 23 No. 69-60, tel. 1/423-3630, www.terminaldetransporte.gov.co) is well organized and clean, and is divided into three "modules," each generally corresponding to a different direction: Module 1 is south, Module 2 is east/west, and Module 3 is north. There are two other modules, 4 and 5, corresponding to long-distance taxi services and arrivals, respectively. All modules are in the same building.

Each module has an information booth at the entrance, with an attendant who can point you in the right direction.

In the arrivals module, there is a tourist information office (PIT), where the helpful attendants can give you a map of the city and assist you in getting to your hotel. There is also an organized and safe taxi service and plenty of public transportation options available.

During the Christmas and Easter holidays, the bus terminal is a busy place with crowds and packed buses. This is also true on *puentes* (long weekends).

To take a cab from La Candelaria to the terminal, a trip that takes about 30 minutes, expect to pay COP$15,000.

PORTAL DEL NORTE

The **Portal del Norte** (Autopista Norte with Cl. 174), part of the TransMilenio station of the same name, may be more convenient if you are arriving from nearby destinations such as Tunja or Villa de Leyva.

TERMINAL DEL SUR

The **Terminal del Sur** (Autopista Sur with Cra. 72D) is near the Portal Sur of TransMilenio. This station serves locations in the south of Cundinamarca, such as Tequendama, and then travels farther south to Girardot, Ibagué, Neiva, Popayán, Armenia, and Cali, continuing all the way to Mocoa in Putumayo.

GETTING AROUND

Bus

To ride TransMilenio or SITP buses, you must first purchase a refillable **Tullave card.** One card can be used by multiple passengers. Cards are available for purchase at TransMilenio stations and at *papelerías* (mom-and-pop stationery stores) located near TransMilenio and SITP bus routes. It's easier to purchase the cards at *papelerías* (look for the Tullave decal on storefronts), as lines at TransMilenio stations can be insufferably long. Buying or refilling Tullave cards is cash-only.

TRANSMILENIO

TransMilenio (www.transmilenio.gov.co) is the bus rapid transit (BRT) system that serves Bogotá. Begun in 2000, it has transformed the city, and is the largest BRT system in the world. Over two million Bogotanos use the system each day, and it can be a useful and inexpensive way for visitors to get around. There are more than 100 stations covering much of the city on 12 lines.

There are three TransMilenio lines that are especially useful to visitors. First are the red hybrid TransMilenio buses on Carrera 7 (the Séptima). These are regular-looking buses, not the massive buses commonly associated with TransMilenio. This is the **M line**, and it is the best way to get from downtown to the north. This line has a modern terminal at the Museo

Nacional. Going south toward La Candelaria, the M line morphs into the **L line.**

Second is the original **B line** on Avenida Caracas. This extends from downtown to the Portal del Norte bus terminal at Calle 170. An offshoot, the J line, makes a detour toward the Museo del Oro.

The third line of importance is the **K line** along Avenida El Dorado (Av. Cl. 26), which serves the airport.

The system operates 5am-midnight Monday through Saturday and 6am-11pm on Sunday and holidays. A ride (paid for a with a Tullave card) typically costs about COP$2,000, and transfers (within 75 minutes) on TransMilenio or SITP cost only COP$300.

While riding the buses, keep your wallet in your front pocket and watch your belongings, especially during rush hour. When attempting to board or disembark TransMilenio buses, don't expect other passengers to make room for you. Call out "*permiso, por favor*" and move with purpose.

SITP

Bogotá is gradually modernizing with **Sistema Integrado de Transporte Público** (SITP, www.sitp.gov.co). Most useful for visitors are the blue SITP buses, which cost COP$2,000 per ride. Like the TransMilenio, you'll need a Tullave card to ride. SITP covers pretty much the entire city, so it's helpful to use apps like Moovit to find a bus that can take you where you want to go (but times are usually inaccurate on the app, so don't rely on them). Once you're at a bus stop and you spot your bus coming, you must flag it down by waving your card at the driver.

Taxis

It's estimated that over a million people take a cab each day in the city. There are around 50,000 taxis (mostly yellow Hyundais) circulating the streets of Bogotá. If you plan on taking a cab, either call one (or have one called) or, better yet, use an app like Easy Taxi, Tappsi, or Uber.

A *taximetro* calculates units, which determine the price. The rates are listed on a *tarjetón* (large card) with the driver's information. That card should always be visible. There are surcharges for cab services ordered by phone, for nighttime rides, and for going to the airport. Taxi drivers do not expect tips, but you can always round up the fare if you'd like. During end-of-year holidays, drivers may ask for a holiday tip.

Walking

You get a real feeling for the city and its frenetic energy by walking its streets. The neighborhoods that make up downtown (La Candelaria, Centro Internacional, and the Macarena) are accessible on foot, and walking is often the best way to get around. The same holds true for the upscale shopping and residential areas in Northern Bogotá.

The worst thing about walking in the city is crossing its streets. Protected crosswalks are rare, and many drivers have little respect for pedestrians or cyclists. Even if a pedestrian light is green, that doesn't guarantee that traffic will yield. Also, note that when traffic lights turn yellow, drivers may not actually slow down. Finally, keep in mind that, when there is no traffic, like on a peaceful Sunday evening, drivers tend to speed.

Biking

Bogotá has one of the most extensive bike path networks in Latin America, with over 340 kilometers of *ciclorutas* (bike lanes). Bicyclists should take extra care when using the *ciclorutas,* as vehicles may not yield for bikes. A popular, easy, and protected bike path extends along Carrera 11 between Calles 82 and 100.

Ciclovía is a weekly event (occurring on Sundays and holidays) during which usually traffic-filled streets are closed to vehicles, and bicycles take their places. Helmets are not essential in the Ciclovía, but they are advisable on the *ciclorutas.* Never leave a bike unattended.

Car Rental

With more than a million (usually aggressive) drivers on the clogged streets of Bogotá, renting a vehicle is a bad idea for visitors. However, if you are planning to travel to nearby places like Villa de Leyva or would like to take your time touring parks or villages, renting might be a solid option.

National (Cra. 7 No. 145-71, www.nationalcolombia.com), **Avis** (Av. 19 No. 123-52 Local 2, tel. 1/629-1722, www.avis.com), and **Hertz** (Av. Caracas No. 28A-17, tel. 1/327-6700, www.rentacarcolombia.co) have offices in Bogotá. Foreign driver's licenses are accepted in Colombia. It's important to find out your car's vehicle restriction days, which mean you can't drive during business hours for two predetermined days of the week, based on the last digit of your license plate.

Vicinity of Bogotá

ZIPAQUIRÁ

A favorite day trip for visitors to Bogotá is the city of **Zipaquirá** (pop. 112,000). About 40 kilometers (25 miles) from Bogotá, Zipaquirá is known for its Catedral de Sal—a cathedral built in a salt mine. Zipaquirá is named for the the Zipa, the Muisca leader of the Bacatá confederation. The Muisca settlement was very close to the mines, and they traded salt for other commodities with other indigenous groups.

Sights

The **Catedral de Sal** (tel. 1/852-3010, www.catedraldesal.gov.co, 9am-5:30pm daily, COP$20,000) is part of the Parque del Sal. The original cathedral was built by miners in 1951, but due to safety concerns at that site, a new and larger cathedral was built and opened in 1995. The cathedral is

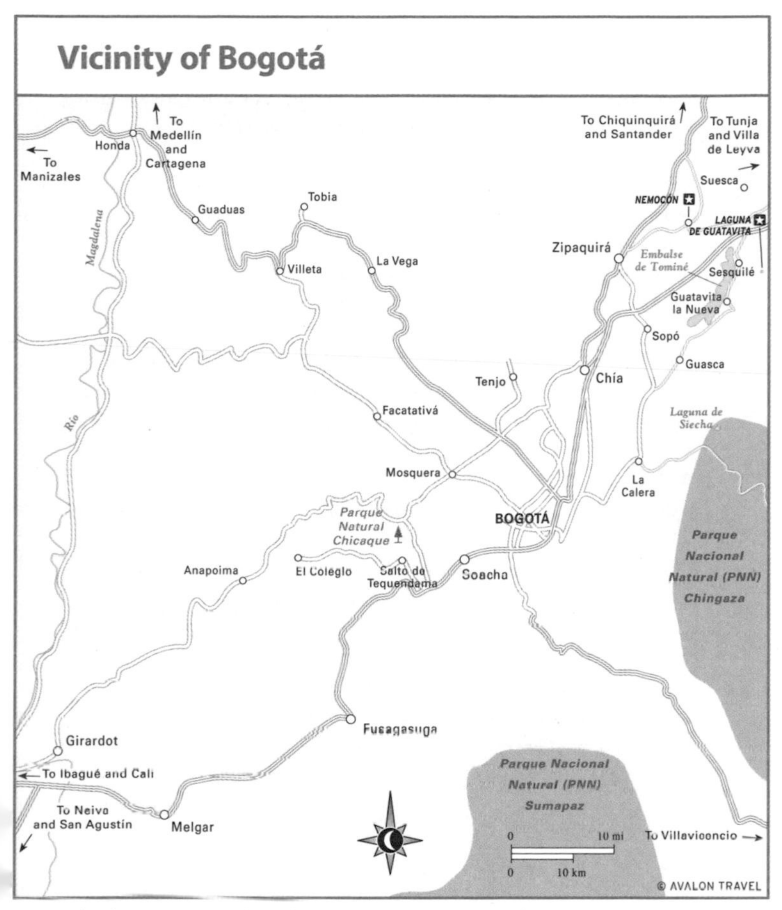

indeed an impressive feat of engineering. Tours are obligatory, but you can stray from the group. Masses take place here on Sundays, and they attract many faithful. Other features include a museum, a rock-climbing wall, and a children's 3-D film, which you could skip.

The picturesque main plaza in Zipaquirá, with palm trees rising against a backdrop of green mountains, is always the center of activity in town. Here locals gather to gossip, get their shoes shined, or munch on an *oblea* (wafer) oozing with caramel. Dominating the plaza is a cathedral designed by Friar Domingo de Petrés, who also designed the Bogotá and Santa Fe de Antioquia cathedrals. Construction began in 1805; 111 years later, in 1916, it was completed and dedicated.

Getting There

Zipaquirá is an easy day trip from Bogotá. On weekends, families and tourists alike take the Turistren from the **Usaquén train station** (Cra. 9 No. 110-08, tel. 1/316-1300) at 8:15am or the **Estación de la Sabana** (Cl. 13 No.

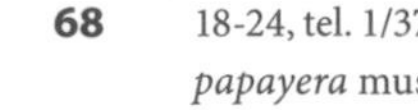

18-24, tel. 1/375-0557) near La Candelaria at 9:15am. Bands play Colombian *papayera* music as you slowly chug through the savanna of Bogotá on the three-hour trip. The train returns to Bogotá in the late afternoon, giving you more than enough time to visit the salt mines. Only round-trip train tickets (COP$52,000) are sold.

The company Alianza runs buses (1 hour, COP$4,800) to Zipaquirá's **Terminal de Transportes** (Cras. 6C-7 and Clls. 10-12) from Bogotá's **Portal del Norte TransMilenio station** every 20 minutes or so, all day long. Upon arriving at Portal del Norte, take a left from where you get off the TransMilenio bus and you will see signs pointing the way for "Zipa" buses; the attendants can also direct you. You'll pay the Zipa bus driver directly. The trip takes about an hour and costs COP$6,000.

You can either walk or take a short taxi ride to the Parque del Sal from Zipaquirá's train or bus station.

★ Nemocón

With only 10,000 residents, the sleepy pueblo of **Nemocón** (www.nemocon-cundinamarca.gov.co) is 15 kilometers (9 miles) from Zipaquirá and just 65 kilometers (40 miles) from Bogotá. It is a cute, compact colonial-era town, also home to salt mines, but it does not attract nearly the same number of visitors that Zipaquirá does. That's part of its allure. In pre-Columbian times, this was also a Muisca settlement devoted to salt extraction.

On the plaza, a church is set against a backdrop of eucalyptus-covered hills that are the result of some sort of reforestation effort. There is a small salt museum on the corner, and students will be happy to give you a tour in Spanish. About a 10-minute walk toward the hills are the **salt mines** (www.minadesal.com, 9am-5pm daily, tours COP$22,000). Tours take about 90 minutes. The beautifully renovated section of the mines that you visit is no longer used for salt extraction. In the depths of the mines you will see stalactites and stalagmites. The pools where salt and water were

the sleepy pueblo of Nemocón

mixed to pump out the salt are a highlight. The reflection of the illuminated vaults on the surface of the pools, combined with the cool lighting, is quite something.

There are simple restaurants with names like the **Venado de Oro** (the Golden Deer) on the plaza or **La Casa de la Gallina** (the Hen House) on Calle 2 (No. 4-24). There's not much in the way of accommodations in Nemocón; most visitors make it a day trip.

The bus company Alianza offers service to Nemocón (1.5 hours, COP$6,700) from the Portal del Norte bus station in Bogotá.

★ LAGUNA DE GUATAVITA

The El Dorado myth, which became an obsession for gold-thirsty Europeans in the New World, is based on a Muisca Indian ritual that took place in this perfectly round mountain lake.

Following the death of the Muisca *cacique* (chief), a nephew would be chosen to succeed him. The day of the ceremony, the nephew would be sequestered in a cave. Then, stripped naked and covered with mud and gold dust, he would be rowed to the center of the sacred lake with incense and music filling the air. Once there, gold, silver, emeralds, and other tributes were tossed into the cold waters, and the *cacique* would dive in.

When Europeans arrived in Guatavita, they drained the lake at least three times, looking for treasure at the bottom of the lake. A giant cut in the lake can be still seen today.

Today **Laguna de Guatavita** (cell tel. 315/831-1086, www.car.gov.co, 9am-4pm Tues.-Sat., non-Colombian adults COP$16,000, free for seniors) is being given the respect it deserves. An environmental agency maintains the park, which is located close to the town of Sesquilé. In order to preserve the lake, the agency has forbidden direct access to it. The lake is much better appreciated from above, on the well-maintained path along the top of the crater. On Saturdays, you must join a tour group (included in admission) to see the lake. Tours leave every 30 minutes and last less than an hour. Guides are knowledgeable and passionate about their work. English tours are possible, especially for larger groups, but those should be reserved in advance. During the week you can amble along the path at your own pace.

While much of the brick path is flat, there is a fairly steep climb, making it difficult for those with physical limitations. At the end of the walk, you can walk or hop on a minibus to the entrance of the park. When Monday is a holiday, the park is open Wednesday-Monday.

Getting There

Getting to Laguna de Guatavita via public transportation is fairly straightforward. The bus company Águila offers service (1.5 hours, COP$8,000) to the town of Nueva Guatavita. At the TransMilenio Portal del Norte station in Bogotá, take a bus bound for Nueva Guatavita. Upon arrival in Nueva Guatavita, contract a taxi driver to take you to the park, wait for you, and bring you back to Nueva Guatavita. Expect to pay COP$60,000 for this service. On weekends, there is a bus service (COP$10,000) from Nueva Guatavita directly to the park that departs at 11am and 1pm.

Another option is to hire a driver out of Bogotá to make the trip to Laguna de Guatavita and back. This trip takes 1.5-2 hours each way. Your hotel or hostel in Bogotá can recommend a private car service, and may even assist with negotiating a price.

PARQUE NACIONAL NATURAL CHINGAZA

Some 75 kilometers northeast of Bogotá, the **Parque Nacional Natural Chingaza** (tel. 1/353-2400, www.parquesnacionales.gov.co, 8am-4pm daily, non-Colombian adults COP$39,500) extends over 76,000 hectares (188,000 acres) and makes for an excellent day trip of hiking among armies of *frailejón* plants through the misty *páramo* (highland moor).

The park limits the number of visitors, so it is best to request an entry permit in advance by calling **Parques Nacionales** (tel. 1/353-2400, www.parquesnacionales.gov.co). They will ask you to send the names of the members of your group in an email and confirm the reservation. They will also provide contact information for the local association of guides. You can save a lot of money, and help the local economy, if you do it this way rather than through an organized private tour. Plan on hiring an experienced guide (COP$50,000/day), as trails are often not obvious. The guides are generally very knowledgeable and friendly. However, they may not speak English.

The hike to the sacred **Lagunas de Siecha,** three mountain lakes called Suramérica, Siecha, and Guascatakes, takes about 3.5 hours. Other excursions within the Parque Nacional Natural Chingaza can be made from different entry points.

Pack rubber boots, as you will be hiking along muddy paths—sneakers

frailejones at the Parque Nacional Natural Chingaza

just won't do. A light raincoat or windbreaker and sweatshirt are essential, as well as a packed lunch, snacks, and water.

Practicalities

In the town of Guasca you can relax, eat, and stay at the **Posada Café La Huerta** (cell tel. 315/742-0999, www.cafelahuerta.com), where they make great corn bread. If you decide to stay with them for a weekend, they can arrange your transportation and visit to PNN Chingaza.

Getting There

It's challenging, but possible, to get to PNN Chingaza via public transportation. From Bogotá, take a bus to Guasca. Buses to Guasca leave from the Portal del Norte bus terminal as well as from an informal bus pickup area between Calles 72 and 73 at Carrera 14. Once there, ask any taxi or bus driver where to find the right bus.

From Guasca, take a *buseta* (minivan) toward Paso Hondo, about 15 kilometers away. This 20-minute ride (COP$2,000) will leave you at the intersection that leads to the park. From there, you must walk six kilometers (about 90 minutes) to reach the park entrance. *Busetas* leave at 6:30am, 7:30am, and 9:30am. Leave Bogotá by around 7am to make the 9:30am *buseta*.

If you travel with private transportation, it is possible to drive closer to the park, but only with a four-wheel-drive vehicle. **Hansa Tours** (tel. 1/637-9800, www.hansatours.com) hires out drivers for the day to do this trip.

SUESCA

It's all about rock climbing in Suesca. On the weekends, Bogotanos converge on this little town and head to the rocks. Most climbing takes place along two kilometers' worth of cliffs, called ***las rocas,*** just behind the town. Some of the cliffs are up to 250 meters (820 feet) high. It's a beautiful setting, and the fresh smell of eucalyptus trees and mountain mist add to the atmosphere.

Several outdoors shops in Suesca rent equipment and organize rock-climbing classes and excursions. **Explora Suesca** (Cra. 6 No. 8-20, cell tel. 311/249-3491 or 317/516-2414) rents rock-climbing gear, teaches classes, and rents out bikes. At **Monodedo** (Cra. 16 No. 82-22, Bogotá, tel. 1/616-3467, cell tel. 316/266-9399, www.mondodedo.com) in Bogotá, expect to pay around COP$60,000 for a three-hour rock-climbing excursion with a guide.

Food

After all that rock climbing, it's time for some Thai food. Check out **Restaurante Vamonos Pa'l Monte** (Km. 5 Vía La Playa-Suesca, cell tel. 320/856-8992, www.vamonospalmonte.com, 8am-8pm Fri.-Sun., COP$14,000) for Phuket vegetables or pad Thai. It's on the main road and within walking distance of *las rocas*.

Another popular place is **Rica Pizza** (Km. 5 Vía La Playa-Suesca, cell tel.

312/379-3610), on the main road, close to *las rocas*. They serve pizza and more typical Colombian fare.

Accommodations

Many folks make a visit to Suesca a camping weekend. The most popular campground is **Campo Base** (1 km east of Vía La Playa-Suesca, cell tel. 320/290-8291, campsite COP$20,000, tent rental COP$15,000). They've got hot water and a place for cooking, and they rent out tents. They're laid-back here.

The luxurious nine-room bed-and-breakfast **Casa Lila** (cell tel. 320/204-8262 or 300/835-9472, patriciavalenciaturismo@gmail.com, COP$150,000-220,000 d) is so cozy, with fireplaces all around and its own restaurant, that it may be hard to leave. It's right next to an old train station at kilometer 3.

Getting There

Buses from Bogotá regularly serve Suesca (1.5 hours, COP$10,000) from the Portal del Norte station. The bus will drop you at the center of town, near *las rocas*.

You can also contact a Bogotá-based tour company that specializes in rock climbing, such as **Ecoglobal Expeditions** (tel. 1/616-9088, www.ecoglobalexpeditions.com, from COP$130,000), who can also arrange for transportation.

HONDA

The steamy town of Honda, known as the City of Bridges for its 29 spans, rests on the banks of the Río Magdalena, almost exactly halfway between Bogotá and Medellín. Founded in 1539, it was the country's first and most important interior port. From the 16th century until the mid-20th century, the Río Magdalena was the main transportation route connecting Bogotá to the Caribbean coast and the rest of the world. Quinine, coffee, lumber, and slaves were loaded and unloaded along the banks, and steamships would ply the route toward the coast.

In 1919, the Barranquilla-based SCADTA airlines became the first airline of the Americas, bringing seaplane service to Honda. (SCADTA would later become Avianca Airlines.)

Honda and its sleepy streets now make for a nice stopover between Bogotá and Medellín. The steamships and seaplanes no longer make their appearances, but if you head down to the river's edge you can ask a local angler to give you a quick jaunt along the river in his boat. Be sure to walk across the bright yellow **Puente Navarro,** a pedestrian bridge built by the San Francisco Bridge Company in 1898. Check out the **Museo del Río Magdalena** (Cl. 10 No. 9-01, tel. 8/251-0129, 10am-6pm Tues.-Sun., COP$3,000) on the way. It puts the historical and geographical importance of the Río Magdalena into context within the development of Colombia.

A popular weekend destination for Bogotanos in need of *tierra caliente* (hot country) relaxation, the town has some good hotel options. For pampering, try the **Posada Las Trampas** (Cra. 10A No. 11-05, tel. 8/251-7415, www.posadalastrampas.com, COP$230,000 d). For a friendly welcome, stay at the ★ **Casa Belle Epoque** (Cl. 12 No. 12A-21, tel. 8/251-1176, cell tel. 312/478-0173, www.casabelleepoque.com, COP$80,000-110,000 d), a moderately priced hotel popular with international travelers. The staff can arrange boat trips on the Magdalena for guests.

There is plentiful public transportation to Honda. From the Terminal de Transportes in Bogotá it is about a five-hour journey (COP$20,000). The bus station in Honda is outside of town, and it costs COP$4,000 for a taxi from there to town.

Boyacá and Santanderes

The mountainous departments of Boyacá, Santander, and Norte de Santander are rich in history, natural beauty, and outdoor activities.

The countryside is dotted with historic colonial towns, including two of the most beautiful and well preserved in Colombia: Villa de Leyva and Barichara. The scenery of the region runs the gamut from the desert landscape near Villa de Leyva to the bucolic rolling hills and pastures of agriculturally rich Boyacá, and from the awe-inspiring Río Chicamocha canyon to the dramatic snowcapped peaks of the Sierra Nevada del Cocuy.

Outdoor activities are the draw here, like trekking in the Sierra Nevada del Cocuy and white-water rafting, caving, and paragliding near San Gil. In most of the region, a refreshingly slow pace prevails. The pueblos of Boyacá are easily accessed from Bogotá and can even be visited on a long weekend. It will take a little more time to discover Santander, located between Bogotá and the Caribbean coast. Although most people only stop in Cúcuta on their way to Venezuela or on a visa run, the sultry city is a pleasant surprise. The historic pueblo of Pamplona is the most chilled-out place in all of Norte de Santander.

HISTORY

Before the Spanish conquest, Boyacá was part of the Muisca heartland. Hunza, where present-day Tunja is located, was the seat of the Zaque, one of the Muisca leaders. The Sun Temple, one of the Muiscas' sacred sites, was in Sogamoso, northeast of Tunja.

Boyacá and the Santanderes played a major role in the struggle for independence. In 1811, Boyacá became the seat of the Provincias Unidas de la Nueva Granada (United Provinces of New Granada), the first Republican independent government. It was in Boyacá in 1819 that the two decisive

---

Previous: cobblestone streets in the colonial village of Guane; Villa de Leyva.

Look for ★ to find recommended sights, activities, dining, and lodging.

Highlights

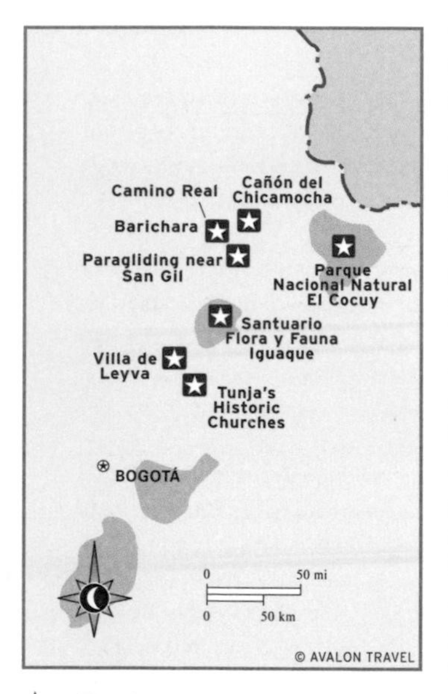

★ **Villa de Leyva:** One of Colombia's most visited and beloved colonial pueblos, relaxed Villa de Leyva is just a couple of hours away from Bogotá (page 79).

★ **Santuario Flora y Fauna Iguaque:** Hike through Andean forest and mysterious *páramo* to a sacred Muisca lake (page 87).

★ **Tunja's Historic Churches:** Glimpse the splendor of Tunja's colonial past in its beautiful churches (page 91).

★ **Parque Nacional Natural El Cocuy:** Stunning scenery greets you at every turn in this remote park of snowcapped peaks (page 106).

★ **Paragliding near San Gil:** Soar through the air with the greatest of ease in Colombia's recreational capital (page 121).

★ **Cañón del Chicamocha:** Experience the blue skies and deep canyons of this photogenic park not far from Bucaramanga and San Gil (page 124).

★ **Barichara:** Decompress and rejuvenate in one of the most beautiful pueblos in the country (page 125).

★ **Camino Real:** Follow in the footsteps of indigenous Guane traders and Spanish colonists on this meandering path through the Santander countryside (page 126).

battles of independence were fought: the Batalla del Pantano de Vargas (Battle of the Vargas Swamp) and the Batalla del Puente de Boyacá (Battle of the Bridge of Boyacá). These battles marked the end of Spanish domination in Colombia.

Santander was one of the more dynamic regions in 19th-century Colombia, with an export economy based on the cultivation of quinine, coffee, cocoa, and tobacco. In the early 20th century, Norte de Santander became the first major coffee-producing region in Colombia.

The mid-20th-century fighting between Liberals and Conservatives was particularly acute in Santander and Norte de Santander. In 1960, the guerrilla group Ejercito de Liberación Nacional (National Liberation Army), or ELN, was born in rural Santander.

The region has experienced steady economic growth since the early 2000s. Bucaramanga, the capital of Santander, has become a prosperous center of manufacturing and services. Cúcuta, in the neighboring Norte de Santander department, is a center of commerce whose fortunes are linked to Venezuela's.

While poverty is widespread in the Boyacá countryside, the area is an important agricultural center and supplies Bogotá with much of its food. The departmental capital of Tunja has also become a major center of learning: It is home to 10 universities.

PLANNING YOUR TIME

There are three main draws in Boyacá and Santander: the lovely colonial town of Villa de Leyva, the snowcapped wonderland of the Sierra Nevada del Cocuy, and, in Santander, the action-packed area around San Gil, including the nearby town of Barichara.

Villa de Leyva can be visited in a short two-day excursion from Bogotá, but you could easily spend a couple more relaxing days seeing all the sights, including a hike to Laguna Iguaque. Add on a day to visit the churches of Tunja. To further explore Boyacá, extend your visit for a couple of days to the area around Sogamoso, particularly the postcard-perfect Iza, Monguí, and Lago Tota. There are good public transportation links throughout Boyacá, but this is also a fairly easy place to drive.

Getting to the Sierra Nevada del Cocuy is a schlep (11 hours by bus from Bogotá), so a trip there requires a minimum of 4-5 days to make it worthwhile. To do day hikes into the park, base yourself in the gateway towns of Güicán or El Cocuy, or nearer to the park in one of several lodges. To do the six-day circuit around the park, plan on 10 days so as to include a day or two of acclimatization before you embark. This is a remote area and there are fewer public transportation options, although buses do depart for the area from Tunja. Roads are in good shape, for the most part.

Beginning in 2013, local U'wa indigenous leaders blocked access to the park; after negotiations with the community (and with aid from the United Nations), the park service reopened the park with the blessing of the U'wa leaders. It's a good idea to contact the park service ahead of

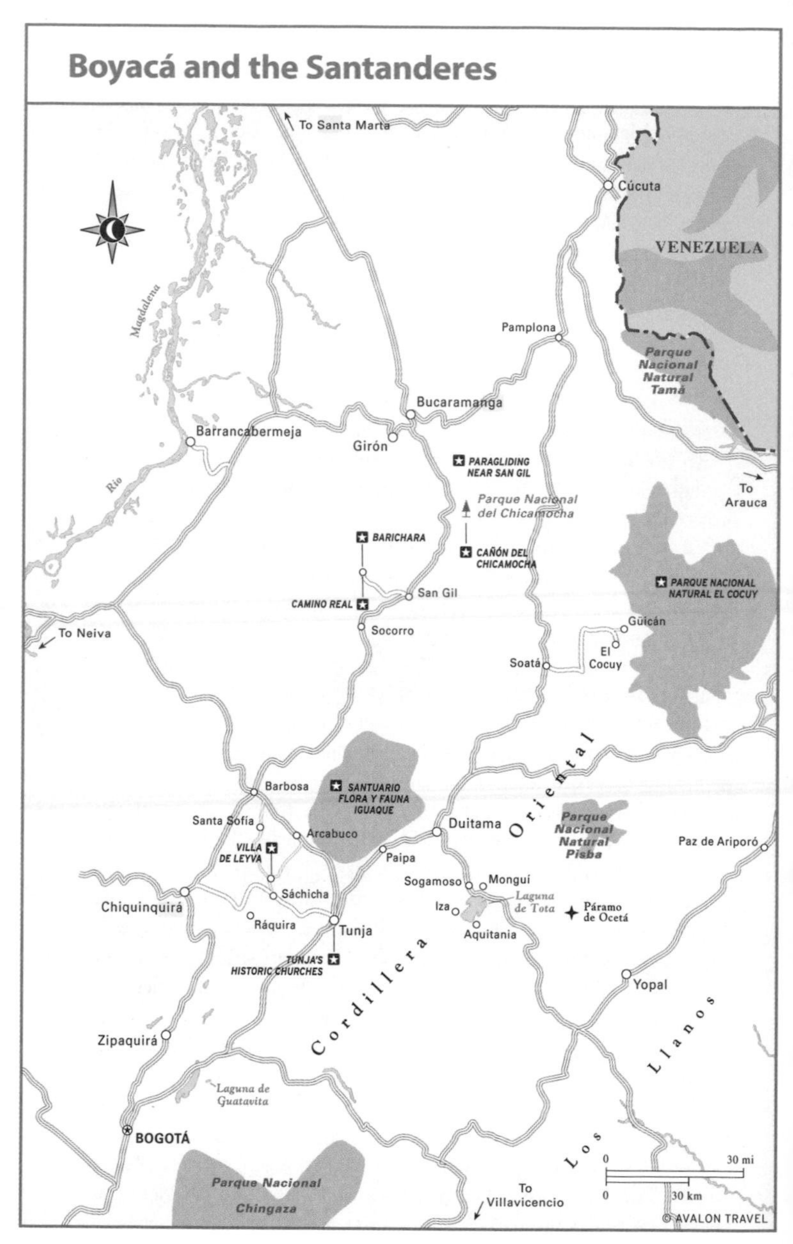

your trip and confirm that the park remains open. For the latest information, contact one of the two national park offices in the area: El Cocuy (Cl. 5 No. 4-22, tel. 8/789-0359, 7am-11:45am and 1pm-4:45pm daily) or Güicán (Transversal 4A No. 6-60, tel. 8/789-7280, 7am-11:45pm and 1pm-4:45pm daily).

In Santander, San Gil and Barichara have a lot to offer, so plan on spending at least three days in the area. Barichara is a more beautiful base for exploring the region, but San Gil is home to the main adventure sport tour operators. There are good public transportation links between Bucaramanga and San Gil and between San Gil and Barichara. However, getting from Bucaramanga and San Gil to Tunja or Villa de Leyva is slow going, as the highway is often saturated with big trucks and buses. On holidays it can be difficult to snag a seat on a bus to or from San Gil, as it's also a stop between Bogotá and Bucaramanga, in the northern part of Santander.

The bus ride between Villa de Leyva and San Gil takes 6-7 hours, with a change of bus in Barbosa and/or Tunja. Even though San Gil and the Sierra Nevada del Cocuy are only 75 kilometers (47 miles) apart as the crow flies, to get from one to the other, you must transfer buses in Tunja, requiring more than 15 hours on multiple buses.

There's frequent bus service between Bucaramanga and Pamplona and Cúcuta, the two main destinations in Norte de Santander—a day or two will suffice in these towns.

Boyacá

To the northeast of Bogotá, the department of Boyacá is a mostly rural agricultural area of bucolic highlands, home to campesinos (farmers) often dressed in *ruanas* (wool capes) as they tend to their dairy cows and potato crops. Boyacenses are known for their politeness, shyness, and honesty, and will often address you not with the formal *usted* but rather with the super-deferential *sumercé,* a term that is derived from the old Spanish *su merced* (literally, "your mercy").

Boyacá is known for its role in Colombian history: The city of Tunja was effectively the runner-up to Bogotá when the Spaniards sought a capital for their New World territory of Nueva Granada. Tunja's colonial-era importance can be seen today in the number of impressive churches that stand in its historic center. Nearby, Villa de Leyva has the perfect combination of colonial charm, good hotels and restaurants, attractions, and fantastic weather.

★ VILLA DE LEYVA

This enchanting colonial pueblo is set in an arid valley (Valle de Saquencipá) and has been a major tourist destination for decades. The population triples on weekends, when city folk from Bogotá converge on the town. The surrounding desert scenery, a palette of ever-changing pastels, is gorgeous; the typically sunny weather is never too hot nor too cool; and the town's architecture of preserved whitewashed houses along stone streets is picturesque.

The influx of visitors every weekend doesn't diminish the appeal of Villa de Leyva. A surprising number of activities and attractions are in reach, including paleontological and archaeological sites and outdoor activities such as biking and hiking. The nearby Santuario Flora y Fauna Iguaque is one of the most accessible national parks in the country, and you need only a decent pair of boots to hike to its sacred lakes. Villa de Leyva is also a good base from which to explore the Boyacá countryside and towns such as Ráquira.

Sights

PLAZA MAYOR

Villa de Leyva's **Plaza Mayor** is one of the most photographed locations in Colombia. The town's main square, the largest plaza in the country (14,000 square meters/3.5 acres), is hard to fit in one photo. In the middle of the square is a Mudejar-style well, the Ara Sagrada, that was the source of water for the townspeople in colonial times. On the western side of the square is the **Iglesia Parroquial** (Cra. 9 No. 12-68, 8am-noon and 2pm-6pm Tues.-Sat., 8am-noon Sun.), built in the 17th century from stone, adobe, and wood. It features a large golden *retablo* (altarpiece).

On the western side of the plaza is the quirky **Casa Museo Luis Alberto Acuña** (Cra. 10 No. 12-83, tel. 8/732-0422, www.museoacuna.com.co, 9am-6pm daily, COP$4,000), dedicated to obscure Colombian artist Luis Alberto Acuña. The small museum is filled with Acuña's cubist-influenced paintings of pre-Hispanic indigenous culture and his private art collection and antiques. Acuña was instrumental in the restoration and preservation of local colonial architecture.

One of the oldest and best-preserved houses in Villa de Leyva is the **Casa Juan de Castellanos** (Cra. 9 No. 13-11) on the northeast corner of the Plaza Mayor. It serves as the main office of the town government. The house belonged to Spaniard Juan de Castellanos, who came to the New World as a soldier. He was an important chronicler of the time. The house is not open to the public. Across from the Casa Juan de Castellanos is the historic **Casa del Primer Congreso de las Provincias Unidas de la Nueva Granada** (Cra. 9 No. 13-04), which was restored by artist Luis Alberto Acuña in the 1950s.

The **Museo El Carmen de Arte Religioso** (Cl. 14 No. 10-04, 10:30am-1pm and 2:30pm-5pm Sat.-Sun., COP$3,000) presents paintings, crucifixes, manuscripts, and religious figures from the colonial era. The museum is on the southwest corner of the grassy **Plazoleta de la Carmen.** The complex, which dates to around 1850, also includes a monastery and convent.

The **Casa Museo Antonio Nariño** (Cra. 9 No. 10-25, tel. 8/732-0342, 9am-noon and 2pm-5pm Thurs.-Tues., free) is the house in which independence figure Antonio Nariño lived and died. It was built in the 17th century, and the museum displays some of Nariño's manuscripts as well as items from everyday life in the 19th century, such as a giant mortar used to mill corn. The small but good museum often puts on temporary art exhibits, which may have a small admission fee.

OTHER SIGHTS

On the northeastern edge of town is the **Museo Paleontológico de Villa de Leyva** (Cra. 9 No. 11-42, tel. 8/732-0466, www.paleontologico.unal.edu.co, 9am-noon and 2pm-5pm Tues.-Sat., 9am-3pm Sun., COP$4,000). Run by the Universidad Nacional, this museum explains the fossils that have been found in the area, some as old as 130 million years. On display are ammonites, spiral-shelled marine fossils, and fossils of prehistoric animals that roamed the area. The museum has an arboretum with gardens of palms, oaks, and an Andean forest. It's about a 15-minute walk from the Plaza Mayor to the museum. It's popular with school groups on weekday mornings.

On **Plaza Ricaurte,** the 19th-century **Convento de San Agustín** houses the **Instituto Humboldt** (Cra. 8 No. 15-98, tel. 8/732-0791, www.humboldt.org.co, free), a research institute dedicated to conservation and environmental education. There are occasional exhibitions in the institute and the former convent's chapel.

The **Casa Museo Capitán Antonio Ricaurte** (Cl. 15 No. 8-17, no phone, 9am-noon and 2pm-5pm Wed.-Sun., free) is in the small house where independence figure Antonio Ricaurte was born in 1786. One room is filled with uniforms and memorabilia of the Colombian air force, of which Ricaurte was a part. Ricuarte died heroically, sacrificing his life by detonating a cache of gunpowder so that it would not fall into the hands of Spaniards.

Entertainment and Events

The most popular place in the evenings is the Plaza Mayor, where the thing to do is buy a couple of beers and hang out. But there are other watering holes in town. **La Cava de Don Fernando** (Cra. 10 No. 12-03, tel. 8/732-0073) is a spot for a cocktail where the music is often rock.

There are two weekly markets at the **Plaza de Mercado** (Clls. 12-13 and Cras. 5-6, 7am-3pm Thurs., 5am-4pm Sat.). The Thursday market is all organic fruits and vegetables, while the Saturday market is the larger of the two, during which local farmers sell produce and handicrafts. Locals and tourists alike delight in this weekly tradition.

The dark, crystal-clear skies above Villa de Leyva make for great stargazing. In February each year the town hosts the **Festival de Astronómica de Villa de Leyva** (www.astroasasac.com, Feb.), during which people are invited to view the stars from powerful telescopes in the Plaza Mayor.

During the breezy days of August, hundreds of colorful kites soar above the plaza during the **Festival del Viento y Cometas** (www.villadeleyva-boyaca.gov.co, Aug.).

Shopping

For centuries, farmers and craftspeople in Villa de Leyva have specialized in woven goods. In fact, the symbol of this part of Colombia could very well be the *ruana,* a warm, woolen cape worn by both men and women. This and other woolen goods can be found on nearly every street corner in Villa de

Leyva. The town is home to many creative types; small jewelers, galleries, and handicraft shops are common throughout town.

Alieth Tejido Artesanal (Cl. 13 No. 7-89, tel. 8/732-1672, www.alieth.8m.com) is an association of about 35 women who weave woolen sweaters, *ruanas* (wool capes), *mochilas* (handwoven purses), gloves, scarves, and colorful, psychedelic bags. A tour, the "Ruta de la Lana," can be taken to nearby farms to learn about the process from sheep to sweater. It costs COP$48,000 per person and lasts for about five hours, and snacks and a souvenir are included. Alieth Ortíz, the head of this interesting program, requests reservations be made a few days in advance so that they can organize things with the artisans.

An excellent store to browse wool items is **Creaciones Dora** (Cra. 10 No. 10-02, 9am-7pm Mon.-Fri., 9am-9pm Sat.). **La Libélula** (Cra. 9 No. 14-35, tel. 8/732-0040, 10am-7pm daily) specializes in leather: handbags, belts, and accessories.

The friendly Italian owner, Luciano, takes the mystery out of emeralds at **Misterio** (Cl. 14 No. 9-85, tel. 8/732-0418, cell tel. 313/4891-9315,10am-8pm daily), where emeralds and quartz from mines in Boyacá are sold. He also sells handmade jewelry. Luciano enjoys educating visitors on how to choose an emerald.

Recreation

HIKING

Close to town, sporty locals regularly take a brisk morning hike up to the **Santo,** a statue on the eastern side of Villa de Leyva. The walk takes about an hour in total, and it is a steep climb. Hikers are rewarded with quite a view of the Plaza Mayor. To get to the path, walk east along Calle 11 to the tennis court and soccer field, north of the Hotel Duruelo. The path entrance is marked. It's best to make the climb early in the morning, before the midday heat envelops the valley. Although the view is nice, you'll be better off leaving your camera at your hotel—not necessarily for safety reasons, but because you may not want to be loaded down as you climb. At times you may need both hands free to scramble over rocks.

BIKE RENTAL

Renting a bike to see the sights in the valley near Villa de Leyva is a great way to spend a day and get some good exercise as you huff and puff up the hill to the Convento del Santo Ecce Homo. **Ciclotrip** (Cra. 9 No. 141-101, tel. 8/732-1485, cell tel. 317/435-5202, www.ciclotrip.com) rents mountain bikes and can organize biking tours in the area. Many hostels also have bikes for rent.

Food

COLOMBIAN

★ **MiCocina** (Cl. 13 No. 8-45, tel. 8/732-1676, cell tel. 320/488-2452, 1pm-10pm daily, COP$25,000) has earned a name for itself as a slightly upscale restaurant serving the best of Colombian cuisine. After a *calentado bogotano,* a beloved hangover cure made with fried eggs and potatoes, save room for the cheese ice cream from Paipa. They serve mostly Colombian meat-based dishes here, but there are a few vegetarian plates. There's a cooking school here as well.

Locals tend to steer clear of the overpriced restaurants on the Plaza Mayor. Close to the Terminal de Transportes, **Los Kioscos de los Caciques** (Cra. 9 No. 9-05, cell tel. 311/475-8681, noon-3pm and 6pm-8pm daily, COP$6,000) specializes in filling local dishes such as *mazamorra chiquita* (beef stew with potatoes, corn, and other vegetables) and *cuchuco con espinazo* (stew with a base of pork spine and potatoes). It's an atmospheric place where you dine in thatched kiosks.

At the Saturday market, those in the know go to **Donde Salvador** (Plaza de Mercado, Clls. 12-13 and Cras. 5-6, 5am-4pm Sat.) for *mute rostro de cordero,* a hearty corn-based soup with lamb. Salvador is well known, and he's one of the first at the marketplace on Saturdays, serving late-night carousers at 4am and more typical shoppers throughout the day. The big market takes place on Saturday, but there is also a smaller organic fruits and vegetables market on Thursdays.

Every day there is a different set lunch menu at **La Cocina de la Gata** (Cl. 11 No. 9-23, cell tel. 310/766-7980, noon-10pm daily). Vegetarian meals are served on Tuesdays and Fridays.

Popular with locals, **Donde Tere** (Cl. 10 No. 8-73, cell tel. 316/542-0387, 8am-8pm Mon. and Wed.-Sat., 8am-5pm Sun., COP$12,000), also called Tienda de Teresa, specializes in breakfast and *cazuela boyacense,* a milk-based soup.

INTERNATIONAL

★ **Mercado Municipal** (Cra. 8 No. 12-25, tel. 8/732-0229, 1pm-10pm daily, COP$22,000) has one of the coolest settings in Villa de Leyva: It's set in a courtyard (that was once part of a parsonage) overflowing with herb gardens in which a traditional Mexican barbecue wood-burning oven is built into the ground. In this oven, they slow-cook their famous barbecued goat. International dishes on the menu include pastas and several vegetarian offerings. It's open for breakfast on the weekends, and there is a nice bakery in front. The set lunch special is a good deal. For a drink and tapas, get comfortable at their adjacent swanky bar, **Bolívar Social Club,** which is open in the evenings.

French cuisine is served at **Chez Remy** (Cra. 9 No. 13-25, tel. 311/848-5000, noon-10pm Fri.-Sat., noon-4pm Sun., COP$24,000), including *quenelle de mar* (COP$28,000), which combines myriad tastes from the faraway sea: salmon, hake, shrimp, and lobster. On chilly nights, the French onion soup (COP$9,000) really hits the spot.

Casa Quintero (Cra. 9 No. 11-75, hours vary by restaurant), on the corner of the Plaza Mayor, holds several restaurants under one roof, like an upscale food hall. There is a little something for everyone here, including a Lebanese restaurant, an arepa joint, and a pizza place.

VEGETARIAN

Savia (Casa Quintero, Cra. 9 No. 11-75, cell tel. 312/435-4602, noon-9pm Thurs.-Mon., COP$25,000) has an extensive menu of both vegetarian and meaty entrées, like lentil stew, rice pilaf, and fish and chicken dishes. They also sell locally produced jams and other items in their storefront.

CAFÉS, BAKERIES, AND QUICK BITES

Flor de Maiz (Cra. 7 No. 11-83) specializes in corn arepas, tamales, and fresh juices. It's a cute hole-in-the-wall.

Panadería Astral (Cl. 12 No. 7-56, tel. 8/732-0811, 9:30am-7pm Mon.-Sat.) is the best place for fresh-baked bread and cakes.

They serve good coffee at **Sybarita Caffe** (Cra. 9 No. 11-88, cell tel. 316/481-1872, 8am-8pm daily), where the owners are on a mission to bring coffee appreciation to the masses. If you want your latte sourced from the coffee region—Quindío to be specific—then **Café Los Gallos** (Cra. 8 No. 13-55, cell tel. 300/851-4714, 9am-8pm daily) is the place.

The pizza at friendly, family-run **Gelatería Pizzería Santa Lucia** (Cra. 10 No. 10-27, cell tel. 313/880-1022, 11am-9:30pm daily) gets accolades. They also serve delicious homemade ice cream and frozen yogurt.

Accommodations

Villa de Leyva lives on tourism, so there are many accommodation options. Rates bump up on weekends and holidays like Christmas and Holy Week. During the week discounts may be possible, especially if you pay in cash.

UNDER COP$70,000

★ **Renacer** (Av. Cra. 10 No. 21, tel. 8/732-1201, www.renacerhostel.com, COP$35,000 dorm, COP$120,000 d) is the best-known hostel in town and is popular for good reason. Set at the foot of a mountain, it's about a 15-minute walk from town—but guests will be reimbursed for the initial taxi ride from the bus station. Facilities are well kept and there are ample open-air common spaces. There are seven rooms and *cabañas* for varying numbers of guests, some with private bathrooms. There is also a place for those arriving in campers or vans. The on-site restaurant has a range of comfort-food options. Through **Colombian Highlands** (www.colombianhighlands.com), Renacer arranges outdoor expeditions to nearby attractions and can even assist in excursions outside of the Villa de Leyva area. They have very good information on how to hike or bike the area solo. This is an excellent place to swap travel tips with backpackers from around the world.

Run by an Austrian-Colombian couple, ★ **Casa Viena** (Cra. 10 No. 19-114, tel. 8/732-0711, cell tel. 314/370-4776, www.hostel-villadeleyva.com, COP$60,000 d) is a quiet and relaxed guesthouse on the same road as Renacer. It has just four rooms, three of which have shared baths.

A low-key hostel option is **Hostal Rana** (Cl. 10A No. 10-31, tel. 8/732-0330, cell tel. 311/464-2969, www.hostal-rana.com, COP$20,000 dorm, COP$40,000 d). It has one dorm room and four private rooms. Rooms are clean and beds are firm. There is a small kitchen for use in the back behind a pleasant patio space.

If you ask locals for a less expensive hotel option, many will tell you to check out **Hospedería Don Paulino** (Cl. 14 No. 7-46, tel. 8/732-1227, cell tel. 313/394-2507, www.donpaulino.co, COP$35,000 s, COP$65,000 d). It's not a fancy place by any means, but the price can't be beat. The 16 rooms all have wireless Internet and TV. Go for a room on the 2nd floor that has a balcony overlooking the patio. Each morning they provide coffee and a voucher for breakfast at a nearby restaurant.

COP$70,000-200,000

Family-run **Hospedería La Roca** (Cl. 13 No. 9-54, COP$90,000 d) has been a cheapie quietly overlooking the Plaza Mayor for years, but it's no longer a budget option. More than 20 rooms with high ceilings surround two interior courtyards that are filled with greenery. Try for one on the 2nd floor with a very distant view of the mountains. Around the corner is the welcoming **Posada de Los Ángeles** (Cra. 10 No. 13-94, tel. 8/732-0562, COP$110,000 d), a lovely option overlooking the Plazoleta de Carmen. Some rooms have balconies with views of the church. Take your American-style breakfast in the cheerfully painted patio filled with potted plants and flowers. There's no wireless Internet available.

The inviting ★ **Hospedería El Marqués de San Jorge** (Cl. 14 No. 9-20, tel. 8/732-0240, www.hospederiaelmarquesdesanjorge.com, COP$130,000-200,000 d) is just a block from the Plaza Mayor, has two interior patios that are filled with greenery, and has clean and comfortable modern rooms (despite having been around since 1972). It's a bargain compared to other luxury hotels in town.

On the outskirts of town, but only about a ten-minute walk from the Plaza Mayor, is **Hotel Santa Viviana** (Diag. 8 No. 12A-76, tel. 732-0818, cell tel. 313/885-1072, www.hotelsantaviviana.com, COP$109,000 d), a spacious hotel with ample green spaces and an open-air restaurant where breakfast is served.

COP$200,000-500,000

The location of the ★ **Hotel Plaza Mayor** (Cra. 10 No. 12-31, tel. 8/732-0425, www.hotelplazamayor.com.co, COP$243,000 d), with a bird's-eye view of the Plaza Mayor from its western side, is unrivaled. The hotel's terrace is a great place to watch goings-on in the plaza and to take a photo of the cathedral bathed in a golden light in late afternoon. Rooms are spacious, some have a fireplace, and all are tastefully decorated. Breakfast is served in the pleasant courtyard.

Two other upscale options face parks. On the cute Parque Nariño, the elegant **Hotel La Posada de San Antonio** (Cra. 8 No. 11-80, tel. 8/732-0538, cell tel. 310/280-7326, www.hotellaposadadesanantonio.com, COP$238,000 d) is lavishly decorated and has spacious rooms, a pleasant restaurant, a cozy reading room, a pool, an art gallery, a billiards room, and even a small chapel. Built in 1845, it was originally home to a wealthy family. On the Plaza de Ricaurte, the ★ **Hotel Plazuela de San Agustín** (Cl. 15 No. 8-65, tel. 8/732-2175, www.hotelplazuela.com, COP$300,000 d) is a cozy hotel with fewer than a dozen enormous carpeted rooms. One room has four beds and a fireplace. Mornings start off with breakfast served near a fountain in the lovely courtyard. The hotel is two blocks from the Plaza Mayor.

Hotel Boutique Candelaria (Cl. del Silencio 18 No. 8-12, tel. 8/732-0534, cell tel. 313/837-4230, www.hotelcandelaria.villadeleyva.com.co, COP$220,000 d) serves cheese and wine and is a very cozy option with wooden floors, antiques, and personal touches. It's next door to the **Hostería El Molino de Mesopotamia** (Cra. 8 No. 15A-265, cell tel. 311/278-8688, www.lamesopotamia.com, COP$200,000 d). Built in the 16th century, this is one of the oldest constructions in Villa de Leyva. It's set in a quiet and lush corner of the town, with babbling brooks and even a chilly pool.

Information and Services

The Villa de Leyva **tourist office** (corner Cra. 9 and Cl. 13, tel. 8/732-0232, 8am-12:30pm and 2pm-6pm Mon.-Sat., 9am-1pm and 3pm-6pm Sun.), off Plaza Mayor, has free tourist maps and brochures.

There are several **ATMs** in Villa de Leyva, particularly along the southern end of the Plaza Mayor.

An efficient and inexpensive laundry service in town near the bus terminal is **Lava Express** (Cra. 8 No. 8-21, cell tel. 320/856-1865, 8am-noon and 2pm-7pm Mon.-Fri., 8am-7pm Sat.).

Transportation

Thanks to a recently expanded four-lane highway that bypasses Tunja, Villa de Leyva is easily accessible by private car or by public bus from Bogotá, as well as from Tunja. Renting a car in Bogotá and driving to Villa de Leyva gives you a lot of flexibility to visit enchanting pueblos to your heart's content. Nearly all hotels have parking lots.

The bus terminal in Villa de Leyva is the **Terminal de Transportes** (Cra. 9 between Clls. 11-12). The bus ride from Tunja to Villa de Leyva takes about 45 minutes, and deposits riders at the bus terminal.

There are a few direct buses to Villa de Leyva (3.5 hours, COP$22,000) from both the Terminal de Transportes and the Portal del Norte in Bogotá. However, it's often quicker and easier to take a bus from the Portal del Norte to Tunja (2-2.5 hours, COP$20,000) via a bus company such as Autoboy. In Tunja, ask your bus driver where to transfer to the *buseta* (small bus) that will take you onward to Villa de Leyva. These leave roughly every 15 minutes (until 8pm). This leg takes about 45 minutes and costs COP$7,000.

Several companies offer two daily return trips to Bogotá, with buses that depart between 5am and 6am and again at around 1pm. There are many more options on Saturdays, Sundays, and Monday holidays. These tend to leave in the late afternoon at around 3pm.

To get to Villa de Leyva from Bucaramanga or San Gil in Santander, you'll have to hop on a bus to Tunja (COP$45,000). The highway that extends from Bogotá to Venezuela is a busy one, and the journey can take five or six hours.

Once in Villa de Leyva, it is easy and pleasant to walk everywhere. A few streets around the Plaza Mayor, including the main drag, Calle 13, are pedestrian-only. Even on non-pedestrian streets it's hard for vehicles to zoom along.

VICINITY OF VILLA DE LEYVA

The countryside near Villa de Leyva, the undulating desert of the Valle de Saquencipá, is a playground for tourists. Many of the region's sights can be visited by bike from Villa de Leyva, although the country roads are hilly.

★ Santuario Flora y Fauna Iguaque

One of the country's most accessible national parks is about 13 kilometers from Villa de Leyva. The **Santuario Flora y Fauna Iguaque** (www.parquesnacionales.gov.co, 8am-4pm daily, last entrance 10am, COP$42,000 non-Colombians, COP$16,000 Colombian residents, COP$8,500 students and children) is an excellent place to experience the unique landscape of the Andean *páramo* (highland moor) as well as dry tropical forest. The protected area extends for some 6,750 hectares. It is also a park of several *lagunas* (mountain lakes). Laguna Iguaque is known as a sacred lake for the Muisca people. They believed the goddess Bachué was born out of the blue-green waters of this lake, giving birth to humanity.

Most day-trippers based in Villa de Leyva visit the park to make the hike up to Laguna Iguaque. The climb, which takes you through three ecosystems—Andean forest, sub-*páramo*, and *páramo*—begins at the Centro Administrativo Carrizal at an elevation of 2,800 meters (9,185 feet) and ends 4.6 kilometers (2.6 miles) later at Laguna Iguaque (3,650 meters/11,975 feet). The enjoyable hike takes about 3-4 hours. Along the way you may be able to spot different species of birds and perhaps some deer or foxes. At the mist-shrouded Laguna Iguaque, you'll be surrounded by hundreds of *frailejones*, unusual cactus-like plants found only in this special ecosystem.

It is best to make the hike during the week, as the trails get crowded on weekends. You do not need a guide for the hike to Laguna Iguaque. During particularly dry spells the threat of forest fires forces the park to forbid entry to visitors. That is most likely to occur in January or August. Ask beforehand at your hostel or hotel to find out if the park is open to visitors.

If you are interested in exploring other paths in the park, consider overnighting at the **Centro de Visitantes Furachiogua,** the park's basic accommodations facility, which caters mostly to student groups. Seven rooms have 6-8 beds each (COP$39,500 pp), and the restaurant is open to day-trippers as well. The facility is about 700 meters beyond the Centro Administrativo Carrizal visitors center. There are camping facilities near the cabins (COP$10,000 pp). To inquire about accommodations or to make a reservation, contact the community organization **Naturar-Iguaque** (cell tel. 312/585-9892 or 318/595-5643, naturariguaque@yahoo.es). A guided walk to Laguna Iguaque costs COP$80,000 for a group of 1-6.

GETTING THERE

Buses bound for the town of Arcabuco leave from the bus station in Villa de Leyva and will stop at the Casa de Piedra (8 km from Villa de Leyva), a local landmark that is a house made of stone. Buses depart at 7am, 10am, and 1:30pm. It's about a 30-minute ride to the Casa de Piedra, which costs COP$5,000. From there it's about an hour-long walk (3 km/2 mi) east to the Centro Administrativo Carrizal visitors center, which is also the park entrance. This walk, along a dirt and gravel road, is an attraction in itself.

For transportation back to Villa de Leyva there are four buses each day: at 8:30am, 10:30am, 1pm, and 4:30pm, which all depart from the Casa de Piedra.

Paleontological Museums

During the Cretaceous period (66-145 million years ago), the area around Villa de Leyva was submerged in an inland sea. Some of the marine species that lived here included the pliosaurus, plesiosaurus, and ichthyosaurus.

Toward the end of this period, many species became extinct. Simultaneously the Andes mountains were created when the earth shifted. As the waters gave way to mountains, the bones of these species became embedded in rock, guaranteeing their preservation. Today this region has a handful of paleontological sites where you can view fossils of everything from parts of massive dinosaurs to small ammonites, of which there are thousands. Excavations continue throughout the valley.

In 1977, locals made a fantastic discovery: a distant relative of carnivorous marine reptiles from the pliosaurus family, to be classified as a *Kronosaurus boyacensis Hampe*. It roamed this part of the earth some 110 million years ago. The first-ever find of this species can be seen, fixed in the earth extending for about 10 meters, in the location of its discovery at the **Museo El Fósil de Monquirá** (Km. 4 Vía Santa Sofía, Vereda Monquirá, COP$6,000). Guides give a brief tour of the museum, which has hundreds of other animal and plant fossils on display. This is a major tourist sight, and there are souvenir shops and juice stands nearby.

Across the street from Museo El Fósil de Monquirá is the **Centro de Investigaciones Paleontológicas** (Km. 4 Vía Santa Sofía, Vereda Monquirá, cell tel. 314/219-2904 or 321/978-9546, 9am-noon and 2pm-5pm Mon. and Wed.-Thurs., 8am-5pm Fri.-Sun., COP$8,000). On view here are parts of a *Platypterygius boyacensis,* as well as a *Callawayasaurus colombiensis,* which were all unearthed nearby. An informative 20-minute tour (in Spanish) of the center is included.

GETTING THERE

You can visit the museums on bike, by taxi, or by public transportation. **CoomultransVilla** has hourly buses (Santa Sofía-bound, COP$2,500) in the mornings from the Terminal de Transportes in Villa de Leyva departing at 6:45am, 8am, 9am, and 10am. The driver can let you off within easy walking distance of all the museums.

There are also buses in the afternoon. The last bus departing Santa Sofía bound for Villa de Leyva leaves at around 4pm and arrives in Villa de Leyva 30 minutes later. You'll have to be on the lookout for it on the road between Santa Sofía and Villa de Leyva and flag it down. It's best to confirm all the bus schedules in advance. If you miss the bus, staff at the museums can call a taxi, which will cost about COP$15,000 to Villa de Leyva.

All hostels and hotels can arrange for a taxi to take you to the museums, wait for you, and deposit you back in town afterward. Negotiate an acceptable price for this; around COP$70,000 for two sights and round-trip travel is considered a fair price.

Convento del Santo Ecce Homo

The **Convento del Santo Ecce Homo** (8 km northwest of Villa de Leyva, tel. 1/288-6373, 9am-5pm Tues.-Sun., COP$5,000) is set idyllically atop a hill overlooking Villa de Leyva. Dominican monks founded this monastery in 1620. The site is a delight to visit. The beautifully preserved baroque chapels and the museum, part of which is dedicated to indigenous cultures, are open to the public. A monk's cell, library, and dining hall area provide a glimpse into monastery life. Surrounded by stone columns, the courtyard is awash in a rainbow of colors, with flowers always in bloom.

GETTING THERE

You can reach the convent on bike, by taxi, or by public transportation. **CoomultransVilla** has hourly buses in the mornings from the Terminal

Convento del Santo Ecce Homo

de Transportes in Villa de Leyva, bound for Santa Sofía (COP$2,500) and departing at 6:45am, 8am, 9am, and 10am. They can let you off within walking distance of the convent.

The last bus departing Santa Sofía bound for Villa de Leyva leaves at around 4pm, and arrives in Villa de Leyva about 30 minutes later. You'll have to be on the lookout for it and flag it down on the road between these two towns. Confirm the bus schedule in advance.

All hostels and hotels can arrange for a taxi to take you to the convent (and other sights), wait for you while you visit, and then return you to town. Negotiate an acceptable price; around COP$70,000 for two sights and round-trip travel is fair.

RÁQUIRA

This town, 28 kilometers (17 miles) from Villa de Leyva, is synonymous with *artesanías* (handicrafts). The main drag is lined with colorful shops, and in one stop you can pick up handicrafts of every size and shape and from across the country: hammocks, *mochilas* (handbags), and row after row of trinkets.

Ráquira is the capital of Colombian **ceramics** and has been since before the arrival of the Spaniards. In fact, it is said that the name Ráquira means "city of clay pots" in the Chibcha language of the Muiscas, who lived in the area. All those reddish flowerpots and planters you may have seen in other parts of the country most likely came from here. It's estimated that some 500 families in the area make their living harvesting the clay in nearby areas or firing the pottery in their own workshops. A dwindling number of women in the area do things the old-fashioned way—with their hands. They make mostly decorative items like candlestick holders and piggybanks with imperfections—telltale signs of their artisan origins.

One large shop specializing in pottery is **Todo Ráquira** (Cra. 5 No. 3A-05, tel. 8/735-7000, www.todoraquira.com, 9am-6pm daily), about two blocks from the pleasant Parque Principal (Cras. 3-4 and Clls. 3-4). The front of the store is filled with a variety of Colombian handicrafts (but note that some are made in China). If you meander to the back, you'll see the workshop where you can check out bowls, flowerpots, and other items.

If you'd like to observe the ceramic-making process, you can visit the workshop of **Isaias Valero** (no phone, hours vary, COP$5,000 suggested donation), which is on the main road near the Casa de la Cultura. You can watch him at work, and he can show you the steps that go into creating a piece. If he is there, Isaias will gladly welcome your visit. To get to the workshop, walk up about 70 steps from the main road, just before the Casa de la Cultura.

Getting There

Buses to Ráquira (45 minutes, COP$7,000) depart from Villa de Leyva's Terminal de Transportes, leaving between 7am and 8:30am daily. Passengers are dropped off at the main plaza, in the center of town.

You may prefer to hire a cab for the day, especially if you're traveling in a small group. Cab drivers typically charge COP$80,000 to drive to Ráquira and the Convento de la Candelaria, with a couple of stops along the way. Drivers will wait for you to visit each stop. Be specific about destinations and price at the beginning (put things in writing) to avoid unpleasant surprises later.

Convento de la Candelaria

One of the oldest monasteries in Latin America, and one that is still in use today, is the **Convento de la Candelaria** (9am-noon and 2pm-5pm daily, COP$5,000), seven kilometers outside of Ráquira. A pair of Augustinian missionaries arrived in this desert area in 1588 with the mission of bringing Christianity to the native Muisca people. They lived in caves (which you can visit) until the monastery was constructed.

The complex includes two cloisters that hold a chapel and a museum. The museum is a hodgepodge of religious art and objects, examples of technological advances through the years—from a *reloj borracho* (drunken clock) to an early Apple computer—and a display on the Colombian saint Ezequiel Moreno y Díaz, who is said to have healed cancer victims.

Adjacent to the monastery is a modern hotel, **Posada San Agustín** (cell tel. 313/852-1882, vocaciones@agustinosrecoletos.com.co, COP$168,000 d), which often hosts yoga and meditation retreats. Rooms are immaculately clean and completely free from clutter. Some even have hot tubs. At night you can sit around a fire in the common area and sip hot spiced wine. Meals are served in the restaurant, and they can also prepare vegetarian food. It's a quiet and peaceful place.

A taxi ride from Ráquira to the convent will cost about COP$20,000-30,000 round-trip; it's a 15-minute drive each way. Specify if you want the driver to wait while you explore the convent. There is also a bus that runs daily from the Parque Principal in Ráquira (COP$2,500), which leaves passengers at an intersection with a dirt road that winds to the monastery.

TUNJA

This university town (pop. 178,000), home to the Universidad de Boyacá, boasts some spectacular churches. Make sure you arrive during church visiting hours, as the city does not have much else to offer. Because there are frequent bus connections with Bogotá and Santander, Tunja is a good base from which to explore Boyacá.

Sights

Everything you need to see in Tunja is in its *centro histórico,* which is between Calles 13 and 24 and Carreras 7 and 12.

★ HISTORIC CHURCHES

Tunja is a city of churches, with over a dozen that date to colonial times. Hours of visitation can be irregular, but they are always open for mass, which is a good time to take a look. Most churches celebrate mass at about 7am and 5:30pm daily, with more frequent masses on Sundays.

On the eastern side of the **Plaza de Bolívar** (Cl. 19 at Cra. 9), **Catedral Santiago de Tunja** (Cra. 9 at Cl. 19) is a 16th-century construction, originally built out of wood and earthen *tapia pisada,* which is an adobe technique. It was the first cathedral to be built in Nueva Granada. It has three naves, four side chapels, and two front chapels.

Santa Clara La Real (Cra. 7 No. 19-58, Cl. 21 No. 11-31, tel. 8/742-5659 or 8/742-3194, 8am-11:30am and 3pm-4:30pm Mon.-Fri., 8am-11:30am Sat., masses 7am and 5pm Mon.-Sat., 7am, 11am, and 5pm Sun.) was built between 1571 and 1574 and was the first Clarisa convent in Nueva Granada. It has one nave, noteworthy for the spectacular decorations adorning its presbytery including golden garlands, grapes, pineapples (which were a sacred indigenous symbol), pelicans, an anthropomorphic sun, and other symbols of nature. Also look for the seal of Tunja, the double-headed eagle, modeled on the seal of Emperor Charles V, who gave the city its charter. In the choir is the tiny cell where Madre Josefa del Castillo lived for over 50 years in the late 17th and early 18th centuries. While there she wrote two books and several poems, with themes of sexual repression and mystical descriptions of heaven and hell. Near her cell are some frescoes made with coal, an abundant resource in the area.

The sky-blue interior of the **Iglesia de Santa Bárbara** (Cra. 11 No. 16-62, between Clls. 16-17, tel. 8/742-3021, 8:30am-12:30pm and 2pm-6pm daily, masses 5:30pm and 6pm Mon.-Fri., 7am, 9am, 10am, and 11am Sat., noon, 5pm, 6pm, and 7pm Sun.) and its Mudejar ceiling designs make this one of the prettiest churches in Tunja. The single-nave structure, with two chapels making the form of a cross, was completed in 1599. When it was built, it was raised at the edge of Tunja, near an indigenous settlement.

Built in the 1570s, the **Templo de Santo Domingo de Guzmán** (Cra. 11 No. 19-55, tel. 8/742-4725, 8am-11:30am Mon.-Fri., masses 7am and 6pm

a decorative church ceiling in Tunja

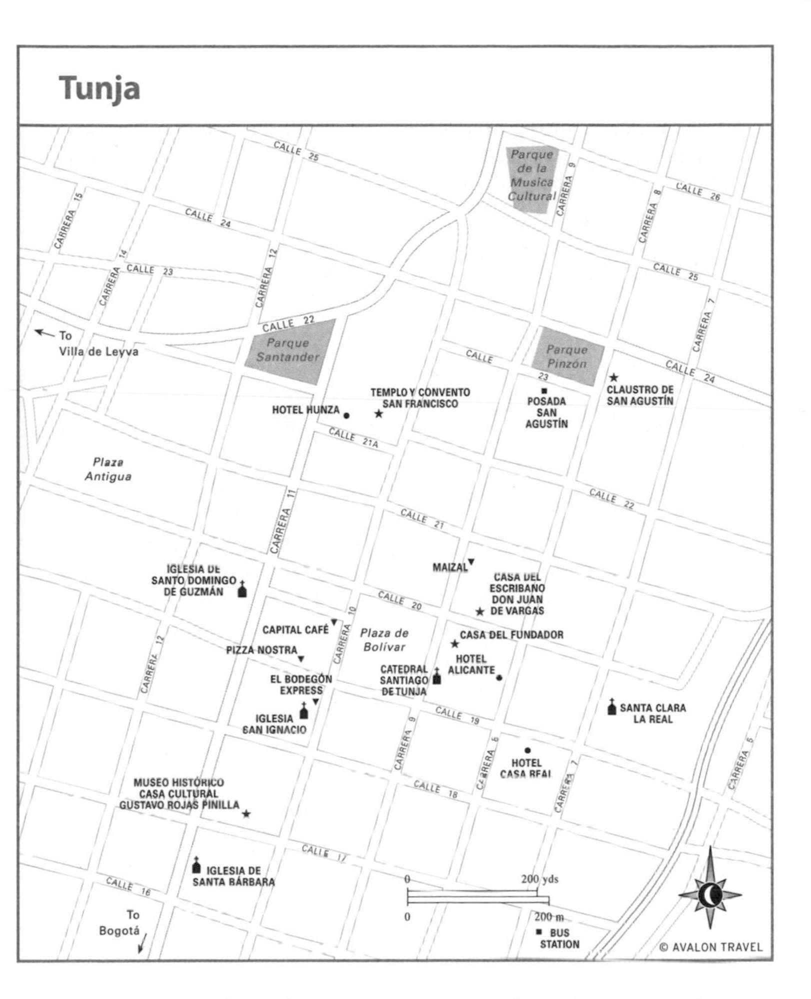

Mon.-Fri., 7am and 6pm Sat., 7am, 10am, noon, and 6pm Sun.) is one of the most elaborately decorated churches in Colombia. Visitors have been known to audibly gasp at their first sight of the spectacular Capilla del Rosario, a chapel constructed of wood painted in red and gold-plated floral designs. It's considered the Sistine Chapel of baroque art in Latin America. Figures of El Nazareno and El Judío Errante are part of the collection of paintings and woodcarvings in this church with several chapels. If you have time to visit just one church in Tunja, make it this one.

The **Claustro de San Agustín** (Cra. 8 No. 23-08, tel. 8/742-2311, ext. 8306, www.banrepcultural.org/tunja, 8:30am-6pm Mon.-Fri., 9am-1pm Sat., free) dates to the late 16th century. It served as an Augustinian convent until 1821, when it was taken over by the government. The friars were sent to another convent, and the building would become the home of the Colegio de Boyacá and was later transferred to the Universidad de Boyacá.

Adorning the corridors around the patio are several colonial-era murals. The *claustro* (cloister) is administered by the Banco de la República, which often holds cultural events here. You can settle down with a book or work on your computer in the gorgeous reading rooms (free Wi-Fi is available). Be sure to check out the gallery space on the 2nd floor.

Other religious sights worth visiting include the 17th-century **Iglesia San Ignacio** (Cra. 10 No. 18-41, tel. 8/742-6611, 8am-noon and 2pm-5pm Wed.-Sat.), which now serves as a theater, and the **Templo y Convento San Francisco** (Cra. 10 No. 22-32, tel. 8/742-3194, 10:30am-12:30pm and 3pm-5:30pm daily, masses 7am, 11am, noon, and 7pm Mon.-Fri., 11am, noon, 6pm, and 7pm Sat., 8am, 10am, 11am, noon, 5pm, 6pm, and 7pm Sun.), one of the oldest churches and monasteries in Tunja. It was an important base for evangelization of nearby indigenous communities.

MUSEUMS

The Mudejar-Andalusian-style **Casa del Fundador Gonzalo Suárez Rendón** (Cra. 9 No. 19-68, Plaza de Bolívar, tel. 8/742-3272, museocasadelfundador@yahoo.com, 8am-noon and 2pm-6pm daily, COP$2,000) was built in the middle of the 16th century. The most remarkable aspects of the house are the frescoes of mythological creatures, human figures, exotic animals, and plants. These whimsical paintings date from the 17th century, although not much else is known about them. Guides will show you around.

Casa del Escribano del Rey Don Juan de Vargas (Cl. 20 No. 8-52, tel. 8/74-26611, 9am-noon and 2pm-5pm Tues.-Fri., 9am-noon and 2pm-4pm Sat.-Sun., COP$2,000) was owned by the scribe to the king, an important post in colonial Tunja. The scribe's jurisdiction covered all of present-day Boyacá, Santander, Norte de Santander, and parts of Venezuela and Cundinamarca. Student guides will give you a thorough tour of the museum. The house showcases furniture and other examples of colonial life, but the highlight of this Andalusian-style house is the unusual painted ceilings portraying exotic animals and mythological creatures, similar to the frescoes that can be found in the Casa del Fundador.

The childhood home of former president Gustavo Rojas Pinilla is now a museum: **Museo Histórico Casa Cultural Gustavo Rojas Pinilla** (Cl. 17 No. 10-63, tel. 8/742-6814, 8:30am-noon and 2pm-6pm Mon.-Fri.). Rojas, after seizing power in 1953, became the only dictator that Colombia has ever had. Upstairs are two exhibition spaces, one with memorabilia of Rojas and the other with portraits of 12 presidents that hailed from Boyacá. Despite his antidemocratic credentials, Rojas is revered in Tunja as the man who brought an end to the mid-20th-century violence between Liberals and Conservatives.

Food

Comida típica (Colombian fare) rules the day in this city lacking in restaurant options. For a really local, greasy-spoon-type experience, try **Restaurante Maizal** (Cra. 9 No. 20-30, tel. 8/742-5876, 7am-8:45pm

Mon.-Sat., 9am-4:45pm Sun., COP$12,000). It has been serving *sancocho* (beef stew), *mondongo* (tripe stew), and *ajiaco* (chicken and potato soup) to Tunja for over 50 years. Another old-timer is **El Bodegón Express** (Cra. 10 No. 18-45, cell tel. 321/221-4460, 8am-4pm Mon.-Sat., COP$10,000). It's next to the Iglesia San Ignacio. It specializes in trout dishes and *cocido boyacense* (COP$6,000), which has a variety of meats and some of the unusual tubers from the area, such as *cubios, ibias,* and *rubas.*

Pizza Nostra (Cl. 19 No. 10-36, tel. 8/740-2040, 11am-8pm daily, COP$18,000) has a few locations in and around town. The most famous one is at the Pozo de Donado (tel. 8/740-4200, 11am-11pm daily), a small park and Muisca archaeological site surrounding a lake.

It's a tradition in Tunja to while away the hours in cafés. It must be the chilly weather. While the actual coffee around town may disappoint, the atmosphere, with groups of retirees dressed in suits brushing shoulders with bevies of college students, does not. Try **Capital Café** (7am-7pm daily), which is at the entrance of the *pasaje* (passage) close to the Plaza de Bolívar.

Accommodations

Most overnight visitors stay in the decent hotels in the *centro histórico* within easy walking distance of the Plaza de Bolívar and sights of interest.

Two blocks from the Plaza de Bolívar is ★ **Hotel Casa Real** (Cl. 19 No. 7-65, tel. 8/743-1764, www.hotelcasarealtunja.com, COP$95,000 d), a colonial-style house with 10 rooms surrounding a divine courtyard. That's where a very nice breakfast is served for an additional cost. The courtyard walls feature lovely tile paintings (by artist Adriano Guio) depicting Boyacá country scenes. You can order your breakfast the night before and even request it to be delivered to your room. Rooms are tastefully decorated and comfortable, and prices here are astoundingly low. Owned by the same people, **Hotel Alicante** (Cra. 8 No. 19-15, tel. 8/744-9967, www.hotelalicantetunja.com, COP$95,000 d) caters to business clientele. This small hotel may not have the charm of Casa Real, but it's clean.

A warm and welcoming guesthouse, the ★ **Hotel Posada de San Agustín** (Cl. 23 No. 8-63, tel. 8/742-2986, www.posadadesanagustin.co, COP$100,000 d) is in a historic, wood-floored house just a few blocks from the Plaza de Bolívar.

The classy address in town is, as it has been for decades, the **Hotel Hunza** (Cl. 21A No. 10-66, tel. 8/742-4111, www.hotelhunza.com, COP$228,000 d). The hotel boasts luxurious king-size beds and card keys. Amenities include a decent-sized indoor pool and a steam room. Its neighbor is the Templo de Santo Domingo. The hotel is a popular place for wedding banquets. There is a lively bar near the entrance, but it shouldn't keep you up at night.

Transportation

Situated 150 kilometers (93 miles) northeast of Bogotá and 20 kilometers (12 miles) southeast of Villa de Leyva, Tunja is easy to get to by car or by bus. Buses to Bogotá, other towns in Boyacá, and to all major cities in Colombia depart from Tunja's **Terminal de Transportes** (Cra. 7 No. 16-40). Buses to Tunja's Terminal de Transportes from Bogotá cost about COP$18,000 and from Villa de Leyva are COP$6,000.

The best way to get around the *centro histórico* is on foot.

Puente de Boyacá

The **Puente de Boyacá war memorial** about 20 kilometers (12 miles) southwest of Tunja celebrates a decisive battle, the **Batalla del Puente de Boyacá,** which effectively ended Spanish control of Nueva Granada. At this site today there are several memorials and statues, including the Plaza de Banderas, where flags from all the departments of Colombia fly. There is also a sculpture of Gen. Francisco Paula de Santander and a large sculpture of Gen. Simón Bolívar surrounded by angels representing the South American countries that he liberated (Bolivia, Colombia, Ecuador, Peru, and Venezuela). There is a small bridge on the memorial grounds, but it dates from the 1930s; the original Puente de Boyacá is long gone.

Santander and Bolívar achieved immortality as heroes of Colombian independence for their victory here. After defeating the Spaniards at the Batalla del Pantano de Vargas on July 25, 1819, revolutionary troops under their command marched toward Bogotá. South of Tunja, they engaged with the main Spanish army, defeating it decisively on August 7 at the Batalla del Puente de Boyacá. The engagement was a small affair with fewer than 3,000 soldiers on each side, with about 100 royalists and only 13 rebels losing their lives. Bolívar marched onward to Bogotá, which he took without a fight, ushering in independence.

At 6pm every day there is a short flag-lowering ceremony; during this time, you can have your picture taken with Colombian soldiers.

Buses passing between Bogotá and Tunja can drop you off here (COP$5,000), or you can contract a taxi (COP$12,000) from Tunja. The journey takes about 15 minutes.

SOGAMOSO AND VICINITY

Sogamoso, a city of over 100,000 inhabitants, is about 75 kilometers (46 miles) east of Tunja and is known for being an important pre-Hispanic Muisca center. It was originally known as Suamoxi. It's a city of little charm; however, the Museo Arqueológico de Sogamoso is worth a stop, and there are several worthy day-trip destinations in the area. There are a number of atmospheric haciendas in the region. Many hotels and lodges have their own restaurants.

Visit Sugamuxi (www.visitsugamuxi.com) offers information on the region and travel tips in English.

For visitors with a little time and who want more independence, it may make sense to rent a car in Bogotá, rather than rely on buses. From Bogotá to Sogamoso it's about a 2.5-hour drive.

Sogamoso

Run by the Universidad Pedagógica y Tecnológica de Colombia (UPTC) in Tunja, the **Museo Arqueológico de Sogamoso** (Cl. 9A No. 6-45, tel. 8/770-3122, 9am-noon and 2pm-5pm Mon.-Sat., 9am-3pm Sun., COP$5,000) has an extensive collection of artifacts of the Muisca civilization, the main indigenous group of Colombia. Muiscas lived in the area that is today the departments of Boyacá, Santander, and Cundinamarca; it was the seat of power for a confederation led by the Iraca. The most memorable sight on the museum grounds is the fantastic Templo del Sol, a re-creation of a Muisca temple that was burned to the ground by the Spaniards in the late 16th century. The museum is worth visiting, even though the exhibition spaces are drab and the sequence of exhibits does not flow very lucidly. That is a shame because there is an interesting history to tell and the collection is impressive. If you have the time and speak Spanish, hire a guide. (Inquire at the ticket office.) Look for the exhibit on *ocarinas,* which are whistles, usually ceramic, that are often zoomorphic in form. Visitors should also see the stunning black-and-white geometric designs of *torteros,* which are spindles used in spinning yarn, as well as remarkably well preserved red-and-white ceramic vessels and urns.

FOOD AND ACCOMMODATIONS

It's said that Simón Bolívar stayed at ★ **Hacienda Suescún** (Km. 4 Vía Sogamoso-Tibasosa, cell tel. 313/853-5384 or 315/648-8985, www.hotel-suescun.com, COP$260,000 d) before he headed off to face the Spaniards at the decisive Batalla del Puente de Boyacá. This hacienda, surrounded by tall trees covered with Spanish moss, has 18 gorgeous rooms, an elegant dining area, no televisions in the rooms, and wonderful grounds you can meander about. Horses can be taken out for a spin in the countryside for an additional fee. Like many hotels in the area, the hacienda fills up on weekends with wedding parties and business groups. During the week, it's very quiet. It's about five kilometers northwest of Sogamoso.

The wonderful ★ **Hotel Finca San Pedro** (Km. 1 Vía Lago Tota, tel. 312/567-7102, www.fincasanpedro.com, COP$25,000 dorm, COP$80,000 d), which is also home to a friendly family, is a lush refuge amid lovely gardens full of fruit trees, vegetables, and flowers. It offers both private and dorm accommodations, all of which are comfortable. They also have a hammock room, a kitchen for guest use, a breakfast area where farm fresh eggs, goat's milk yogurt, and fresh juices are available for an additional cost, and common areas (both indoor and outdoor). Those traveling in motor homes are welcome too. What sets San Pedro apart is the owners: They know this region better than anyone, and they promote sustainable community-based tourism projects. It's easy to find, just off the main highway from Sogamoso to Lago Tota. A cab ride from the Sogamoso bus station costs COP$5,000.

Sogamoso's **Terminal de Transportes** (Cra. 17 between Clls. 11-11A, tel. 8/770-330) is downtown. Many buses connect Sogamoso with Paipa, Monguí, and Aquitania, the main town of Lago Tota.

From Bogotá to Sogamoso it's over 200 kilometers (124 miles), with regular bus service (3 hrs., COP$26,000) from the Portal del Norte bus terminal in Northern Bogotá. From Tunja the bus ride takes about one hour and costs COP$15,000.

Paipa

LOS LANCEROS MONUMENT

On the site of the **Batalla del Pantano de Vargas** (Battle of the Vargas Swamp) stands Colombia's largest sculpture, ***Los Lanceros*** (9 km south of Paipa on Paipa-Pantano de Vargas road, free), close to the town of Paipa. The massive monument was designed by Colombian sculptor Rodrigo Arenas Betancourt and built in commemoration of 150 years of Colombian independence. Bronze sculptures show the 14 *lanceros* (lancers on horseback) charging into battle, fists clenched in the air, with fear and defiance depicted on their faces. Above them is an odd triangular concrete slab that points into the heavens. It is 36 steps up to the platform of the monument, the age of Simón Bolívar on that fateful day.

The Batalla del Pantano de Vargas was a decisive battle during Simón Bolívar's independence march on Bogotá in 1819. After crossing the Llanos from Venezuela and climbing up the Andes via the Páramo de Pisba, the revolutionary army under Bolívar engaged a contingent of Spanish troops at the Pantano de Vargas on July 25, 1819. Exhausted after their long slog over the Cordillera Oriental mountains, the revolutionary troops were nearly defeated. However, a charge by 14 armed horsemen led by Juan José Rendón saved the day. Soldiers from the British Foreign Legion, under

the memorial of the Batalla del Pantano de Vargas, *Los Lanceros*

the command of Irishman James Rooke, also played a decisive role in this battle. The royalists lost 500 men in the battle, while 350 revolutionaries perished.

Across from the monument is the **Casa Museo Comunitario Juan Vargas** (COP$2,000), a small museum mostly about the military campaigns of Simón Bolívar. It was in this house that Juan Vargas, his wife, and their 12 children were executed by the Spaniards for supporting the rebel troops.

FOOD AND ACCOMMODATIONS

The ★ **Hacienda El Salitre** (Km. 3 Vía Paipa-Toca, tel. 8/785-1510, www.haciendadelsalitre.com, COP$350,000 d) is set in the countryside under towering eucalyptus trees, and you'll pass grazing cows to get there. At the hotel, go for one of the rooms with a thermal bathtub. You'll be treated to a thermal bath three times a day (staff come in and change the water each time). Rooms are cozy, warm, and spacious, but not quite luxurious. Here you can get a massage, or you can take a horse out for a trot to a nearby lake. From Sunday to Friday there is a 30 percent discount, so guests only pay full price for a Saturday-night stay. It's a popular location for wedding banquets and honeymoons on the weekends. The hacienda served as a barracks during the Batalla del Pantano de Vargas in 1819. The hotel has a very nice restaurant with outdoor seating, plus a café and a bar. Also open to nonguests, the restaurant, with its lovely setting, is the best around. It serves international and Colombian cuisine.

Overlooking Lago Sochagota is the **Estelar Paipa Hotel y Centro de Convenciones** (Lago Sochagota, Paipa, tel. 8/785-0944, www.hotelesestelar.com, COP$286,000 d). This upmarket chain hotel is modern, service oriented, and well maintained. The main attraction here is a spa with thermal baths, and there are other facilities on-site to keep you busy, such as a pool, tennis court, and a golf course. They also offer horseback riding. With over 100 rooms, this is a popular place for large groups.

Monguí

The chilly highland colonial village of **Monguí** was founded in 1601 and was a strategic post for the Spaniards thanks to its location between Tunja and the vast Llanos, the eastern plains. It is considered one of the most beautiful towns in Boyacá. Its narrow cobblestone streets are lined with white and green houses, many of which are multiple centuries old.

Three colonial constructions in Monguí have been declared national monuments. The stone **Basílica y Convento de Nuestra Señora de Monguí** stands on the Plaza de Bolívar. The adjacent Franciscan convent today houses the **Museo de Arte Religioso** (tel. 8/778-2050, 8am-noon and 2pm-5pm daily, free), which highlights the work of the famous 17th-century Colombian baroque painter Gregorio Vásquez de Arce y Ceballos. Other historic structures are the **Capilla de San Antonio de Padua,** which was the town's first church, and the photogenic stone bridge, the **Puente de Calicanto.**

Today Monguí is almost as famous for its soccer ball-making industry as for its colonial beauty. Around 70 percent of the town works in about 20 small factories. They churn out some 30,000 balls each month. More are produced during World Cup years. You can pick one up for about COP$25,000 at **Balones Hurtado** (Cl. 7 No. 3-60, tel. 8/778-2021, www.baloneshurtado.com, 9am-6pm Mon.-Sat.).

FOOD AND ACCOMMODATIONS

Monguí has a handful of lodging options. The reliable and comfortable choice is **La Casona de San Francisco de Asis** (Cra. 4A No. 3-41, tel. 8/778-2498, cell tel. 311/237-9823, COP$40,000 pp d). Rooms have a view over the Río Morro canyon, and the hotel is quite tidy. The restaurant, which has been in service for over two decades, is also one of the best in town, specializing in *cocido boyacense,* which has a variety of meats and some of the unusual tubers from the area, such as *cubios, ibias,* and *rubas.*

The **Calicanto Real** (Puente de Calicanto, Monguí, cell tel. 311/811-1519, calicantoreal.hostal@gmail.com, COP$25,000 pp) is an old house with five rooms overlooking the Puente de Calicanto. It was once the home of a wealthy emerald miner. Rooms are spacious with nice views and have a lot of character, but the beds are on the soft side. Within the hotel is a quirky tavern (hours vary) filled with decorations like cowboy hats, animal heads, and an homage to Monguí's most famous poet, El Indio Romulo.

TRANSPORTATION

There are two roads between Sogamoso and Monguí. The old but scenic route is partly unpaved and winds through eucalyptus forests and the pueblo of Morca. It's about 20 kilometers (12 miles) and makes for a challenging bike ride. On the new road, a bus ride to Monguí costs about COP$5,000 and takes about 45 minutes. The bus leaves from the intersection of Carrera 14 and Calle 16 in Sogamoso.

Lago Tota

One of the most popular destinations in Boyacá is **Lago Tota,** Colombia's largest lake, covering 55 square kilometers (21 square miles). The views are spectacular here, with mountains, valleys, and fields surrounding the lake. Over 145 species of birds have been seen in this area. The main town on the lake is Aquitania, and it's a rather dreary and surprisingly rough-and-tumble place. Most visitors choose to stay at one of the cozy lakeside lodges nearby.

The lake and surrounding countryside, a patchwork of fields of green onions and potatoes, is beautiful. However, the lake is in peril. The dumping of fertilizers and pesticides from lakeside farms has been the primary reason that this lake, which provides drinking water for hundreds of thousands of people, has been declared one of the top five most threatened wetlands in the world by the World Wetlands Network. There are other culprits as well, such as large caged trout farms. The threat of oil drilling in the lake was thwarted by environmental activists in 2012. Despite these environmental challenges, the lake remains a recreational draw for boaters. The water is very cold, so it's not considered a good place to swim.

Playa Blanca (COP$3,500 entry), a chilly lakeside beach, is the main draw at Lago Tota, as it's the only beach and gathering place here. At the water's edge is usually a local hawking boat rides on the lake. If you have a mountain bike, a nice ride is along the western side of the lake, along a mostly dirt road. This is also a pleasant route for a walk.

FOOD AND ACCOMMODATIONS

Along the shore of Lago Tota are many rooms with a view. Bargains can be had during the week, when you will have your lodge (if not the lake) blissfully to yourself. On long weekends, it's especially lively with visitors from Bogotá. Most lakeside lodges offer all meals. You may feel a little stuck here, due to lack of regular public transportation.

The Decameron all-inclusive hotel chain has agreements with two hotels in the area. The nicer of the two is **Refugio Santa Inés** (Km. 29 Vía Sogamoso-Aquitania, tel. 1/628-0000, cell tel. 313/261-2429, santaineshotel@gmail.com, www.decameron.com, COP$99,000 pp d), a comfortable lodge-style hotel with 13 rooms and two cabins. Wood ceilings and floors add to the atmosphere. Set on the eastern side of the lake, the hotel has a terrace, an ideal vantage point from which to watch the sunset with a drink (also open to nonguests). Beds are very comfortable, there is wireless Internet access, and breakfast is included. The restaurant offers other meals as well. Hiking, horseback riding, and taking a boat around the lake are other activities on offer, all of which require being accompanied by a guide. The other Decameron location is **Hotel Refugio Rancho Tota** (Km. 21 Vía Sogamoso-Aquitania, cell tel. 311/273-7863, www.hotelranchotota.

Playa Blanca, Lago Tota

com, COP$80,000 pp d), with similar pricing and facilities. It also has a small spa, and some rooms have fireplaces.

For charm and a view, there are two long-standing stone lodges. ★ **Pozo Azul** (Lago Tota, Bogotá tel. 1/620-6257, cell tel. 320/384-1000, www.hotelrefugiopozoazul.com, COP$196,000 d), set on an inlet, was one of the first nice hotels on the lake, and it retains its charm. You'll often see guests gathered by a circular fireplace in the lobby area. The hotel has 15 rooms and two *cabañas* (COP$340,000) that sleep four and feature their own fireplaces. Some beds are on the soft side. Getting from the parking lot to the lodge requires descending 80 steep steps, which could be difficult for those with physical limitations. The lodge can arrange a boat excursion around the lake for an additional cost. **Rocas Lindas** (Lago Tota, cell tel. 310/349-1107, www.hotelrocaslindas.wordpress.com, COP$85,000 pp d) is a cozy lodge with 10 rooms and one cabin. There's no wireless Internet here, and this hotel could use some upgrading.

TRANSPORTATION

To get to Playa Blanca from Sogamoso, there are two bus options that take different routes around the lake. Each ride takes about an hour and costs COP$5,000-6,000. One route goes through Iza and the other takes you to Aquitania, which requires transferring to a minivan at Aquitania's market, four blocks from the town's Plaza Principal. This second leg takes 10 minutes and costs COP$1,500.

Another option is to hire a car in Sogamoso for about COP$25,000 each way.

SIERRA NEVADA DEL COCUY

The Sierra Nevada del Cocuy, the highest mountains within the Cordillera Oriental (Eastern Range) of the Andes mountain chain, are 260 kilometers (162 miles) northeast of Bogotá in northern Boyacá. The entire mountain range is contained within and protected by the Parque Nacional Natural El Cocuy, the country's fifth-largest national park. With its 11 jagged snow-capped peaks, massive glacier-formed valleys, extensive *páramos* (highland moors) studded with exotic *frailejón* plants, and stunning crystalline mountain lakes, streams, and waterfalls, it is one of the most beautiful places in Colombia. The sierra appeals to serious mountaineers and rock climbers, but it is also a place that nature lovers with little experience and no gear can explore by doing easily organized day hikes.

PLANNING YOUR TIME

Getting to the Sierra Nevada del Cocuy entails a long, grueling trip, albeit through the beautiful, verdant countryside of Boyacá. Ideally you want to spend at least four days here, taking in the spectacular mountain landscapes.

The park has three sectors: the Northern, Central, and Southern Sectors, each with many options for day hikes, more strenuous ascents to the snowcapped peaks, or highly technical rock-climbing expeditions. There is also a spectacular six-day trek along a valley between the two main ridges of the sierra. It is not a highly technical trek but requires good high-altitude conditioning. For many visitors, this is the main reason to visit the sierra.

The gateway towns of El Cocuy and Güicán are convenient arrival and departure points for visiting the area. In both you can find basic tourist services, tour operators and guides, and stores to stock up on food, though not trekking equipment (which can be rented from local tour operators). Both have a few interesting sights and are departure points for day hikes. El Cocuy is better located to access the Southern Sector of the park and Güicán the Northern Sector. However, because both these towns are around 20 kilometers (12 miles) from the park and there is limited public transportation, a good option is to base yourself nearer to the park boundary in one of several pleasant lodges or campsites. You could easily spend a few days in each one of the three sectors, setting off on beautiful day hikes from your accommodations.

The only way to do the six-day hike around the park is with an organized tour, as the trails are not marked. If you are planning to do this trek, you may want to arrive a few days earlier to do some high-altitude acclimatization hikes. Many peaks are more than 5,000 meters (16,000 feet) high.

The only dependable time to visit the Sierra Nevada del Cocuy is from December to March, during the *verano* (summer dry season) in the Cordillera Oriental. At other times, there may be permanent cloud cover and much rain. High season, when Colombian visitors flock to the mountains, is from mid-December to mid-January, and again in Holy Week (late March or April).

The best available topographical maps of the Sierra Nevada de Cocuy can be viewed and downloaded online at www.nevados.org.

Sierra Nevada del Cocuy

GETTING THERE

The towns of El Cocuy and Güicán are served from Bogotá by three bus companies. The trip takes 11 hours; it stops at El Cocuy and terminates at Güicán. The most comfortable option is with the bus company **Libertadores** (COP$50,000), which operates a big bus that leaves Bogotá at 8:30pm. The return trip departs El Cocuy at 7:30pm. Bus line **Fundadores** (COP$45,000) has two buses; they leave Bogotá at 5am and 4:30pm, returning from El Cocuy at 7:30am and 8:30pm. **Concord** (COP$45,000) also has two services, leaving Bogotá at 3am and 5pm and leaving El Cocuy for Bogotá at 5:30am and 7:30pm.

El Cocuy

El Cocuy is a charming colonial town nestled in the lower folds of the Sierra Nevada del Cocuy at an altitude of 2,750 meters (9,022 feet). The town is meticulous, its whitewashed houses painted with a band of aquamarine. El Cocuy offers decent accommodations, a few tour operators, and some stores to stock up for a visit to the park, though no specialized mountaineering stores.

The only sight to check out is in the Parque Principal, where there is a large **diorama** of the Sierra Nevada del Cocuy. This will allow you to understand the mountain geography, with its multitude of snowcapped peaks, lakes, and valleys.

RECREATION

For a spectacular panoramic view of the entire sierra, take a hike to **Cerro Mahoma** (Mahoma Hill), to the west of town. It is a strenuous six- to seven-hour excursion often used by people who are acclimatizing before trekking in the Sierra Nevada del Cocuy. The trailhead is outside of El Cocuy on the road that leads to the town of Chita. Because the trail is not marked and splits several times, it is best to go with a guide.

For an experienced local guide, contact the local guide association, **ASEGUICOC** (Asociación de Prestadores de Servicios Ecoturísticos de Güicán y El Cocuy, cell tel. 311/557-7893, 311/236-4275, or 313/371-9735, aseguicoc@gmail.com).

FOOD AND ACCOMMODATIONS

Hotels like Casa Muñoz generally offer the best food, but don't expect to be amazed come dinnertime. Vegetarians may want to travel with a can of emergency lentils to hand over to kitchen staff to warm up for you.

Hotel la Posada del Molino (Cra. 3 No. 7-51, tel. 8/789-0377, www.elcocuycasamuseo.blogspot.com, COP$50,000 d) is a friendly guesthouse. Rooms in this old house are set around two colorful interior patios. The house has a little history to it as well. It is said that during the deadly feuds between Güicán and El Cocuy (Güicán was conservative and El Cocuy was liberal), the famous Virgen Morenita image was taken from its shrine in

Güicán and hidden away in the house where the hotel is located. You can see the room that hid this secret.

Casa Muñoz (Cra. 5 No. 7-28, tel. 8/789-0328, www.hotelcasamunoz.com, COP$25,000 pp d) has a great location overlooking the main plaza in town. It offers a restaurant in the patio on the main floor. Rooms are fine, though somewhat small, with firm beds and wooden floors.

INFORMATION AND SERVICES

At the offices of the **Parque Nacional Natural El Cocuy** (Cl. 5 No. 4-22, tel. 8/789-0359, cocuy@parquesnacionales.gov.co, 7am-noon and 1pm-4:45pm daily), you can obtain a park entry permit (COP$37,500 non-Colombians, COP$14,000 residents, COP$7,500 children/students) and general information.

There is an **ATM** at the Banco Agrario at Carrera 4 and Calle 8.

Güicán

Long before its foundation in 1822, Güicán was a place of significance for the U'wa indigenous people. The U'wa fiercely resisted the Spanish conquest, and, rather than submit to domination, their chief Güicány led the people to mass suicide off a nearby cliff known as El Peñón de los Muertos.

The town, damaged by fires and civil war, is a mix of modern and old buildings, without much charm. However, it is a convenient base for visiting the Northern Sector of the park. It has good accommodations, several tour operators, and is the starting point for numerous beautiful day hikes.

Folks in Güicán resent that the national park carries the "El Cocuy" name. They feel that this natural wonder is just as much theirs as it is their rivals in the town of El Cocuy. You can score points with them by referring to the park as Parque Nacional Natural El Güicán.

SIGHTS

The main sight in town is the image of the Virgen Morenita de Güicán, located in the **Iglesia de Nuestra Señora de la Candelaria** (Parque Principal). This image of the Virgin, with strong indigenous traits, appeared to the survivors of the U'wa mass suicide and ushered in their conversion to Christianity.

At the entrance to the town on the road from El Cocuy is the **Monumento a la Dignidad de la Raza U'wa** (Monument to U'wa Dignity), a large statue that depicts the culture and history of the U'wa people. It was designed by a local artist with input from the community.

RECREATION

There are several pleasant day hikes to be done from Güicán. A mildly strenuous three-kilometer (two-mile), two-hour round-trip hike takes you to the base of **El Peñón de los Muertos** (3,800 meters/12,500 feet), site of the U'wa mass suicide. The 300-meter (985-foot) cliff is imposing, and the thought of hundreds of people jumping off in defiance is sobering. From the Parque Principal, follow the road east toward the Vereda San Juan sector of the park. Several signs for El Peñon de los Muertos indicate the way, so you will not need a guide.

A longer and more strenuous 11-kilometer (7-mile), six-hour hike leads northeast along the **Sendero del Mosco** (Mosco Trail) up the Río Cardenillo, passing sheer cliffs to a spot called Parada de Romero, which is the initial (or ending, depending on which way you go) segment of the six-day circuit around the Sierra Nevada del Cocuy. The hike ends at an altitude of 3,800 meters (12,500 feet) and is a good acclimatization walk. The trailhead is off the road that leads from Güicán to PNN El Cocuy. Because the trail is not marked, it is best to take a guide.

To book a guide, contact the association of local guides, **ASEGUICOC** (Asociación de Prestadores de Servicios Ecoturísticos de Güicán y El Cocuy, cell tel. 311/557-7893, 311/236-4275, or 313/371-9735, aseguicoc@gmail.com).

FOOD AND ACCOMMODATIONS

The **Brisas del Nevado** (Cra. 5 No. 4-57, tel. 7/789-7028, cell tel. 310/629-9001, www.brisasdelnevado.com, COP$35,000 pp) has the best accommodations and restaurant in town. Four rooms in the original house sleep 2-4 people each. Outside is a nicer cabin with two rooms. The only problem is its location next to a rowdy bar. The restaurant, which serves Colombian cuisine, has varied hours, so inquire beforehand to make sure they'll be open.

El Eden (Transversal 2 No. 9-58 Urbanización Villa Nevada, cell tel. 311/808-8334, www.guicanextremo.com, COP$30,000 pp) is in a residential neighborhood about 10 minutes from the main plaza. It's a friendly place with lots of basic but clean rooms, and you can use the kitchen. Rabbits and parakeets are caged in the garden below.

Just outside of town is the **Hotel Ecológico El Nevado** (road to El Cocuy, cell tel. 320/808-5256 or 310/806-2149, www.hoteleconevado.jimdo.com, COP$60,000 d), which occupies a spacious and green setting. There are two parts to the hotel: the original quaint farmhouse with an interior patio, and a modern wing. The farmhouse has more character, but the modern wing is more comfortable.

INFORMATION AND SERVICES

At the Güicán office of the **Parque Natural Nacional El Cocuy** (Transversal 4 No. 6-60, tel. 8/789-7280, 7am-noon and 1pm-4:45pm daily), you can obtain a park entry permit (COP$55,000 non-Colombians, COP$28,000 residents, COP$13,500 children/students) and general information.

★ Parque Nacional Natural El Cocuy

Located about 20 kilometers (12 miles) east of the towns of El Cocuy and Güicán, the **Parque Nacional Natural El Cocuy** (tel. 8/789-0359, cocuy@

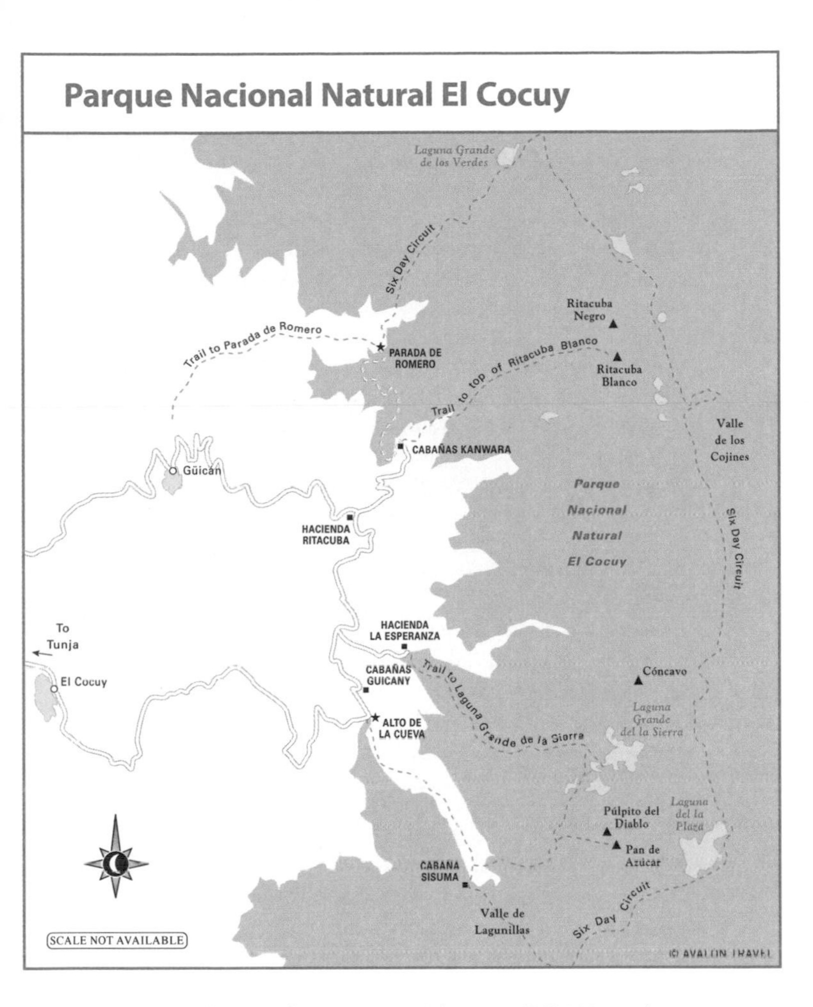

parquesnacionales.gov.co) covers 306,000 hectares (760,000 acres) spanning the departments of Boyacá, Arauca, and Casanare.

Entry permits (COP$55,000 non-Colombians, COP$28,000 residents, COP$13,500 children/students), which include entry fees, are required and can be easily obtained at the park offices in El Cocuy (Cl. 5 No. 4-22, tel. 8/789-0359, cocuy@parquesnacionales.gov.co, 7am-noon and 1pm-4:45pm daily) or Güicán (Transversal 4 No. 6-60, 7am-noon and 1pm-4:45pm daily). In peak season from mid-December to mid-January and during Holy Week, it is better to obtain the permit several weeks in advance through the Park Service in Bogotá. Call (tel. 1/353-2400) or email (ecoturismo@parquesnacionales.gov.co) to request a permit. You will be asked to submit the names of visitors, passport numbers, and expected dates of your arrival. The Park Service will provide instructions for paying and will send the permit by email.

The Sierra Nevada del Cocuy, consisting of two parallel ranges 30 kilometers (19 miles) long with 11 peaks higher than 5,000 meters (16,400 feet), is the centerpiece of the park. However, the park extends far north and east from the sierra and includes extensive tracts of temperate and tropical forests. It also includes 92,000 hectares (230,000 acres) of U'wa indigenous *resguardos* (reservations), which are not open to tourism.

The Sierra Nevada del Cocuy is home to the largest expanse of glaciers in Colombia, extending 16 square kilometers (6 square miles); what are usually referred to as *nevados* (snowcapped mountains) are in fact glacier-capped mountains. Unfortunately, all the glaciers in Colombia, including those of the Sierra Nevada del Cocuy, are rapidly melting due to global warming. A 2013 report by the Colombian Hydrological, Meteorological, and Environmental Studies Institute (IDEAM) forecasts that, by 2030, all the glaciers in Colombia will have disappeared.

The sierra's highest peak is **Ritacuba Blanco** (5,380 meters/17,650 feet). Other notable glacier-capped peaks are **Ritacuba Negro** (5,350 meters, 17,550 feet), **San Pablín Norte** (5,200 meters, 17,060 feet), **Cóncavo** (5,200 meters/17,060 feet), and **Pan de Azúcar** (5,100 meters, 16,730 feet). One of the most striking peaks in the Sierra Nevada del Cocuy is the **Púlpito del Diablo** or Devil's Pulpit (5,100 meters, 16,730 feet), a massive rectangular flat-topped rock formation. Ritacuba Blanco, Cóncavo, and Pan de Azúcar can be ascended by anyone in good physical shape and do not require mountain-climbing skills.

At the bases of the peaks are numerous glacier-formed valleys supporting *páramos,* unique tropical high-altitude ecosystems of the Andes. The *páramos* are covered with beautiful *frailejones,* plants that have imposing tall trunks and thick greenish-yellow leaves. Other *páramo* vegetation includes shrubs, grasses, and *cojines* (cushion plants).

Erwin Krauss, a Colombian of German descent, was the first modern explorer of the sierra in the 1930s. In the 1960s and 1970s, Colombian and European expeditions climbed most of the peaks. During the 1980s and 1990s, there was significant ELN and FARC presence and tourism all but disappeared. In the past decade, the army has reestablished control of the area around the Sierra Nevada de Cocuy, and tourists have started to come back. In the 2012-13 season, there were an estimated 9,000 visitors. The Park Service has been scrambling to deal with the influx of visitors.

There are three separate sectors where you can do spectacular one- to two-day hikes into the park. Each of these sectors has lodges and campgrounds that serve food and make convenient starting points for these hikes. You can get to any of these lodges by getting a ride on the morning *lechero* (milk truck) from either El Cocuy or Güicán.

HIKING TOUR OPERATORS AND GUIDES

Whether you decide to do a couple of day hikes or the six-day trek, securing a reliable, professional guide will greatly increase your enjoyment. For day hikes, contact the local guide association **Asociación de Prestadores**

de Servicios Ecoturísticos de Güicán y El Cocuy (ASEGUICOC, cell tel. 311/557-7893, aseguicoc@gmail.com). Expect to pay about COP$80,000-100,000. If you ascend to the top of a glacier, the daily rate goes up to COP$130,000-150,000 and includes necessary gear.

One of the leading trekking operators in the Sierra Nevada del Cocuy is **Colombia Trek** (Cra. 4 No. 6-50, Güicán, cell tel. 320/339-3839, arias_rodrigo@hotmail.com, www.colombiatrek.com), run by knowledgeable veteran Rodrigo Arias. It is one of the few operators offering English-speaking guides.

Another tour company based in El Cocuy is **Servicios Ecoturísticos Güicány** (Cra. 5 at Cl. 9, El Cocuy, cell tel. 310/566-7554), run by Juan Carlos Carreño, son of the owner of Cabañas Güicány, one of the park's lodges.

Avoid horseback rides through the park. Horses and cattle have caused significant damage to the flora of the park, and both are officially illegal. Unfortunately, many lodge owners do not agree with this environmental policy and refuse to adhere to it.

SOUTHERN SECTOR

This sector is accessed from **Alto La Cueva,** a stop outside the park on the *lechero* (milk truck) route. There are two good lodging options in this area, and they serve as points of reference: **Cabañas Güicány,** a lodge at Alto La Cueva, and **Cabaña Sisuma,** a facility 10 kilometers (6 miles) from Alto La Cueva inside the park.

One popular day hike in the Southern Sector goes up to **Lagunillas** through a wide glacier-formed valley strewn with different types of *frailejones* and passing four large lakes. From Alto La Cueva it is a six- to seven-hour round-trip hike to an altitude of 4,300 meters (14,100 feet). From the Cabaña Sisuma lodge within the park, it is a four- to five-hour round-trip hike. It's a good idea to hire a guide for this excursion.

A strenuous hike takes you to the **Pan de Azúcar.** From the Cabaña Sisuma lodge it is a six-hour round-trip hike to the border of the glacier that covers Pan de Azúcar, or 10 hours round-trip to the top of the glacier. Along the way you will pass the **Púlpito del Diablo** (Devil's Pulpit). From the top of Pan de Azúcar there are spectacular views of Laguna Grande de la Sierra, Púlpito del Diablo, and Cóncavo. A guide is required for this hike.

CENTRAL SECTOR

The starting point for visits to the Central Sector is the working farm and hotel **Hacienda La Esperanza,** which is on the edge of the park and a stop on the daily *lechero* (milk truck) route. From there, it is a strenuous six-hour round-trip hike to **Laguna Grande de la Sierra,** a beautiful lake nestled between the Cóncavo and Púlpito del Diablo peaks. It's best to go with a guide on this excursion. It's possible to continue and ascend the **Cóncavo** (5,200 meters/17,060 feet), **Concavito** (5,100 meters, 16,730 feet), or **Toti** (4,900 meters/16,075 feet) peaks, though doing so requires camping a night at the lake. Each ascent involves a strenuous four- to five-hour round-trip hike and should be done with a guide. From Laguna Grande de la Sierra, it is also possible to reach Cabaña Sisuma, in the Southern Sector, in nine hours. A guide is necessary because this trail is not well marked.

NORTHERN SECTOR

The starting point for hikes in the Northern Sector is **Cabañas Kanwara,** a lodge that's about a 90-minute walk from the closest stop on the *lechero* (milk truck) route, Hacienda Ritacuba. A short and moderate three- to four-hour round-trip hike takes you to the **Alto Cimiento del Padre,** a mountain pass at 4,200 meters (13,800 feet). This hike offers spectacular views of Ritacuba Negro peak. It's a good idea to hire a guide for this hike.

Cabañas Kanwara is also the starting point for hikes to the gently sloping **Ritacuba Blanco,** the highest peak in the Sierra Nevada del Cocuy. The ascent to the top can be done in one grueling 9- to 10-hour excursion, leaving at 2am or 3am in order to reach the peak in the morning, when conditions are best for climbing on the glacier. Most people split the trek into two days, camping at the Playitas camp halfway up the mountain. A guide is necessary for this trek.

SIX-DAY CIRCUIT

An unforgettable experience is to do the six-day trek through the glacier-formed valleys lying between the two ranges of mountains. Along the entire route you will have glacier-capped mountains on both sides. There are a few mountain passes, but generally the altitude is 4,000-4,500 meters (13,100-14,800 feet). You do not need to be an expert mountaineer, but in addition to being in good physical condition, you need to be acclimatized to the altitude. You may be required to complete a few day hikes prior to this trek. Do not attempt this trek without a knowledgeable guide, as it's easy to get lost in this treacherous landscape. The basic tour, which involves carrying all your own gear, will cost on average COP$700,000 per person. Don't pay less than that because it means the operator is skimping on the guide's salary. High-end tours, with porters and a cook, will cost COP$1,500,000 per person.

ACCOMMODATIONS

While not luxurious by any means, the lodging options in and around the park are homey. The proprietors are all attentive and friendly.

The best-located accommodation in the Southern Sector is ★ **Cabaña Sisuma** (cell tel. 311/236-4275 or 311/255-1034, aseguicoc@gmail.com, COP$35,000 pp), a cozy cabin inside the park run by the local tour guide association ASEGUICOC. It has six rooms, good food, and fireplaces to keep warm. The cabin is a two-hour hike into the park from Alto La Cueva, a stop on the daily *lechero* (milk truck) route. Another pleasant and comfortable option is rustic **Cabañas Güicány** (Alto La Cueva, cell tel. 310/566-7554, cab_guaicany@yahoo.es or guaicany@hotmail.com, COP$70,000 pp with meals, COP$40,000 pp without meals, COP$10,000 pp camping), in Alto La Cueva. The *lechero* (milk truck) can drop you off at the lodge. The owner, Eudoro Carreño, is a delight to chat with over a hot drink in the kitchen.

In the Central Sector, ★ **Hacienda La Esperanza** (cell tel. 314/221-2473, haciendalaesperanza@gmail.com, COP$50,000 pp with meals, COP$35,000 pp without meals), a working farm on the edge of the park, provides accommodations in a rustic farmhouse oozing character. The family running the hotel is very hospitable, and the host is a trained chef who enjoys pampering his guests. Nothing beats hanging out by the fireplace in the late afternoon with a warm drink after a day of mountain climbing. The *lechero* (milk truck) makes a stop at the hacienda.

The most conveniently located place to stay in the Northern Sector is **Cabañas Kanwara** (cell tel. 311/231-6004 or 311/237-2260, infokanwara@gmail.com, COP$35,000 pp). This lodge of cute wooden A-frame houses also serves good food. To get here, you must get off the *lechero* (milk truck) at the farm Hacienda Ritacuba and walk 90 minutes toward the park.

TRANSPORTATION

To get to any of the three sectors of the park from gateway towns El Cocuy and Güicán, there are three possibilities: hiking 4-5 hours uphill to the park, taking an express service (COP$80,000-100,000), or riding an early-morning *lechero* (milk truck). This is a working truck that picks up milk from farms along a set route. Merchandise and passengers share the back of the truck, which is covered with canvas. The *lechero* leaves Güicán from the intersection of Carrera 5 and Calle 6 every morning at 5:30am and stops at El Cocuy around 6am. Around 7:30am it arrives at Alto La Cueva, where you can get off to visit the Southern Sector. Around 9am it pulls up to Hacienda La Esperanza, a lodge and farm in the Central Sector. Around 10:30am it reaches Hacienda Ritacuba, from where you can walk up to Cabañas Kanwara, a lodge in the Northern Sector.

Santander

Beautiful, lush scenery, a delightful climate, well-preserved colonial pueblos, and friendly, outgoing people—this is the Santander department. Located in northeast Colombia, Santander lies to the north of Boyacá and southwest of Norte de Santander. Bucaramanga is the modern capital city, but you'll probably be drawn to the countryside. San Gil and the Cañón del Chicamocha will keep you busy with a smorgasbord of outdoor adventures, while nearby Barichara will seduce you with its tranquil ambience.

BUCARAMANGA

Known as the Ciudad Bonita (Beautiful City), Bucaramanga is a busy and growing city with a young and vibrant population and an agreeable climate that ensures the flowers are always in bloom. Its central location makes for a strategic launching point for visits to the Santander countryside, and the city is midway between Bogotá and Santa Marta on the Caribbean coast as well as Cúcuta in the far east. Including neighborhoods that are an extension of Bucaramanga (Floridablanca, Girón, and Piedecuesta), the population exceeds one million.

ORIENTATION

Most of your time will probably be spent in **Cabecera** (the upscale shopping and residential area), the **city center** (between Cras. 9-17 and Cl. 45 and Av. Quebrada Seca), and in nearby municipalities such as Girón and Floridablanca.

Carreras (avenues) run north to south, increasing in number from west to east. The main *carreras* are 15, 27, and 33. *Calles* (streets) run east to west and increase in number from north to south.

Sights

Bucaramanga's main sights are contained within the walkable city center. If you're staying in the Cabecera neighborhood it's a long, hot walk to the city center, so you're better off taking a cab.

Bucaramanga prides itself on its parks, and one of the most famous is the **Parque García Rovira** (Cras. 10-11 and Clls. 36-37). Filled with towering palms, it doesn't provide much shade, but with the pale yellow and white 19th-century **Catedral San Laureano** (Cra. 12 No. 36-08) standing prominently on the park's eastern side, it is rather photogenic. On the west side of the park is Bucaramanga's oldest church, the **Capilla de los Dolores** (Cra. 10 No. 36-08). This unassuming whitewashed structure dates to 1748 and is generally not open to the public. Across from it is **La Casa del Libro Total** (Cl. 35 No. 9-81, tel. 7/634-3558, www.ellibrototal.com, 8am-10pm Mon.-Fri.), a cultural center with gallery space and reading rooms. They have a free digital library of over 50,000 titles, and they publish and sell gorgeously bound and illustrated books, mostly classics in various languages. The on-site café serves free coffee.

The Libertador, Simón Bolívar, stayed in what's now known as the **Museo Casa de Bolívar** (Cl. 37 No. 12-15, tel. 7/630-4258, 8am-noon and 2pm-6pm Mon.-Fri., 8am-noon Sat., COP$2,000) for about 70 days in 1828 while he awaited news from the Convención de Ocaña. (The convention ended with a rift between Bolívar and Santander growing wider, and Bolívar's self-declaration as dictator.) The museum has personal belongs of Bolívar, a diary from the first Expedición Botánica led by José Celestino Mutis, and an exhibit on the Guane indigenous people from the area.

A few blocks to the east is the lively **Parque Santander** (Cras. 19-20 and Clls. 35-36), in the middle of the bustle of modern Bucaramanga. The Romanesque revival **Catedral de la Sagrada Familia** (Cl. 36 No. 19-56, 7am-10pm daily) took more than a hundred years to complete. It was finished in 1865. Its striking interior features include many stained glass

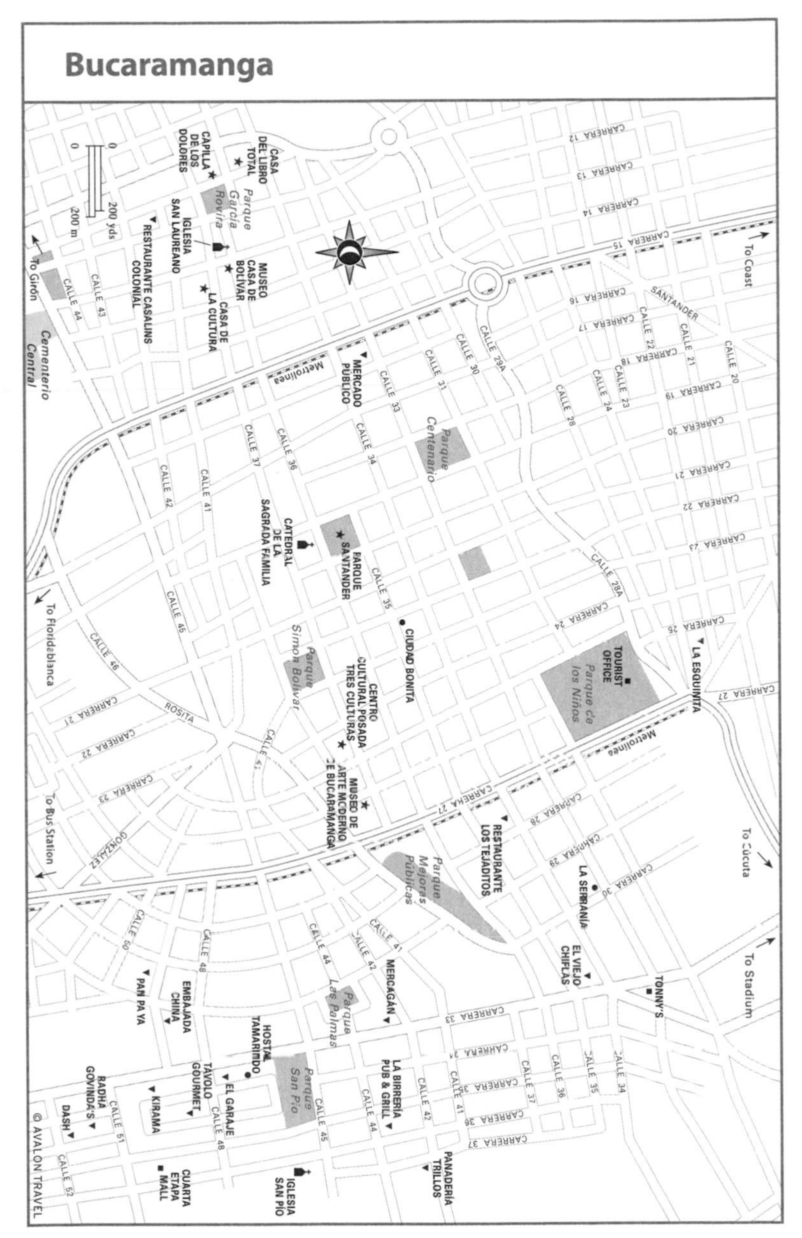

windows. Nearby is the **Banco de la República** (Cra. 19 No. 34-47, tel. 7/630-3133, www.banrepcultural.org/bucaramanga, 8am-11:30am and 2pm-6pm Mon.-Fri., free), which always has an art exhibit on. They also have a public library space.

The **Museo de Arte Moderno de Bucaramanga** (Cl. 37 No. 26-16, tel.

7/645-0483, www.museodeartemodernodebucaramanga.blogspot.com, 8:30am-noon and 2pm-5:30pm Mon.-Fri., 8am-noon Sat., COP$2,000) is worth checking out, but it's only open when there is an exhibit. The **Centro Cultural Posada Tres Culturas** (Cl. 37 No. 24-62, tel. 7/634-4859, www.fusader.org, 9am-noon and 2pm-7pm Mon.-Sat.) is near the museum and often hosts cultural events. It has a small on-site bookstore.

The **Parque San Pío** (between Cras. 33-35 and Clls. 45-46) is a vibrant green space near the Cabecera neighborhood. At the western end stands the Fernando Botero sculpture *Mujer de Pies Desnuda*.

Nightlife

Exuberant is a good word to describe the nightlife scene in Bucaramanga. Most bars and clubs are open Thursday through Saturday, closing at 2am or 3am.

La Birrería 1516 Pub & Grill (Cra. 36 No. 43-42, tel. 7/657-7675, noon-midnight Sun.-Thurs., noon-2am Fri.-Sat.) serves sports bar-type food (although there are some healthy selections) and beer. This open-air place is where locals gather to watch big *fútbol* matches. **La Esquinita de los Recuerdos** (Cl. 22 No. 25-55, tel. 7/632-0640 or 7/645-6861, hours vary Tues.-Sat.) is a beloved bar and a good place to have a beer. The bar has been around since 1965.

As you might imagine from its name, **Dash** (Cl. 48 No. 34-12, cell tel. 315/624-6905) is a high-energy club popular with the college-aged crowd.

Food

Want to eat like a local? Look for these Santanderean specialties: *cabrito con pepitoria* (goat fricassee), *carne oreada* (dried meat), and *mute santandereano* (a corn-based meaty stew). And don't forget the ants: fried big-bottom ants or *hormigas culonas*. These queen ants are harvested throughout Santander, typically after Holy Week. After months of hibernation, on one prickly hot day, the queens leave their colony, at which point they are caught. The practice of eating ants dates back hundreds of years to the Guane culture.

★ **Casalins Colonial** (Cl. 41 No. 10-54, tel. 7/696-0539, 11am-9pm daily, COP$15,000) is a seafood restaurant popular with government bureaucrats on their lunch break. There is always a set lunch menu (plus a la carte items), and frequently you'll have to wait a bit to be seated. Tables are set around a pleasant, sunny patio. It is behind the Gobernación building.

One of Bucaramanga's favorite restaurants is ★ **El Viejo Chiflas** (Cra. 33 No. 34-10, tel. 7/632-0640, 9am-midnight Mon.-Wed., 24 hours Thurs.-Sun., COP$23,000). The atmosphere here is cowboy style with wooden tables and interiors, and the menu features local specialties, such as goat and the Santander classic *carne oreada* (dried meat). An arepa (cornmeal cake) accompanies every meal. Portions can be huge.

Los Tejaditos (Cl. 34 No. 27-82, tel. 7/634-6028, www.restaurantelostejaditos.com, 11am-10pm Tues.-Sat., 11am-5pm Sun., COP$23,000) is an old-fashioned restaurant with a popular lunch menu. **Mercagán** (Cra. 33 No. 42-12, tel. 7/632-4949, www.mercaganparrilla.com, 11am-6pm Mon. and Thurs., 11am-11pm Tues.-Wed. and Fri.-Sat., 11am-4pm Sun., COP$25,000) is a legendary steak house in Bucaramanga that has multiple locations, but this one, with the best atmosphere, faces the Parque San Pío.

Radha Govinda's (Cra. 34 No. 51-95, tel. 7/643-3382, lunch Mon.-Sat.) is a long-running and popular vegetarian restaurant that is open only for lunch. It's on a quiet street in Cabecera.

The Chinese restaurant **Embajada China** (Cl. 49 No. 32-27, tel. 7/647-1931, 10am-10pm daily, COP$15,000) is run by a Chinese family, and they serve generous portions. It's in Cabecera near the Kasa Guane hostel.

Stir-fries, salads, and pastas are on the menu at slightly fancy **Tavolo Gourmet** (Cra. 35 No. 48-84, tel. 7/643-7461, www.tavologourmet.com, 11am-10pm Tues.-Sun., COP$18,000). It's a bright and airy place in an upscale shopping area.

★ **Toscana** (Av. Jardín Casa 1A, tel. 7/647-6666, www.toscanarestaurante.com, 11am-11pm daily, COP$24,000) is an elegant Italian restaurant with outdoor seating. It regularly receives high marks, especially for the atmosphere.

Pan Pa Ya (Cl. 49 No. 28-38, tel. 7/685-2001, 8am-10pm Mon.-Sat, 9am-noon and 5pm-8pm Sun.) is a Colombian chain that's a reliable place for a decent cup of coffee, pastries, and an inexpensive breakfast of eggs and fresh fruit.

Accommodations

Bucaramanga has a number of standard business hotels, including familiar international names like Holiday Inn and Ramada. Rates tend to dip substantially on weekends.

UNDER COP$70,000

Kasa Guane (Cl. 11 No. 26-50, tel. 7/657-6960, cell tel. 313/274-2199, www.kasaguane.com, COP$25,000 dorm, COP$80,000 d) remains the top choice of international backpackers passing through town. This busy yet friendly place has both dorms and private rooms, hosts activities, and provides insider information. The guys here will get you hooked up with paragliding and give you expert insider tips on all the Bucaramanga party spots.

COP$70,000-200,000

Antigua Belén Bed and Breakfast (Cra. 31 No. 17-22, tel. 7/634-9860, www.hotelantiquabelen.com, COP$100,000 d with a/c) has 13 rooms in a modern house full of antiques. It's located in a quiet part of town. Breakfast is served in a pleasant patio in the back.

★ **Ciudad Bonita** (Cl. 35 No. 22-01, tel. 7/635-0101, www.hotelciudadbonita.com.co, COP$174,000 d) is one of the best-known traditional hotels in the city center. It has 70 rooms, two restaurants, a café, a pool, gym, and sauna, and there's live music Thursday, Friday, and Saturday evenings. Take a cab in this area at night; the surrounding streets empty out in the evenings. There's a Pacific coast-themed seafood restaurant in the lobby.

Hotel Tamarindo (Cra. 34 No. 46-104, tel. 7/643-6502, cell tel. 316/696-5241, www.hoteltamarindobucaramanga.com, COP$195,000 d) has seven rooms, air-conditioning, private baths, and a delightful patio around a mango tree.

Located in an upscale neighborhood above the Parque San Pío, ★ **Serenity Suites Casa Boutique** (Cra. 48B No. 53A-10, cell tel. 316/875-2224, www.serenitysuitescolombia.com, COP$190,000 d) is a small, family-run hotel with 10 spacious rooms (many with balconies overlooking the city), a small pool, and a Jacuzzi. It's the calmest option in town. Although the Cabecera neighborhood is a short distance away, down the hill, it's best to take a cab to and from this hotel in the evenings.

Information and Services

The **tourist office** (Cl. 30 No. 26-117, tel. 7/634-1132) is parkside at the Parque de los Niños.

Police can be reached by dialing 123, the **Hospital Universitario González Valencia** (Cra. 33 No. 28-126, 7am-10pm daily) by calling tel. 7/634-6110.

Transportation

The **Aeropuerto Internacional de Palo Negro** (BGA, Vía Lebrija), Bucaramanga's airport, is 25 kilometers (15 miles) west of town. **Avianca** (Cl. 52 No. 35A-10, tel. 7/657-3888, www.avianca.com, 8am-6pm Mon.-Fri., 8am-1pm Sat.), **EasyFly** (tel. 7/697-0333, www.easyfly.com.co), **VivaColombia** (tel. 1/489-7989, www.vivacolombia.com.co), and **LATAM** all serve BGA. Taxis between the airport and Bucaramanga cost COP$32,000.

Frequent long-distance bus service is offered between Bucaramanga and all major Colombian cities as well as small locales in Santander. The **Terminal de Transportes** (Km. 2 Tr. Metropolitana, tel. 7/637-1000, www.terminalbucaramanga.com) is modern, clean, and open-air. It is off Calle 70 on the way toward Girón.

The **MetroLínea** (www.metrolinea.gov.co) is the Bucaramanga version of Bogotá's TransMilenio. These green buses are clean and efficient, and the system covers just about the entire city, although it can be difficult to figure out. Maps of the system are hard to come by, obligating you to ask fellow travelers for information. You can purchase cards for the regular buses (ones that do not have dedicated lanes) at kiosks on the streets.

Reliable taxi-hailing and ride-sharing companies, such as EasyTaxi, Tappsi, and Uber, operate in Bucaramanga.

The city center and Cabecera area are easily visited on foot, although the streets are often clogged with traffic.

Floridablanca

Floridablanca has evolved to become essentially a southeastern suburb of Bucaramanga, five kilometers away.

There aren't many reasons to make a special trip here, but a good one is to take a bite out of one of their famous *obleas,* crisp paper-thin wafers filled with gooey and delicious *arequipe* (caramel spread). **Obleas Floridablanca** (Cra. 7 No. 5-54, tel. 7/648-5819, 10am-8pm daily) is a famous *oblea* factory that's been around since 1949. There are around 30 types of *obleas* you can order, although the classic is an *oblea* with just *arequipe.* Two of the more popular flavors are the *amor eterno* (eternal love), which has *arequipe,* cheese, and blackberry jam, and the *noviazgo* (courtship), which has *arequipe* and cheese. They also have do-it-yourself *oblea* kits that you can take home with you.

Along the manicured lawns of the **Jardín Botánico Eloy Valenzuela** (tel. 7/634-6100, 8am-5pm daily, COP$4,000), you can wander paths that you'll share with turtles, and view enormous ceibas and other trees. If you look closely at the treetops in this botanical garden, you might even see some sloths. The small Río Frío flows through the gardens, which were revamped in 2012. It's not terribly easy, but you can get to the gardens via MetroLínea from Bucaramanga.

At the time of research, the **Museo Arqueológico Regional Guane** (Casa Paragüitas, 9am-5pm Mon.-Sat., free) was in the process of being moved to the Casa Parguitas, a lovely colonial construction. The collection of ceramics here is impressive and extensive.

Mesa de Ruitoque

A surprisingly quiet and rural area to the southeast of Bucaramanga and Floridablanca, Mesa de Ruitoque sits on a plateau that has perfect conditions for paragliding.

PARAGLIDING

This area is blessed with 350 flyable days per year. It's a great location to take your first tandem paragliding flight or enroll in a 10-day course.

Colombia Paragliding (cell tel. 312/432-6266, www.colombiaparagliding.com) offers tandem flights of different durations from the launch point, **Voladero Las Águilas** (Km. 2 Vía Ruitoque, tel. 7/678-6257, www.voladerolasaguilas.com.co), about 10 kilometers (6 miles) south of Bucaramanga. Instructors are all certified and speak English. The launch site opens each day at 10am, but winds are best in the afternoon, from noon until 4pm. A 10-minute flight costs COP$50,000, 20 minutes costs COP$90,000, and a 30-minute flight costs COP$120,000. The views are quite spectacular from above Bucaramanga, so bring your camera. At the fly site there is also a snack bar. The place gets very crowded on weekends and holidays. For a fee of COP$25,000, you can get a DVD of your flight.

The Kasa Guane hostel (Cl. 11 No. 26-50, tel. 7/657-6960, cell tel.

313/274-2199, www.kasaguane.com) can arrange transportation from Bucaramanga to the launch point.

A 10-day certification course is offered by Colombia Paragliding at the Águilas site, with additional flight time in the Chicamocha area. The course costs COP$3,200,000, including transportation, meals, and lodging.

Next door to the launch site, ★ **Nest Fly Site Hostel** (Km. 2 Vía Mesa de Ruitoque, cell tel. 312/0432-6266, www.colombiaparagliding.com, COP$25,000 dorm, COP$60,000 d) is the place to stay if you're interested in paragliding. It's a quiet and cute place, with a pool and a view, and it's only 20 minutes away from the bustle of Bucaramanga. Nest is run by the same people as Colombia Paragliding and the Kasa Guane hostel.

Girón

While Bucaramanga is a pulsating tribute to modern Colombia, nearby Girón, 12 kilometers (7 miles) west, is a living reminder of the colonial past, at least in the city's historic center. The population of Girón is around 150,000. The main plaza is a vibrant meeting place.

On weekends Girón has a festive air to it as city folk from Bucaramanga and other day-trippers stroll the town's cobblestone streets. Check out the **Parque Las Nieves** (Clls. 30-31 and Cras. 25-26), which houses the **Basílica Menor San Juan Bautista,** and walk along the *malecón* (wharf) of the town's small brook.

FOOD AND ACCOMMODATIONS

Girón makes a good base. It's charming and quiet, and traveling back and forth to neighboring Bucaramanga is easy. The trip takes less than 15 minutes, and a taxi ride will cost only around COP$10,000. You can also get to Girón on the MetroLínea system.

La Casona (Cl. 28 No. 28-09, tel. 7/646-7195, www.lacasona-restaurante.com, noon-8pm Tues.-Sun., COP$16,000) is a spiffy old place, and they have a fun *onces* (tea time) menu for late-afternoon tea, Colombian style: You get a tamale, cheese, bread, and hot chocolate.

In a remodeled colonial house, ★ **Girón Chill Out Hotel Boutique** (Cra. 25 No. 32-06, tel. 7/646-1119, www.gironnchillout.com, COP$144,000 d) is run by an Italian couple (hence the Italian flag). It has a quiet vibe, and they serve authentic Italian food.

Las Nieves (Cl. 30 No. 25-71, tel. 7/681-2951, www.hotellasnievesgiron.com, COP$82,000 d, COP$116,000 d with a/c) faces the plaza. The interior of the hotel is full of palm trees and greenery, and the owner's dog is friendly. There are about 30 rooms, many full of twin beds. It's a standard place.

SAN GIL AND VICINITY

Rafting, paragliding, caving, mountain biking, canyoning, hiking, birding, and rappelling are all within reach in San Gil, Colombia's outdoor adventure capital. Even if your idea of "adventurous" is merely being in

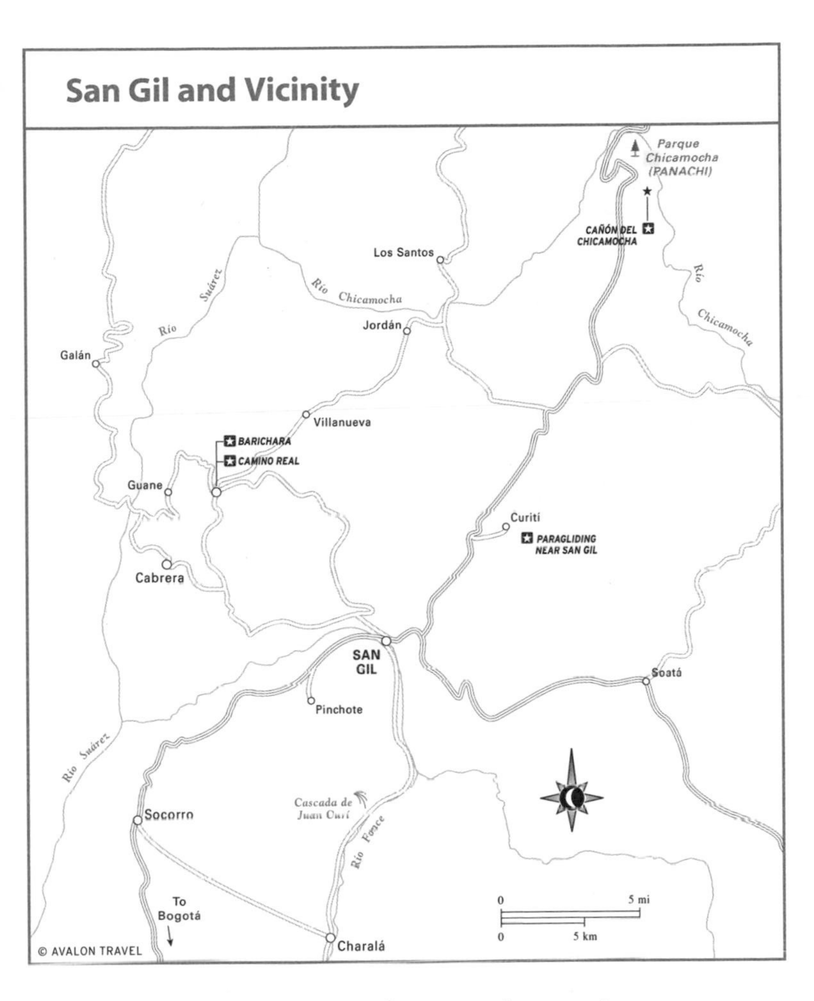

Colombia, the breathtaking Santander scenery of canyons, rivers, waterfalls, and mountains is more than enough reason to warrant a visit.

During the late 19th and early 20th centuries, San Gil and nearby towns built their prosperity on quinine, coffee, cocoa, and tobacco cultivation. Today, old tile-roofed hangars to dry tobacco, known as *caneys,* still dot the landscape. It's a peaceful place to visit and a top tourist destination.

There's no need to stay in bustling San Gil in order to enjoy the many outdoor activities that the area offers. You can easily organize rafting trips or paragliding adventures from quieter and more charming towns such as Barichara, which is 20 kilometers (12 miles) north.

San Gil

This spry city (pop. 43,000) on the steep banks of the Río Fonce is 95 kilometers (59 miles) southwest of Bucaramanga. It caters to international tourists. San Gil can feel claustrophobic, but accommodations here are plentiful, comfortable, and inexpensive.

SIGHTS

On the Río Fonce about a 15-minute walk from town is the **Jardín Botánico El Gallineral** (Cra. 11 No. 21-1, tel. 7/723-7342, 8am-5pm daily, COP$8,000). This used to be just a park, but it has been given a makeover and now it's a botanical garden. There are cute stalls selling handicrafts, sweets, and coffee along the orderly paths. It's a pretty place for a late-afternoon walk among the towering trees. The on-site restaurant is open for lunch.

RAFTING AND KAYAKING

Two rivers near San Gil offer excellent year-round rafting adventures. The **Río Fonce,** whose banks the town stands on, is the closest and one of the best suited for rafting. It's a Class II-III. A 90-minute rafting trip on the Fonce costs about COP$30,000.

The **Río Suárez** is a Class IV-V river. Between March and April and October through November, the water levels are higher, and if there have been excessive amounts of rain this river can be too dangerous to tackle. The starting point for rafting on the Suárez is about an hour's drive from San Gil toward Bogotá. The trip leaves at 10am and returns at 4pm, and costs COP$125,000. You're on the water for about two hours.

Colombia Rafting Expeditions (Cra. 10 No. 7-83, tel. 7/724-5800, www.colombiarafting.com) is considered the best rafting company in town. They focus exclusively on river activities. The walls of their small office are covered with diplomas and certificates earned by their team of experienced guides. They can organize rafting trips on the region's rivers, determining which one is right for you based upon on your skill level and sense of adventure and the rivers' water levels. They also do kayaking trips. This company takes safety very seriously and conducts safety training exercises

The Río Fonce flows through San Gil.

in English. Three-day kayaking courses (four hours per day, starting at 8am) cost COP$400,000 and take place on the Río Fonce. They also rent out kayaks to those with experience.

★ PARAGLIDING

There are two main paragliding areas near San Gil. One is the spectacular **Cañón del Chicamocha,** where 35-minute tandem paragliding trips over the canyon cost around COP$170,000 (including transportation). These flights take place in the mornings.

The other location for paragliding is 16 kilometers (10 miles) from San Gil at the launch site, **Las Vueltas,** in the town of Curití. Here, 20-minute paragliding excursions cost COP$60,000. These flights are held in the afternoon.

Colombian Paragliding (cell tel. 312/432-6266, www.colombiaparagliding.com) has a very good reputation for paragliding certification courses (COP$3,200,000, including transportation, meals, and lodging). The company is based near Bucaramanga at Mesa de Ruitoque.

CAVING

Several caves around San Gil make for good exploring. The **Cueva Indio** is one of the most popular. It's filled with bats, and you don't really have to do much bending over to explore it. It's near the town of Páramo. An excursion including equipment and a guide costs COP$25,000, but that doesn't include transportation. Contact **Páramo Extremo** (Cra. 4 No. 4-57, Páramo, tel. 7/725-8944, www.paramosantanderextremo.com) in the town of Páramo to sign up for an excursion to Cueva Indio.

The **Cueva Vaca,** near the town of Curití, is the most challenging cave in the area. You will be in water and mud the entire time you are underground, and at one point you'll have to swim underwater to get through to the next cave. There are lots of stalactites and stalagmites and bats to see. It's action packed and there are some tight squeezes as well, but the adventure is worth it. It costs COP$25,000, plus about COP$3,000 in bus transportation. **Colombia Rafting** (Cra. 10 No. 7-83, cell tel. 311/283-8647, www.colombiarafting.com) can organize a trip here.

La Antigua cave is on the road toward Barichara. **El Dorado Hostel** (Cl. 12 No. 8-55, tel. 7/723-7588) organizes an extreme trip that includes a visit to La Antigua with canyoning, rappelling, and two waterfall descents. This five-hour trip costs COP$80,000 including transportation.

The Medellín-based outfit **Expedición Adventure** (cell tel. 314/258-9499, expedicionadventure@gmail.com, www.expedicionadventure.blogspot.com) specializes in unique 3- to 20-day caving trips to mostly unexplored and unspoiled areas in the Santander region. The starting point is usually in Barbosa, a town between Tunja and Barichara.

BIKING

Colombian Bike Junkies (Cl. 12 No. 8-35, tel. 7/724-1165, cell tel. 316/327-6101, www.colombianbikejunkies.com) organizes intense downhill day-trip rides and multiday adventures. A single-day trip (COP$100,000) starts at an elevation of 2,000 meters (6,500 feet) on the top of the Cañón del Chicamocha, then goes down through beautiful countryside to the ghost town of Jordan. After a swim and lunch, there is yet one more downhill trip near the town of Curití, for a total of some 50 kilometers (30 miles) of downhill riding, on top-of-the-line mountain bikes.

To rent a cheap bike for the day, go to **Bicicletería El Ring** (Cl. 7 No. 10-14, tel. 7/724-3189, cell tel. 315-648-8543).

SWIMMING

On weekends and holidays, families head to the area's swimming holes. The atmosphere is joyous, and there's usually music and plenty of food and drink as well.

Pozo Azul (Km. 2 Vía San Gil) is a natural pool with small cascades that's surrounded by tress. From San Gil, Pozo Azul is about five minutes by bus or taxi or a 20-minute walk just off the highway. **Pescaderito** is better, with five swimming holes in which to cool off—all of them completely free. It's near the town of Curití, about a 40-minute bus ride (COP$3,000) from San Gil. Both spots are quieter during the week.

TOURS

Planeta Azul (Parque El Gallineral, Cra. 11, tel. 7/724-0000, cell tel. 310/771-7586, www.planetaazulsangil.com) is an agency that organizes rafting trips as well as a host of other activities, like bungee jumping (COP$46,000), caving (COP$40,000), rappelling (COP$40,000), paragliding (COP$60,000), and horseback riding (COP$95,000).

Aventura Total (Cl. 7 No. 10-27, tel. 7/723-8888, cell tel. 316/693-9300, www.aventuratotal.com.co) has a good reputation. They offer all-inclusive packages that include rafting, caving, and other activities as well as hotel accommodations. Aventura Total often organizes activities for large school groups. **Nativox** (Cra. 11 No. 7-14 Malecón, tel. 7/723-9999, cell. tel. 315/842-2337, www.nativoxsangil.com) is similar to Planeta Azul and Aventura Total.

Hostels can also organize activities for guests.

FOOD

Mostly Tex-Mex ★ **Gringo Mike's** (Cl. 12 No. 8-35, tel. 7/724-1695, 8am-11:45am and 5pm-10pm daily, COP$18,000) is paradise for Americans who have been on the road awhile, with guacamole and chips, barbecue burgers, black bean burgers, Philly cheesesteaks, and even breakfast burritos.

To brush elbows with the locals, try **Rogelia** (Cra. 10 No. 8-09, tel. 7/724-0823, 7am-7:30pm daily, COP$12,000) or **Maná** (Cra. 10 No. 9-49, lunch daily, COP$12,000), the latter of which is a popular and inexpensive place for lunch. Try the grilled chicken stuffed with ham and cheese, but don't expect gourmet cuisine or charm.

The best aspect of **Gallineral Restaurante** (Parque Gallineral, Cra. 11, cell tel. 300/565-2653, 8am-5pm daily, COP$20,000) is its lush setting.

ACCOMMODATIONS

Excellent and affordable lodging options are plentiful in San Gil, but they are geared toward international backpackers. If you're looking for fresh air, more luxury, or more privacy, consider staying in nearby Barichara.

One of the first hostels in town to cater to international backpackers, ★ **Macondo Hostal** (Cra. 8 No. 10-35, tel. 7/724-8001, www.macondohostel.com, COP$30,000 dorm, COP$70,000 d w/bath) remains an excellent and reliable choice. Their clean dorm rooms (popular with backpackers) and private rooms fill quickly, so make a reservation in advance. They have a hot tub, small garden, and hammocks for post-adventure relaxing. What sets Macondo apart is its extremely knowledgeable, helpful, and friendly staff, who will organize outdoor activities in the region.

Bacaregua Hostel (Cra. 9 No. 16-77, tel. 724-2241, cell tel. 320/260-6277, COP$25,000 dorm, COP$60,000 d) is a low-key, locally operated hostel in a familial setting with hot showers, high ceilings, and ample common space. There are a couple of dormitory rooms in addition to private rooms.

Sam's VIP Hostel (Cr. 10 No. 12-33, tel. 7/724-2746, www.samshostel.com, COP$17,000 dorm, COP$70,000 d) has a fine location on the town's main plaza. It bustles with activity as international backpackers plot their travels on the sun-soaked terrace or by the small pool. The owner, Sam, has a second place with 11 rooms in an old renovated house: **La Mansion de Sam Hotel Boutique** (Cl. 12 No. 8-71, tel. 7/724-6044, www.hotelmansionsangil.com, COP$70,000-100,000 d), which is set just a block from the main plaza. Inside this hotel is an inviting pub (7:30am-10pm daily) that specializes in steaks, ribs, and beer.

If you'd like to get away from the backpacker scene but still pay backpacker prices, there are several cheap hotels in town. At ★ **Posada Familiar** (Cra. 10 No. 8-55, tel. 7/724-8136, cell tel. 301/370-1323, COP$45,000 pp high season) the name says it all—the lady of the house makes guests feel at home. The patio overflows with flowers and plants, you can cook in the kitchen, and the owner is a warm and generous person.

Almost exactly halfway between San Gil and Barichara on a quiet farm is ★ **La Pacha Hostel and Camping** (Km. 7 Vía San Gil-Barichara, cell tel. 310/221-1515, www.lapachahostel.com, COP$60,000 d), where goats roam free, the common space is a funky old bus, and guests sleep in tents and yurts. It's run by a friendly English-Colombian couple.

To enjoy the peace of the countryside and charm of a colonial town but still be within striking distance of San Gil restaurants and activities, consider staying in the hamlet of Pinchote. ★ **Hotel Boutique Wassiki** (Km. 3 Vía San Gil-Bogotá, tel. 7/724-8386, www.wassiki.com, COP$210,000 d) is an excellent upscale hotel, offering well-appointed and airy rooms, comfortable common areas, a beautiful dining room, lots of hammocks, and a pool. It has a fine view of the valley below and is within walking distance of Pinchote's idyllic Plaza Principal.

TRANSPORTATION

San Gil's main **Terminal de Transportes** (Vía al Socorro, tel. 7/724-5858) is five minutes out of town, on the south side of the Río Fonce. Buses depart there for major cities such as Bucaramanga, Tunja, and Bogotá. Taxis to and from the Terminal de Transportes to the town center cost COP$3,200. Getting to San Gil from Bucaramanga by bus takes 2.5 hours and costs COP$15,000. Getting here from Tunja will take 3-5 hours. From Bogotá, the trip to San Gil (COP$45,000) takes seven hours. From Santa Marta or Medellín, the bus ride takes about 12 hours and costs COP$70,000. From Bucaramanga, the trip takes six hours and costs COP$15,000.

A smaller bus terminal for nearby towns is on Carrera 15 at Calle 11. It serves towns such as Barichara, Charalá, Curití, and Pescadero. It doesn't have an official name, but some refer to it as the **Mini Terminal.** Buses to Barichara depart every 30 mintues from 6am to 6:30pm.

★ Cañón del Chicamocha

The Cañón del Chicamocha is the result of eons of work by the Río Chicamocha, which carved its way through mountains to create a stunning canyon. This area is worth a visit for its breathtaking views, and is also home to an amusement park that holds a cable car offering a unique view of the canyon.

PARQUE NACIONAL DEL CHICAMOCHA

Set in a spectacular location above the Cañón del Chicamocha, the privately run **Parque Nacional del Chicamocha** (Km. 54 Vía Bucaramanga-San Gil, tel. 7/639-4444, www.parquenacionaldelchicamocha.com, 10am-6pm

Cañón del Chicamocha

Wed.-Fri., 9am-7pm Sat.-Sun., COP$50,000 admission) is a cheesy amusement park geared toward Colombian families, but the views are superb. Also known as Panachi, the park has several attractions, like an ostrich farm, areas that celebrate Santander culture and traditions, extreme sports, and a water park. The main point of interest for international travelers is the 6.3-kilometer (3.9-mile) **cable car ride** (10:30am-5:30pm Wed.-Fri., 9am-7pm Sat.-Sun., included with admission) across the canyon over the Río Chicamocha. The trip over the river takes about 12 minutes, and rather than shooting straight across the canyon, it follows the contours of the mountains. Plan to spend about an hour or two here.

Buses leaving from the Bucaramanga bus terminal bound for San Gil can drop you off at the park; this trip takes one hour and costs COP$12,000. The vistas from the road that hugs the canyon high above the Río Chicamocha make the right-hand-side window seat from Bucaramanga worth fighting for. The bus company COTRASANGIL (tel. 7/724-3562) offers regular bus service (30 minutes, COP$6,000) from San Gil's Terminal de Transportes.

MESA DE LOS SANTOS

The village of Los Santos is on the opposite side of the canyon from Parque Nacional del Chicamocha. In this area, known as **Mesa de los Santos,** there are a few places to stay. The area ranks second in the world for annual number of tremors at 390 per month (a rate of about one earthquake every two hours). The tremors are usually short in duration and not very powerful.

Refugio La Roca (Km. 22 in La Mojarra, cell tel. 312/333 1480, www.refugiolaroca.blogspot.com, COP$60,000 d shared bath) overlooks the Chicamocha canyon. Here you can camp for COP$10,000 per night (they have tents and sleeping bags for rent). In addition to private rooms, there is also one dorm room with four beds for COP$80,000.

At the other end of the spectrum from Refugio La Roca is ★ **Hotel Hacienda El Roble** (Vía Piedecuesta-Los Santos, Mesa de los Santos, tel. 1/232-8595, www.cafemesadelossantos.com, COP$325,000 d). This romantic getaway is on a large certified organic coffee farm, set underneath towering oak trees on a property teeming with over 100 species of birds. The rate includes a tour of the on-site plantation where their award-winning organic coffee is grown. The hotel is located after the Mesa toll booth.

★ Barichara

In 1975, when it was declared a national monument, Barichara (pop. 8,000) was named the most beautiful pueblo in Colombia. Despite its popularity with weekenders and a steady stream of international visitors, it hasn't lost its charm. This old tobacco town of sloping cobblestoned streets and whitewashed colonial-era homes is permanently blessed with bright blue skies and warm temperatures. Located 20 kilometers (12 miles) northwest of San Gil, the town is on a plateau that overlooks the Río Suárez. Don't skimp on your time here.

All around town are structures that utilize the technique of adobe block-making called *tapia pisada*. You'll often see a small patch of the mud interior exposed on these brilliantly white walls, purposely done to show passersby that it's authentic *tapia pisada*.

On the serene Parque Principal is the circa 1780 **Templo de la Inmaculada Concepción,** with two grandiose towers that soar 22 meters (72 feet) into the air. The sandstone church is particularly striking when lit up at night. Up picturesque Calle 6, at the top of the hill, is the **Capilla de Santa Bárbara,** a Romanesque-style church that is a popular place for weddings.

There are two other colonial churches to see: the **Capilla de Jesús** (Cra. 7 at Cl. 3), next to the cemetery, and the **Capilla de San Antonio** (Cra. 4 at Cl. 5).

Barichara is the birthplace of Aquileo Parra Gómez, who was the 11th president of the Estados Unidos de Colombia. His childhood home, **Casa Aquileo Parra Gómez** (Cl. 6 at Cra. 2), has been extremely well preserved and is an excellent example of typical 19th-century Barichara architecture. The site is also a handicraft workshop for the elderly, who weave shoulder bags and other items out of the natural fiber *fique*. They are there Monday through Thursday.

★ CAMINO REAL

A must-do activity in Barichara is to take the 5.3-kilometer (3.3-mile) **Camino Real** to the pueblo of Guane. It's a lovely path that zigzags down from the plateau of Barichara through farmland, affording nice views of the countryside. Parts of the path are lined with centuries-old stone walls.

Before the conquest, indigenous tribes throughout what is now Colombia traded crops and goods with each other, utilizing an extensive network of footpaths. These trails meandered through the countryside of present-day Santander, Boyacá, Norte de Santander, Cundinamarca, and beyond.

the Camino Real between Barichara and Guane

During Spanish rule, the paths continued to be a major means of communication between colonial towns, and the networks became known as Caminos Reales. In the late 19th century, a German, Geo von Legerke, restored the Barichara-Guane Camino Real and built a stone bridge across the Río Suárez in order to improve transportation.

The hike to Guane takes two hours, and you don't need a guide: It's well marked, well trodden, and safe. To get to the trailhead, walk west along Carrera 10 to the Piedra de Bolívar, where you'll see the stone path leading down toward the valley.

In Guane you can check out the small **Museo Isaias Ardila Díaz** (Parque Principal, hours vary), which has three rooms: one on paleontology, with fossils; the next on archaeology, with a mummy; and a third on colonial life in rural Santander.

Sabajón, the Colombian version of eggnog, is the sweet specialty in Guane, and it is sold in various shops around Parque Principal.

If you are not up for the hike, a bus (COP$2,000) departs daily from the Parque Principal in Barichara at 6am, 9:30am, 11:30am, 2:30pm, and 5:30pm. The bus returns 30 minutes later from Guane.

FESTIVALS AND EVENTS

Little Barichara proudly hosts two annual film festivals. The **Festival Internacional de Cine de Barichara** (www.ficba.com.co) takes place in June, and the **Festival de Cine Verde** (www.festiver.org), an environmentally themed festival, is held every September in the town's churches.

SHOPPING

Barichara has always been a magnet for artists and craftspeople, many of whom have shops in town.

The **Fundación Escuela Taller Barichara** (Cra. 5 No. 4-26, tel. 7/726-7577, www.tallerdeoficiosbarichara.com, 8am-7pm Mon.-Thurs., 8am-9pm Fri.-Sat., 8am-1pm Sun.) is a gallery, museum, school, shop, and restaurant, all wrapped up in one. Occasional photography and painting exhibitions are held at this lovely cultural center, traditional decorative objects from the area are always on display, ceramics and other items made by students are for sale, and anyone can take a monthlong (or longer) course here. They offer dozens of classes for free. The on-site Restaurante y Café Las Cruces is one of the finest places to eat in town.

The **Taller de Papel de Fique** (Cl. 6 No. 2-68, no phone, 8am-3pm Mon.-Thurs.) makes for an interesting stop. At this workshop, artisans make beautiful paper out of the natural fiber of *fique.* On sale in this small store are cards, stationery, and handicrafts, all produced from *fique.* They also experiment with paper made from pineapple leaves. Short tours explaining the papermaking process are given for a small charge.

One of the best-known ceramic artists in town is **Jimena Rueda** (Cra. 5 No. 2-01, cell tel. 314/400-5071, 10am-6pm Mon.-Sat.). In addition to browsing her work, you can ask Señora Jimena if she has any pieces of the famous rustic handmade pottery of the Guane indigenous people. There is only one person who knows and uses this technique: **Ana Felisa Alquichire.** Doña Ana Felisa has been declared a living national cultural treasure by the Colombian presidency; her plates and bowls are sold in a few different shops in Barichara and Guane.

Galería Anil (Cl. 6 No. 10-46, cell tel. 311/470-1175) is the studio for local artists Jasmín and Carlos.

Formas de Luz (Cl. 10 No. 7-20, tel. 7/726-7279, cell tel. 317/438-4042, www.formasdeluz.com, 8am-noon and 2pm-6pm Mon.-Sat., 9:30am-1:30pm Sun.) is the workshop of talented designer Muriel Garderet.

FOOD

Restaurants in Barichara gear up for the weekend crowd, but opening hours may vary during the week.

★ **Restaurante y Café Las Cruces** (Cra. 5 No. 4-26, tel. 7/726-7577, www.tallerdeoficiosbarichara.com, 6pm-9:30pm Fri., noon-9:30pm Sat., noon-4pm Sun., COP$28,000) is considered the top restaurant in Barichara for its ambience and creative dishes. It's in the beautiful patio of the Fundación Escuela Taller Barichara. Look for signature dishes such as *pernil de cabro* (barbecued goat leg) with an ant sauce or *costillitas de tamarindo* (tamarind ribs). It's not open Monday through Thursday.

La Puerta (Cl. 6 No. 8-51, tel. 7/726-7649, www.baricharalapuerta.com, lunch and dinner daily high season, COP$22,000) is a beautiful place, with candlelit tables at night. They serve tasty pastas and use local, organic ingredients when possible.

Shimbala Shanti (Cra. 7 No. 6-22, cell tel. 318/391-3124) serves big stir-fries, both vegetarian and nonvegetarian, as well as salads and fresh juices.

Don Juan (Cra. 6 No. 6-13, cell tel. 318/775-5691, COP$12,000) is famous for its set lunches, but it only serves 20 each day, so arrive early. Don Juan also serves delicious Venezuelan arepas. In the evening, ask for balcony seating.

Overlooking the Parque Cementerio, **Al Cuoco** (Cra. 6A No. 2-54, cell tel. 312/527-3628, noon-9pm or 10pm daily, COP$22,000) is an authentic Italian place with a small menu of homemade pasta served up by its Roman chef. Try the parmesan ice cream.

For pizza, check out **7 Tigres Pizza & Pita** (Cl. 6 No. 10-24, cell tel. 312/521-9962), a funky favorite serving thin-crust personal pizzas and grilled meat pitas.

Locals flock to **El Balcón de Mi Pueblo** (Cl. 7 No. 5-62, cell tel. 318/280-2980, noon-5pm daily, COP$12,000) for good, meaty Colombian food like *cabro* (grilled goat), *carne oreada* (sun-dried steak), and *churrasco* (steak). It's a cute place up on the 2nd floor.

Another favorite is the lunch-only **Misifú** (Cra. 6 No. 6 31, tel. 7/726-7321, noon-6pm daily, COP$12,000). Their specialty is *carne oreada,* a dry and toothsome steak that is reminiscent of beef jerky.

For a coffee or the popular *galletas de cuajada* (cheese cookies), head to

Panadería Barichara (Cl. 5 No. 5-33, tel. 7/726-7688, 7am-1pm and 2pm-8pm daily). They've been around since 1954.

ACCOMMODATIONS

With Barichara's growth in popularity, accommodation options to fit all budgets and styles have popped up in the town. Weeknight rates will be lower.

Backpackers and budget travelers have several options in Barichara. The ★ **Color de Hormiga Hostel** (Cl. 6 No. 5-35, cell tel. 315/297-1621, http://colordehormiga.com/hostel.html, COP$45,000 d) used to house teachers from a neighboring school. It's decorated with institutional furniture that was left behind, and it still has its original groovy tiled floors. There are seven small rooms for one or two people, each with its own private bath. The kitchen is open for use by guests.

On an old tobacco farm, the ★ **Reserva Natural** (Vereda San José Alto, cell tel. 315/297-1621, COP$70,000 pp d), from the same owner as the Color de Hormiga Hostel, is a step up, with more luxury and more solitude. Birds representing all colors of the rainbow appear like clockwork every morning to munch on pieces of banana and papaya, to the delight of guests enjoying their breakfasts. This spot is about a 10-minute walk from town. The staff is incredibly friendly. The property also has dorm rooms and campsites.

At **Tinto Hostel** (Cra. 4 No. 5-39, tel. 7/726-7725, www.tintohostel.com, COP$30,000 dorm, COP$120,000 d) there's a ton of open green space, a pool, and perfectly fine rooms, making it a backpacker favorite. Dorm rooms have either four or six beds.

On the edge of town, peaceful **Artepolis** (Cra. 2 No. 2-2, cell tel. 300/203-4531, www.artepolis.info, COP$85,000 d) has eight minimalist rooms overlooking the countryside. Artist workshops are held here occasionally. Breakfast is sold by the woman who runs the kitchen.

The peaceful **Posada Sueños de Antonio** (Cra. 9 No. 4-25, tel. 7/726-7793, www.suenosdeantonio.com, COP$135,000 d) has five spacious rooms surrounding an interior patio that attracts birds every morning.

Casa Oniri (Cl. 6 No. 7-55, tel. 7/726-7138, cell tel. 312/300-8870, www.casaoniri.com, COP$196,000 d) is one of the swankiest options around, with rooms surrounding two courtyards and an upstairs lookout to boot.

Hicasua Hotel Boutique & Centro de Convenciones (Cl. 7 No. 3-85, tel. 7/726-7700, cell tel. 312/419-7154, www.hicasua.com, COP$285,000 d) offers very comfortable medium-sized rooms, satellite TV, and an inviting pool that is perfect after a long, active day.

The wonderful ★ **Posada del Campanario** (Cl. 5 No. 7-49, tel. 7/726-7261, www.posada-campanario.com, COP$290,000 d), one of the first hotels in Barichara, has seven rooms that are comfortable, but not overly luxurious. It's surrounded by gardens, and has an open-air dining area and a divine *mirador* (lookout) with a view of the Templo de la Inmaculada Concepción. Church bells may awaken you early in the morning.

La Nube (Cl. 7 No. 7-39, tel. 7/726-7161, cell tel. 310/334-8677, www.lanubeposada.com, COP$276,000 d) was boutique before the word entered the Colombian hotel industry's lexicon. It's a comfortable choice with 11 rooms and a good restaurant (breakfast not included). The patio is a sublime place for relaxing to the soothing sound of a fountain.

GETTING THERE

Most visitors to Barichara arrive either in their own transportation or by bus. To get to Barichara from Bogotá, head to Bogotá's Portal del Norte bus terminal. The journey to Barichara takes six hours or more, and you'll have to transfer in San Gil. It costs COP$30,000.

From Bucaramanga, from the Terminal de Transportes, a CONTRASANGIL bus leaves for Barichara at 4:45pm Monday-Friday, 9:15am on Saturday, and 7:30pm on Sunday. It takes three hours and costs COP$18,000.

Busetas leave San Gil every half hour (daily) from the Terminal de Transportes starting at 5am, with the last bus departing at 6:45pm. The 20-kilometer (12-mile) journey to Barichara takes 45 minutes and costs less than COP$5,000.

Norte de Santander

This department in the northeast of the country borders Venezuela to the east and Santander to the south. The main places of interest are Pamplona and Cúcuta, two very different cities. Pamplona is a charming and cool highland town that was important during the colonial era, though much of its period architecture has disappeared due to earthquakes and the march of progress. To the north, the departmental capital of Cúcuta is a hot and busy commercial city and gateway to Venezuela. Both cities are easily accessed by road from Bucaramanga. The southernmost area of Norte de Santander and the northernmost area of Catatumbo have been plagued with guerrilla and paramilitary activity in recent years and are best avoided.

PAMPLONA

Set in a lush, agriculturally rich valley at 2,300 meters (7,500 feet), this historic colonial town is a refreshing change from the heat of Cúcuta and Bucaramanga. In addition to colonial remnants like the Casa de las Tres Marías (now Museo de Arte Moderno Eduardo Ramírez Villamizar), Pamplona is known for being the home of abstract expressionist artist Eduardo Ramírez, and for being a surprisingly lively college town that hosts the Universidad de Pamplona and its thousands of students. Pamplona is also well known for its processions during Semana Santa (Holy Week).

Sights

Pamplona has its share of museums, all easily visited in a day on foot. During the week, when there are few visitors in town, museums may not open as their official hours suggest.

The top museum in town is the **Museo de Arte Moderno Eduardo Ramírez Villamizar** (Cl. 5 No. 5-75, tel. 7/568-2999, www.mamramirez-villamizar.com, 9am-noon and 2pm-5pm Tues.-Sun., COP$3,000), set in a lovingly restored 16th-century house. It features the work of modernist sculptor and painter Eduardo Ramírez Villamizar, and also puts on temporary shows of contemporary Colombian artists. In the courtyard, surrounding a magnolia tree, are many Ramírez sculptures.

Around the corner is the **Museo Arquidiocesano de Arte Religioso** (Cra. 5 No. 4-87, tel. 7/568-2816, 10am-noon and 3pm-5pm Wed.-Mon., COP$2,000). It houses oil paintings from masters such as Gregorio Arce y Ceballos, woodcarvings dating back to the 17th century, and silver and gold ceremonial items.

The town's most interesting churches include the imposing **Catedral Santa Clara** (Cl. 6 between Cras. 5-6, 8am-noon and 2pm-6pm daily), which dates to 1584, and the **Ermita del Señor del Humilladero** (Cl. 2 between Cras. 7-8, 6:30am-noon Mon. and Wed.-Fri., 6:30am-noon and 1:30pm-7pm Sat.-Sun.), which is next to the cemetery and filled with aboveground tombs. It is famous for its realistic carving *Cristo del Humilladero*.

The **Museo Casa Colonial** (Cl. 6 No. 2-56, tel. 7/568-2043, www.casacolonialpamplona.com, 8am-noon and 2pm-6pm Mon.-Fri., free) packs a punch in its 17th-century abode. It includes exhibits on some of the native cultures from the area, touches on the independence movement and struggles of the early Colombian republic, and takes the visitor through to the 20th century. It surrounds a courtyard bursting with color.

Finally, the small **Museo Casa Anzoátegui** (Cra. 6 No. 7-48, 9am-noon and 2pm-5:30pm Mon.-Sat., COP$1,000) examines the life of General José Antonio Anzoátgui and the fight for independence from Spain. It was in this house that the war hero died in 1819. He was the head of Bolívar's honor guard and was promoted to general following the Batalla del Puente de Boyacá.

The **Casa Mercado** (Cl. 6 between Cras. 4-5) stands on the previous location of a Jesuit college; this covered market, where you can buy fruit, vegetables, and much more, was built in 1920, and retains its popularity despite the arrival of supermarkets. The vendors will be happy if you buy some fruit from them.

Food and Accommodations

Pierro's Pizza (Cra. 5 No. 5B-67, tel. 7/568-0160, 5pm-11pm daily, COP$20,000) is the most popular place for pizza and pasta.

Vegetarians will want to head to **Majesvara** (Cra. 3B No. 1C-26, cell tel. 310/267-9307, noon-2pm and 7pm-8:30pm Mon.-Sat., COP$8,000), where you can eat a healthy meal for cheap. They offer a simple lunch menu with soup, a main dish with a vegetable protein and rice or potatoes, salad, and juice. The restaurant is about a 12-minute walk from Parque Águeda Gallardo.

★ **Hostal 1549** (Cl. 8B No. 8-64, Calle los Miserables, tel. 7/568-0451, cell tel. 317/699-6578, www.1549hostal.com, COP$130,000) is the cozy and comfortable option in town. Seven spacious rooms have big, comfortable beds, and many have fireplaces. The hotel has an adjacent restaurant where breakfast is served. At night locals gather to drink, but they are usually shown the door by 11pm.

The quirky **Hotel Ursua** (Cl. 5 No. 5-67, tel. 7/568-2470, cell tel. 311/847-4027, COP$40,000 d) has a fantastic location facing the main plaza, the Parque Águeda Gallardo (Cras. 5-6 and Clls. 5-6), and rooms come in all shapes and sizes. The on-site restaurant serves inexpensive breakfasts and lunches.

Once home to a scribe to the Spanish authorities in the 18th century, ★ **El Solar** (Cl. 5 No. 8-10, tel. 7/568-2010, www.elsolarhotel.com, COP$110,000 d) is one of the most popular accommodation and restaurant options. It has 10 rooms comprising 21 beds. Breakfast at the on-site restaurant is included, as is wireless Internet. The restaurant is open to the public, and at night the bonfire in the center creates the best ambience in town.

Getting There

Pamplona is on the road between Bucaramanga and Cúcuta. Its bus station is the spick-and-span **Terminal de Transportes** (Cra. 9 No. 3-120), about a 10-minute walk from the town center.

The road between Bucaramanga and Pamplona winds through *páramo* (highlands) and meanders through mountains, so the trip between these towns can be slow going. The bus ride to Pamplona from Bucaramanga costs about COP$25,000 and takes less than five hours.

From the bus station in Cúcuta, shared taxis, *busetas*, and buses leave on a regular basis all day long. Shared taxis are quick, but less comfortable than both *busetas* and larger buses, as you're likely to be crammed into the back seat of a small car. The under two-hour trip costs about COP$10,000.

CÚCUTA

The capital of the Norte de Santander department, Cúcuta is a tree-lined, historic, and pleasant city that straddles the border with Venezuela. It's most often visited as a waypoint for travelers headed into Venezuela.

The main tourist attraction, Parque Gran Colombiano, is just outside of the city in Villa del Rosario, on the way to Venezuela. That's where General Francisco de Paula Santander was born and where the first constitution for Gran Colombia was drafted. Simón Bolívar officially became the country's president here.

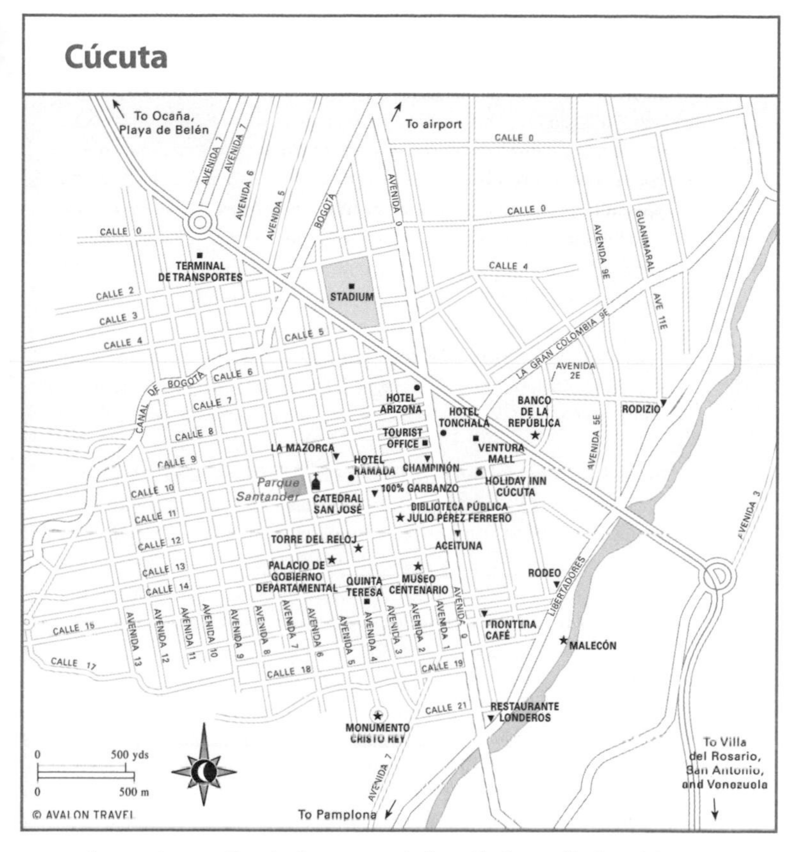

In recent years, the city has seen an influx of refugees fleeing violence in other parts of Norte de Santander and Arauca. During the 1990s there was a bloody turf war between paramilitaries and leftist guerrillas. In 2008, in response to months of simmering tension with Venezuela, Colombian pop singer Juanes organized Paz sin Fronteras (Peace Without Borders), a concert on the border that attracted 300,000 delighted fans. Today, although the situation in neighboring Venezuela is uncertain, Cúcuta is a safe place to visit.

ORIENTATION

The western boundary of Cúcuta is the Avenida Libertadores. Many of the big restaurants are located here, and this is where the Ciclovía is held on Sundays. All the decent hotels and most sights in Cúcuta are in the downtown area between Avenida 0 to the east and Avenida 6 to the west and Calle 8 to the north and Calle 13 to the south. The Aeropuerto Camilo Daza is in the northwest of the city.

Sights

CITY CENTER

There are a handful of cultural sights in downtown Cúcuta that can be easily visited on foot. The small but cool **Museo de Norte de Santander** (Cl. 14 No. 1-03, tel. 7/595-8377, 8am-noon and 2pm-6pm Mon.-Fri., 9am-noon Sat., free) hosts art exhibitions and events.

The beautifully restored **Biblioteca Pública Julio Pérez Ferrero** (Av. 1 No. 12-35, Barrio La Playa, tel. 7/595-5384, www.bibliocucuta.org, 8am-noon and 2pm-6pm Mon.-Fri., 9am-noon Sat., free) served as a hospital in the 19th century. This cultural center has a reading room open to the public and there is an outdoor café (hours vary).

The **Palacio de Gobierno Departamental** (Clls. 13-14 and Avs. 4-5) is noteworthy for its Republican-era neoclassical architecture. It's not open to the public. The neoclassical **Catedral San José** (Av. 5 No. 10-53) faces the shady **Parque Santander** (Avs. 5-6 and Clls. 10-11).

The **Torre del Reloj** (Cl. 13 No. 3-67) stands in what is now the **Casa de la Cultura** (tel. 7/583-2215, 7:30am-noon and 2pm-6pm Mon.-Fri.). This sophisticated early 20th-century Italian-made clock tower houses bells that toll the national anthem. Inquire at the Casa de la Cultura if you want to make the climb. From the top, you can get a nice view of the city with the **Monumento Cristo Rey** (Av. 4 at Cl. 19) in the distance. The Casa de la Cultura complex also hosts art exhibitions.

The **Banco de la República** (Diag. Santander No. 3E-38, tel. 7/575-0131, www.banrepcultural.org/cucuta, 8am-11:30am and 2pm-6pm Mon.-Fri.) always has an art exhibition on view, usually featuring a Colombian artist. Concerts are also held at the facility's theater.

PARQUE GRAN COLOMBIANO

The major historical site in greater Cúcuta is seven kilometers (4.3 miles) outside the city, near the town of **Villa del Rosario** on the road toward San

Parque Gran Colombiano

Antonio del Táchira, Venezuela. The **Parque Gran Colombiano** (Km. 6 Autopista Internacional, no phone, dawn-dusk daily, free), also known as the **Templo Histórico,** is a park set in the middle of the busy highway that leads to the Venezuelan border. Much of the park, which extends for about a kilometer, is green space where couples cuddle below royal palm trees and others jog or walk their dogs.

The **Casa Natal del General Santander** (Km. 6 Autopista Internacional, tel. 7/570-0265, 8am-11am and 2pm-5pm Tues.-Sat., 9am-5pm Sun., free) is a museum that tells the story of important independence figure General Francisco de Paula Santander, known as Colombia's Thomas Jefferson. It's the westernmost structure in the park, and is set in Santander's childhood home. Guides show visitors around for free, but you may wish to give a small tip afterward. Note the brick aqueduct and the tamarind and laurel trees that have been around for centuries.

The photogenic ruins of the **Templo del Congreso** are where Gran Colombia's Constitution of 1821 was drafted and where Simón Bolívar was sworn in as president (and Santander as vice president). Congress met for over a month to draft the constitution, and on their breaks, they would rest under the shade of a huge tamarind tree. The tree is still there, in front of the church. The Templo was badly damaged in the Cúcuta Earthquake of 1875. Only the dome, in a different style altogether, was rebuilt. A marble statue of Bolívar stands amid the ruins. The Templo is within walking distance of the Casa Natal del General Santander.

Across the highway from the Templo is the **Casa de la Bagatela,** which was the seat of the executive branch of Gran Colombia. It was named in honor of independence figure Antonio Nariño, who helmed a revolutionary paper in Bogotá called *La Bagatela.* There's not much more to see up close, so there's no need to cross this busy thoroughfare.

To get to the park, you can take a shared taxi or a *buseta* (small bus) bound for San Antonio del Táchira at the Centro Comercial Ventura Plaza. These cost around COP$2,500. Ask to be dropped off at the Templo Histórico. Private taxis cost about COP$7,500 from downtown Cúcuta.

Food

The most typical food from Cúcuta includes *hayacas cucutenas,* similar to tamales; *mute,* a meaty stew; and *pastel de garbanzo,* a fried garbanzo bean pastry.

For a welcome break from meat, try **Champiñon** (Cl. 10 No. 0-05, tel. 7/571-1561, 8am-8:30pm Mon.-Sat., COP$12,000). This is Cúcuta's best exclusively vegetarian restaurant, highlighted by a generous set lunch.

★ **Aceituna** (Av. 0 No. 13-135, tel. 7/583-7464, cell tel. 320/210-2332, 10:30am-10pm daily, COP$18,000) is a long-standing restaurant run by a Lebanese-Colombian family. They specialize in shawarma and falafels.

When darkness falls in Cúcuta, especially on the weekends, the energy shifts to the *malecón* area, about a 10-minute cab ride west from downtown. That's where many of the big restaurants are located. **Londeros**

Sur (Av. Libertadores No. 0E-60B, tel. 7/583-3335, www.restaurantelondreros.com, COP$25,000) is famous around town for its Argentinian steaks. **Rodizio** (Av. Libertadores No. 10-121, tel. 7/575-1719, www.rodizio.com.co, COP$30,000) is known for its Brazilian-style grilled meats. **Rodeo** (Av. Libertadores No. 16-38, www.rodeogourmet.com, COP$25,000) is another very popular option for carnivores.

For coffee prepared in one of five different ways, head to **Frontera Tienda de Café** (Av. 1E No. 16A-15, tel. 7/589-8979, 7:30am-8:30pm Mon.-Sat.) in the leafy Caobos neighborhood. Breakfast is also served.

Accommodations

There are no true backpacker hostels in Cúcuta. International brands Holiday Inn and Ramada have both set up shop in town, and they are excellent choices.

Hotel Tonchalá (Av. 0 at Cl. 10, tel. 7/575-6444, www.hoteltonchala.com, COP$340,000 d) is a classic big hotel and is popular for business meetings. The lap pool may be its major selling point. It's within a five-minute stroll of Centro Comercial Ventura Plaza. Staff at **Hotel Arizona Suites** (Av. 0 No. 7-62, tel. 7/573-1884, www.hotelarizonasuites.com, COP$148,000) are exceptionally friendly. Rooms are fine, if a little on the small side. The restaurant overlooks a small pool. The location (decent, but not great) is near two busy streets and about a 10-minute walk to downtown.

Information and Services

The **tourist office** (Cl. 10 No. 0-30, no phone, 8am-11:50am and 2pm-6pm Mon.-Fri., 8:30am-noon Sat.) has lots of brochures and maps for Cúcuta as well as the rest of the Norte de Santander department.

In case of an emergency, contact the **Policía Nacional** by dialing 123. A major hospital in town is the **Hospital Erasmo Meoz** (Av. 11E No. 5AN-71, tel. 7/574-6888).

Transportation

The **Aeropuerto Camilo Daza** (CUC, Km. 5 Autopista Panamericana) is a 15-minute cab ride (COP$22,000) from downtown. **Avianca** (Cl. 13 No. 5-22, tel. 7/571-3877, www.avianca.com, 8am-noon and 2pm-6pm Mon.-Fri., 8am-noon Sat.) flies nonstop between Cúcuta and Bogotá and Medellín. **EasyFly** (tel. 7/595-5005, www.easyfly.com.co) connects Cúcuta with Bucaramanga and Medellín. **LATAM** (Aeropuerto Camilo Daza, Km. 5 Autopista Panamericana, tel. 1/745-2020, 5:30am-9:30pm Mon.-Fri., 6:30am-10:30am and 2pm-6pm Sat., 8am-noon and 4pm-8pm Sun.) offers flights from Bogotá.

The bus ride from Bogotá to Cúcuta costs around COP$70,000 and the trip takes 14 hours. From Bucaramanga it costs COP$30,000 and takes six hours, and from San Gil it costs about COP$45,000 and takes eight hours. The **Terminal de Transportes** (Avs. 7-8 between Clls. 1-2) in Cúcuta is dirty, chaotic, and generally unpleasant. When departing from the bus terminal, try to get your ticket in advance so you don't have to be there longer than necessary. If you are waiting for a bus, it's best to wait outside on the curb, away from the claustrophobic station.

If you are staying downtown, all attractions are within relatively easy walking distance. It's always a good policy to call a cab beforehand, and always after dark. The best way to call for a cab is to use a smartphone app such as Easy Taxi or Uber.

CROSSING INTO VENEZUELA

Crossing the border from Cúcuta into San Antonio del Táchira, Venezuela, is theoretically easy. But there is always some uncertainty, depending on the political situation. *Busetas* (shared taxis) depart from in front of Centro Comercial Ventura Plaza in Cúcuta. Expect to pay about COP$2,500 for a *buseta* ticket. Taxis will cost upwards of COP$20,000. Note that there is a 30-minute time difference in Venezuela.

Be sure to get off before the bridge in order to get an exit stamp from immigration officials in your passport. (Making this stop is a standard practice for bus drivers.) Visas are not required for citizens of North America or the European Union.

Hotels in San Antonio del Táchira are dismal, so it's better to either stay in Cúcuta or continue onward in Venezuela.

For more information on visas, visit the **Consulado Venezuelano** (Venezuelan consulate, Av. Aeropuerto Camilo Daza, Sector Corral de Piedra, Zona Industrial, Cl. 17 Esquina, tel. 7/579-1954 or 7/579-1951, 8am-10am and 2pm-3pm Mon.-Thurs., 8am-10am Fri.). It's close to the airport.

Background

The Landscape

Colombia covers a land area of 1.14 million square kilometers (440,000 square miles), roughly the size of Texas and California combined, making it the fourth-largest South American country in area after Brazil, Argentina, and Peru. It is located in the northwest corner of South America, with seacoast on both the Pacific and the Atlantic, and it borders Venezuela, Brazil, Peru, Ecuador, and Panama. The Amazonian departments of Putumayo, Caquetá, Amazonas, and Vaupés in the south of the country straddle the equator.

For a country of its size, Colombia has an astonishing variety of landscapes, including the dense rainforests of the Amazon and the Pacific coast, the vast grassland plains of the Llanos, the lofty Andes Mountains, and the Caribbean islands of San Andrés and Providencia. Colombia's mountainous regions themselves hold a succession of vertically layered landscapes: tropical rainforests at their base, followed by cloud forests at higher elevations, topped by the unique tropical high mountain *páramo* (highland moor) above 3,500 meters (11,480 feet). The country boasts several peaks higher than 5,000 meters (16,400 feet), including Nevado del Ruiz (5,325 meters/17,470 feet) and Pico Cristóbal Colón (5,776 meters/18,950 feet).

GEOGRAPHY

Región Andina

This central part of Colombia is dominated by the Andes mountain range. This region, which is referred to as the Región Andina or simply *el interior* (the interior) is the heartland of the country. It covers roughly 25 percent of the surface of the country and is home to 60 percent of the Colombian population.

The Andes mountain range, 8,000 kilometers (5,000 miles) long, runs the entire length of South America. The Andes are relatively young mountains, and some of the loftiest in the world after the Himalayas, resulting from the collision of the westward-moving South American plate with the Nazca and Antarctic plates starting 145 million years ago. The heavier Nazca and Antarctic plates to the west subducted under the lighter and more rigid South American plate, propelling it upwards and forming the Andes. In Colombia, as a result of a complex pattern of tectonic collisions, three parallel ranges were formed. At the Masizo Colombiano (Colombian Massif), a mountain range 175 kilometers north of the border with Ecuador, the Andes split into the Cordillera Occidental (Western Range), Cordillera Central (Central Range), and Cordillera Oriental (Eastern Range).

The Cordillera Occidental is the lowest and least populated of the three ranges. It runs roughly 750 kilometers parallel to the Pacific coast and ends

---

Previous: Thousands protest for peace in Bogotá; Bogotá skyline.

150 kilometers from the Caribbean Sea. Its highest point is the Cerro de Tatamá (4,250 meters/13,945 feet). Of Colombia's three ranges, it has the least human intervention and is home to some of the world's only pristine high mountain *páramos* ecosystems, notably that covering the Cerro de Tatamá.

The Central Cordillera is the highest of the three ranges and is the continuation in Colombia of the main Andes range. It runs roughly 800 kilometers and tapers off in the northern Caribbean plains, 200 kilometers from the Caribbean coast. Like the Andes in Ecuador, it is dotted with volcanoes. North of the Masizo Colombiano is the Serranía de los Coconucos (Coconucos Range), a range of 15 volcanoes including the Volcán del Puracé (Puracé Volcano, 4,580 meters/15,025 feet). Farther north, the Cordillera Central reaches its maximum elevation at the massive Nevado del Huila (5,750 meters/15,585 feet). Farther north is a large complex formed by the Nevado del Tolima (5,215 meters/17,110 feet), Nevado Santa Isabel (4,950 meters/16,240 feet), and Nevado del Ruiz (5,325 meters/17,470 feet). In its northern part, the Cordillera Central broadens to form the uneven highland that comprises the mountainous heartland of Antioquia with Medellín as its capital.

Several of the volcanoes of the Cordillera Central have seen recent activity, notably Volcán Galeras (4,276 meters/14,029 feet), near the southern city of Pasto, which last erupted in 2005, forcing evacuation of nearby settlements. Volcán Galeras is currently closed to visitors because of the threat of volcanic activity. In 1985, the Nevado del Ruiz erupted unexpectedly, creating a landslide that engulfed the town of Armero, killing more than 20,000 people. Since 2012, the Nevado del Ruiz has seen some activity, which has restricted access to the northern part of the Parque Nacional Natural Los Nevados.

The Cordillera Oriental, which like the Cordillera Occidental is nonvolcanic, extends more than 1,100 kilometers to the border with Venezuela. The range broadens to form a broad high plateau called the Altiplano Cundiboyacense, which extends 200 kilometers north of Bogotá. This is an area of broad valleys with the extremely rich soil of sedimentary deposits. The Sabana de Bogotá, or Bogotá High Plateau, where Bogotá is located, is one particularly broad valley. North of the altiplano is the soaring Sierra Nevada del Cocuy, a mountain range with 11 glacier-covered peaks, including Ritacuba Blanco (5,380 meters/17,650 feet). North of El Cocuy, the Cordillera Oriental loses altitude and splits in two: A smaller western segment forms the Serranía de Perijá on the border between Colombia and Venezuela, and a larger branch continues into Venezuela to form the Venezuelan Andes.

The 1,500-kilometer-long Río Magdalena flows along a broad valley that separates the Cordillera Central and the Cordillera Oriental, making it the main commercial waterway of Colombia. Due to heavy sedimentation, it is now only navigable when waters rise during the rainy seasons in the central part of the country (Apr.-May and Oct.-Nov.). The Río Cauca, which flows parallel to the Magdalena along the much narrower valley between the Cordillera Central and the Cordillera Occidental, is the main tributary of the Magdalena. They join in northern Colombia and flow into the Caribbean.

Andean Colombia is a seismically volatile area, and the country has suffered some major earthquakes in the past. The most deadly measured 7.5 on the Richter Scale and occurred in Cúcuta in 1875. It killed 10,000 and completely destroyed the city. In recent years, around 600 were killed in the Pacific port city of Tumaco during a quake and tsunami in 1979; 300 perished in the 1983 Holy Week earthquake in Popayán; and over 1,100 died in the Armenia quake of 1999.

Caribe

Colombia's Caribbean coast runs 1,760 kilometers (1,100 miles) from the border of Panama to Venezuela, just longer than the California coast. However, the term "Caribe" or "Región Caribe" refers to much more than the narrow strip of coast; it encompasses basically all of Colombia north of the Andes, including a vast area of plains. This region covers 15 percent of the surface of Colombia and is home to 20 percent of the population.

The terrain is mostly low-lying and undulating. Near the border with Panama, the land is covered by dense tropical forests, similar to those on the Pacific coast. Farther east is the Golfo de Urabá, a large, shallow bay. Between the Golfo de Urabá and Cartagena is the Golfo de Morrosquillo, a broad inlet that is 50 kilometers (31 miles) wide. Off the shore of the Golfo de Morrosquillo are two small archipelagos, the Islas de San Bernardo and the Islas del Rosario, with beautiful coral reefs. Inland to the south is a large savanna in the departments of Córdoba and Sucre largely devoted to cattle ranching. This area was once covered by dry tropical forests, which have been largely felled.

Bahía de Cartagena, farther east, is a magnificent deep bay that caught the attention of the early Spanish explorers. To the southeast of Cartagena is the lower valley of the Magdalena and Cauca Rivers, a vast expanse of low-lying lagoons and lands prone to seasonal flooding. The Río Magdalena flows into the Caribbean east of Cartagena at the port city of Barranquilla. Farther to the east along the coast is a major mountain range, the Sierra Nevada de Santa Marta. It was formed by the collision of the South American plate and the Caribbean plate to the north and is entirely independent of the Andes. This range is home to Colombia's two highest peaks, the twin Pico Cristóbal Colón and Pico Bolívar (5,776 meters/18,950 feet), and is considered the highest coastal mountain range in the world. The Sierra Nevada de Santa Marta contains the same range of vertically layered landscapes as the Andes, from low-lying tropical forest through cloud forest, Andean forests, *páramo,* and glaciers. There are eight peaks with elevations greater than 5,000 meters (16,400 feet).

Northeast of the Sierra Nevada de Santa Marta is La Guajira, an arid peninsula jutting into the Caribbean. Punta Gallinas, at the tip of La

Guajira, is the northernmost point in South America. There are a few low-lying mountain ranges in La Guajira, such as the Serranía de la Macuira (864 meters/2,835 feet), which is covered with rainforest. The Sierra Nevada de Santa Marta and Serranía de la Macuira are biological islands, and their upper reaches are home to numerous endemic species that evolved in isolation.

Pacífico

The Pacific coast of Colombia extends 1,329 kilometers from Ecuador to Panama, about the same length as the coast of California. The term Pacífico, as it relates to Colombia, designates all the land—jungle to be more accurate—that lies between the Pacific Ocean and the Cordillera Occidental. This region covers 6 percent of Colombia and is home to about 2 percent of the population.

The topography of this region is mostly flat, with the low-lying coastal Serranía del Baudó (1,810 meters/5,940 feet) providing a mountainous backdrop to the coastal plain and forming an inland basin that is drained by the mighty Río Atrato, which flows northwards into the Caribbean Sea. The coast has a number of bays and inlets, notably the Ensenada de Utría (Utría Inlet), visited by humpback whales traveling every winter from the Antarctic Sea to give birth in the warm waters of the Colombian Pacific. South of Buenaventura, the coast has extensive mangroves, much of which are well-preserved. Offshore are two islands: Isla Gorgona is 35 kilometers off the coast on the continental shelf, and tiny Malpelo is 490 kilometers off the coast. Both of these islands are likely of volcanic origin.

The Colombian Pacific region is one of the wettest places on Earth, with average annual rainfall of 10,000 millimeters (33 feet). Due to the enormous amount of precipitation, the region has a dense river network with dozens of major arteries, such as the Río Baudó, Río San Juan, and Río Patía.

Amazon

The Amazon region of Colombia comprises 400,000 million kilometers, or roughly 35 percent of Colombia's territory, including all the territory east of the Andes and south of the Río Guaviare. The Colombian portion covers only 10 percent of the entire Amazon drainage basin. Total population in the Amazon region is 1.1 million, or 2 percent of the country's population. It is the most sparsely populated area in the country.

Like the Llanos, the Amazon has an undulating terrain, interrupted occasionally with ancient, low-lying mountainous formations of the Guyana Shield, such as the Serranía de Chiribiquete, a series of highly eroded tabletop mountains. The Amazon consists of two distinct but intermingled areas: *terra firme*, the undulated lands that are above the highest flood point, and *varzea*, floodplains along the main rivers, which can extend 50 kilometers from the river.

There are two types of rivers in the Amazon: the predominant white rivers, which carry sediments down from the Andes; and the black rivers, which originate within the rainforest in the Guyana Shield formations that were long ago denuded of soil due to erosion. As these waters travel though the flooded forest, they pick up pigments that give them their characteristic black color. *Igapo* is the name given to jungles flooded by black water rivers. Most of the rivers of the Colombian Amazon are white, such as the massive Río Putumayo, Río Caquetá, Río Apaporis, and Río Vaupés, all of which are more than 1,000 kilometers long. The main black river in Colombia is the Río Guainía, which does originate in the Andes, and which is the headwater of the largest black river of the Amazon—the Río Negro—which flows into the milky Amazon at Manaus, in Brazil.

Los Llanos

The Llanos, Colombia's vast eastern plains, cover an area of 250,000 square kilometers, roughly 25 percent of Colombia's territory. The plains are hemmed in to the west by Cordillera Oriental and to the south by the Amazon rainforest, and extend far into Venezuela. Though the transition between the Amazon and the Llanos is gradual, the Río Guaviare, which flows from west to east at a longitude that is roughly midway between the northern and southern tips of Colombia, is considered the demarcation line between these two areas. The Llanos are home to about 1.5 million inhabitants, or about 3 percent of the population, making it the region with the second lowest population density—after the Amazon region—in the country.

After the genesis of the Andes, water flowing eastward down the mountains accumulated in a vast freshwater lake that was confined on the east by old mountainous formations (now the Guyana and Brazilian highlands). Large amounts of sediments were deposited, forming the basis for the Llanos' undulating topography. Near the Andes, elevations can reach 300 meters and, moving east, slowly decrease in altitude until they reach the north-flowing Río Orinoco, which forms the border between Colombia and Venezuela.

The only significant mountain range in Los Llanos is the Serranía de la Macarena (Macarena Range), a 120-kilometer-long, 30-kilometer-wide range that is 45 kilometers east of the Andes just of the Río Guayabero, a tributary of the Río Guaviare. This range is part of the Guyana Shield complex of ancient, highly eroded remnants of mountains that existed long before the formation of the Andes.

The Llanos are drained by a multitude of large rivers, such as the Río Guaviare, Río Vichada, and Río Meta, which flow down from the Andes and meander east. All the rivers of the Llanos are tributaries of the Orinoco—for this reason, this region is also often called La Orinoquía.

CLIMATE

Colombia has a typically tropical climate, with no change of seasons. Climate is related primarily to elevation, and there are defined annual precipitation patterns.

In the mountainous areas, temperature decreases approximately six

Colombia's National Parks

From undisturbed coral reefs to the Amazonian jungle to snow-covered mountain ranges, Colombia's national park system is a treasure, and making the effort to visit them is worthwhile for any visitor. The country's system of natural parks and protected areas covers more than 14 million hectares (34.6 million acres), around 13.4 percent of the country. It includes 43 Parques Nacionales Naturales (National Natural Parks), which are areas of major ecological interest that have remained largely untouched by human intervention, and 12 Santuarios de Flora y Fauna (Flora and Fauna Sanctuaries), areas that are devoted to the preservation of specific ecosystems. Of the 43 parks, 24 are open for tourism. The rest are officially off-limits, due to lack of infrastructure, security concerns, or in order to respect the territory of indigenous communities.

In 1960, PNN Cueva de los Guácharos, in the southwest, was the first park to be established. The number of parks steadily increased, especially from 1986 to 1990 when President Virgilio Barco doubled the park holdings from roughly 5 million hectares to 10 million hectares (12 million to 24 million acres). In the past few years, the government has again been increasing the number and extension of parks. In 2013 President Juan Manuel Santos doubled the size of the PNN Serranía de Chiribiquete to its present 2.8 million hectares (7 million acres), or three times the size of Yellowstone National Park.

Charged with the considerable task of administering this huge system are a mere 430 rangers—roughly one person for every 33,000 hectares (82,000 acres). Rangers face a great challenge in protecting the parks against threats related to human encroachment, particularly cattle ranching and the planting of illicit crops. There are other threats as well, such as illegal mining and logging. Paradoxically, what has preserved many of the parks until now has been the lack of security due to Colombia's internal conflict. As security conditions improve, there will be increasing pressure on these natural habitats. The Parks Service is actively engaging with the communities that live near the parks and is transferring the operation of much of the ecotourism infrastructure to community-based organizations as part of an effort to enlist local communities in the preservation of the land.

Entry permits and entry fees are only required in a handful of highly visited parks, such as PNN Tayrona, PNN Gorgona, PNN Cocuy, and PNN Los Nevados. At these, you will automatically be charged if you book lodging in advance, or if not, upon arrival. If you want to be meticulous, you can obtain the entry permit and pay entry fees in advance by contacting the **Parques Nacionales** (tel. 1/353-2400, www.parquesnacionales.gov.co) in Bogotá.

degrees Celsius per every 1,000 meters (3,280 feet) of elevation (or three degrees Fahrenheit per every 1,000 feet). The common designations for the altitudinal zones are as follows: *tierra caliente* (hot lands) is anywhere below 1,000 meters of elevation; *tierra templada* (temperate lands) is anywhere between 1,000 and 2,000 meters; and *tierra fría* (cold land) is anywhere above 2,000 meters. Roughly 80 percent of the country is *tierra caliente,* 10 percent is *tierra templada,* and 7 percent is *tierra fría.*

Cartagena, which is at sea level, has an average temperature of 27.5°C (81.5°F); Medellín, which is at 1,600 meters (5,250 feet), has an average temperature of 22°C (71.5°F); and the capital city of Bogotá, which is built at 2,625 meters (8,612 feet), has an average temperature of 13.5°C (56°F).

Precipitation patterns vary throughout the country. In the Andean region, there are generally two periods of *verano* (dry season, literally "summer"), from December to March and from June to September, and two periods of *invierno* (rainy season, literally "winter"), in April and May and from October to November. On the Caribbean coast, the dry period is from December to April and the rainy season is from May to November. In the Pacific it rains almost the entire year, but there is a slight dry spell from December to March. In the Llanos, there are two very marked seasons: a very dry *verano* from November to March and a very wet *invierno* from April to October. In the Amazon, it rains almost the entire year, but there is a slight dry spell from August to October.

Extreme weather in Colombia is rare, but the country is susceptible to weather phenomena such as El Niño or La Niña, when temperatures in the Pacific Ocean rise or fall, respectively. In 2015-2016, the country was affected by a strong El Niño, which brought prolonged drought.

San Andrés and Providencia are occasionally, and the Caribbean mainland of Colombia rarely, in the path of Atlantic hurricanes from August through October. The last storm of significance was Hurricane Beta in 2005. It caused considerable damage in Providencia.

Plants and Animals

When it comes to biodiversity, Colombia is a place of superlatives. Though representing only 0.2 percent of the planet's surface, it is home to about 10 percent of all the species in the world. The country has an estimated 55,000 plant species, including 3,500 species of orchids. Only Brazil, with seven times the land surface, has as many plant species. Colombia is the country with the greatest number of bird species in the world—about 1,800. It's also home to about 3,200 fish, 750 amphibian species, 500 reptile species, and 450 mammal species. No wonder Colombia was designated as one of 17 so-called megadiverse countries, a select club of countries that are home to an outsized proportion of the world's biodiversity. Other megadiverse countries include Australia, Brazil, China, Democratic Republic of Congo, Indonesia, Madagascar, Mexico, the United States, and South Africa.

This enormous biodiversity is the result of Colombia's location in the tropics, where year-round sunlight and high precipitation are conducive to plant growth, plus the country's mountainous topography with numerous climatic zones and microclimates that have created biological islands where species have evolved in relative isolation. Furthermore, the recent ice ages were not as severe in this part of the world, and as a result many ancient species were preserved. Finally, Colombia's location at the crossroads of Central and South America has further enriched the country's biodiversity.

Colombian Fruits

Colombia is a land bursting with exotic fruit. Sold from the back of pickup trucks by farmers on the roadside, overflowing at stalls in colorful markets in every town and village, lined up in neat rows in the produce section at fancy grocery stores and at juice stands—just about anywhere you go, delicious fruit is in reach.

You know pineapple, papaya, mangoes, and bananas, but be sure to try these tropical delights that you may not have encountered outside of Colombia.

- ***Pitahaya*** **(dragon fruit):** Looking like a yellow grenade, *pitahayas* have a sweet white meat inside.
- ***Guanábana*** **(soursop):** By far the strangest-looking fruit, soursop resemble prehistoric dinosaur eggs. Inside the large green spiky fruit is a milky and slimy flesh. *Guanábana* is great in juices and desserts.
- ***Granadilla:*** Crack open this orangey-yellow fruit and slurp down the slimy gray contents, seeds and all. It's delicious.
- ***Higo*** **(prickly pear):** This green fruit comes from cactus plants and has sweet, if tough, orange-colored meat.
- ***Chirimoya*** **(cherimoya):** This green fruit that resembles a smooth artichoke is covered with a smooth, silky skin and filled with delectable, sweet pulp.
- ***Níspero*** **(sapodilla):** A fruit with a deep brown color that tastes like a prepared sweet.
- ***Mangostino*** **(mangosteen):** Crack open a deep-purple mangosteen and enjoy the sweet segments inside. They're full of antioxidants.
- ***Uchuva*** **(Cape gooseberry):** Known in English as Cape gooseberries, these tart yellow berries are a cousin of the tomato and are tasty on their own or in salads, but are often used in jams and sweets.
- ***Mamoncillo:*** Tough-skinned grapes (don't eat the skin), *mamoncillos* are usually sold only at street markets.

RAINFOREST

Rainforests are among the most complex ecosystems on Earth. They have a layered structure with towering trees that soar 30-40 meters high (100-130 feet) to form the forest's canopy. Some of the most common rainforest trees are the ceiba, mahogany, myrtle, laurel, acacia, and rubber trees. Occasionally, particularly high trees known as *emergentes* pierce the canopy, reaching as high up as 60 meters (200 feet). Below the canopy is the *sotobosque*, a middle layer of smaller trees and palms that vie for the sunlight filtering in through the canopy. In the canopy and *sotobosque* there are many epiphytes (plants such as orchids and bromeliads) that have adapted to live on top of trees so as to be nearer to the sunlight. Near the ground live plants that require little sunlight, including ferns, grasses, and many types of fungi. The two main rainforests in Colombia, the Amazon and the Chocó, have the same layered structure, though they have some differences in their flora and fauna.

The Amazon rainforest is home to an impressive array of vertebrates. Over millennia, a large number of canopy-dwelling species evolved. Monkeys, such as the large and extremely agile spider monkey, the woolly monkey, and the howler monkey, evolved prehensile tails that allowed them to move easily from branch to branch. Anteaters, such as the tamandua and the *oso mielero* (giant anteater) and the incredibly cute *kinkajú* (kinkajou), also developed prehensile tails. Other inhabitants of the canopy include sloths, such as the adorable three-toed sloth, whose strategy is not agility but passivity: It eats tree vegetation and is covered with algae that gradually turns the animal green to allow for good camouflage. The canopy is also home to myriad bats and many birds, including exotic eagles, curassows, toucans, woodpeckers, cotingas, and macaws.

Notable is the majestic harpy eagle, with powerful claws and the ability to fly unencumbered through the canopy. It preys on monkeys and sloths, which it kills with the force of its claws. The *tigrillo* (tiger cat) is a small and extremely endangered species. It has a long tail that helps with its balance as it moves from tree to tree.

On the ground, large vertebrates include the extremely endangered tapir, an ancient mammal species that can grow two meters long (over six feet) and weigh 300 kilograms (660 pounds). It is equally at ease on land as in the water. Other land mammals include the giant armadillo, giant anteater, deer, and boars, such as the *saíno* and *pecarí*. Smaller mammals include the *guatín* and *borugo*, both rodents. These animals are often prey to the puma and jaguar, both of which inhabit the Amazon but are difficult to observe in the wild.

The rivers of the Amazon are home to more than 1,500 species of fish, including endangered pirarucu, one of the largest freshwater fishes on Earth. There are also dolphins, both pink and gray. The former evolved separately from the oceangoing dolphins when the Amazon was an inland sea. The Amazonian gray dolphins are sea dolphins that adapted to living in freshwater. Other aquatic mammals include the highly endangered manatee and otters.

The Chocó Rainforest is particularly rich in palms, of which 120 species have been identified. In fact, it is sometimes referred to as the "Land of the Palms." The forest also abounds in cycads, ancient plants that have a stout trunk and crowns of hard, stiff leaves. Chocó is also notable for more than 40 species of brightly colored poisonous frogs, known locally as *ranas kokois*. These small frogs are covered with a deadly poison and have evolved stunning coloration, from bright orange to red, gold, and blue. They are active in the day and therefore relatively easy to spot. Of Colombia's 1,800 species of birds, more than 1,000 have been identified in the Chocó, including a large number of hummingbirds.

Offshore, the Pacific Ocean welcomes the annual migration of Antarctic humpback whales. The beaches of the Pacific coast are popular nesting areas for sea turtles, in particular the *tortuga golfina* (olive ridley) and *tortuga carey* (hawksbill) sea turtles.

CLOUD FOREST

Rainforests that grow at higher altitudes on the flanks of the Andes are known as montane rainforests or cloud forests because they are often enveloped in mist that results from the condensation of warm air against chillier mountain currents. Unlike the lowland rainforest, cloud forests only have two layers, the canopy and ground layer. Generally, the vegetation is less dense than that in the lowland rainforest. However, it is home to many palms, ferns, and epiphytes, particularly orchids.

The type of cloud forest vegetation is dictated by altitude. *Selva subandina* (sub-Andean forest) vegetation grows between the altitudes of 1,000 and 2,300 meters (3,300-7,500 feet), where temperature varies 16-23°C (61-73°F). Plant species include the distinctive Seussian white *yarumo* with its oversized leaves, as well as cedar, oak, and mahogany trees. Many palms grow here, including the svelte wax palm and *tagua*, which produces a nut that resembles ivory. Ferns include the striking *palma boba* or tree fern. Colombia's premier crop, coffee, is grown at this elevation.

At elevations between 2,300 and 3,600 meters (7,500-12,000 feet), the vegetation is described as *selva Andina* (Andean forest). This vegetation is even less dense and at higher elevations the trees are smaller. *Selva Andina* includes many oak, *encenillo*, *sietecuero* (glory bush), and pine trees.

Mammals include the spectacled or Andean bear, the only species of bear in South America, the mountain (or woolly) tapir, anteaters, armadillos, sloths, boars, foxes, and *olingos*, small arboreal carnivores of the raccoon family. In 2013, the *olinguito* (small *olingo*), an incredibly cute animal, was declared a new species. Other unusual animals include the slow-moving *guagua loba* and *guatín*, both of which are rodents. In addition, numerous species of monkeys inhabit the cloud forest, including noisy troops of howler monkeys. Birds include many types of *barranqueros* (motmots), including the spectacular blue-crowned motmot. Other common birds include *tángaras* (tanagers), woodpeckers, warblers, parrots, owls, and ducks, including the beautiful white-and-black torrent duck.

PÁRAMOS

Páramos are unique tropical highland ecosystems that thrive above 3,500 meters (11,500 feet), where UV radiation is higher, oxygen is scarcer, and where temperatures vary from minus-2 to 10 degrees Celsius (28-50°F). Due to frequent mist and precipitation, *páramos* are often saturated with water and have many lakes. They are true "water factories" that provide water to many of Colombia's cities, notably Bogotá. Though *páramos* exist throughout the New World tropics, most are located in Colombia. The Parque Nacional Natural Sumapaz, south of Bogotá, is the world's largest *páramo*.

Páramo vegetation includes more than 50 species of *frailejón* (genus *Espeletia*), eerily beautiful plants that have imposing tall trunks and thick yellow-greenish leaves. Other *páramo* vegetation includes shrubs, grasses, and *cojines* (cushion plants). Mammals include the spectacled bear, *páramo* tapir, weasels, squirrels, and bats. The *páramo* is the realm of the majestic black-and-white Andean condor, which has a wingspan of up to three meters (10 feet). The condor, whose numbers had declined almost to the point of extinction, is found in the national parks of the Sierra Nevada de Santa Marta, Sierra Nevada del Cocuy, and Los Nevados. The *páramo* lakes welcome many types of ducks, including the Andean duck, as well as smaller birds.

TROPICAL DRY FORESTS

Tropical dry forests exist in areas where there is a prolonged dry season. The vegetation includes deciduous trees that lose their leaves during the dry season, allowing them to conserve water. Trees on moister sites and those with access to groundwater tend to be evergreen. Before Columbus, this ecosystem covered much of the Colombian Caribbean coast. However, much of it has since been cut down for cattle ranching. Pockets still exist east of the Golfo de Morrosquillo and at the base of the Sierra Nevada de Santa Marta. Tropical dry forests are the most endangered tropical ecosystem in the world.

Though less biologically diverse than rainforests, tropical dry forests are home to a wide variety of wildlife. They were once the stomping ground of the now highly endangered *marimonda*, or white-fronted spider monkey.

TROPICAL GRASSLANDS

Los Llanos (The Plains) of Colombia are covered with lush tropical grasslands. Vegetation includes long-stemmed and carpet grasses in the drier areas and swamp grasses in low-lying humid areas. There are also thick patches of forest throughout the plains and along the rivers (known as gallery forests). These plains are teeming with wildlife, including deer, anteaters, armadillos, tapirs, otters, jaguars, pumas, and *chigüiros* (also known as capybaras), the world's largest rodent. The Llanos are also home to the giant anaconda and to one of the most endangered species on Earth, the Orinoco crocodile, which reaches up to seven meters (23 feet) long.

History

BEFORE COLUMBUS

Located at the juncture of Central and South America, what is now Colombia was a necessary transit point for the migration of people who settled South America. However, because these peoples left few physical traces of their passage, little is known of them. The oldest human objects found in Colombia, utensils discovered near Bogotá, are dated from 14,000 BC. With the expansion of agriculture and sedentary life throughout the territory of present-day Colombia around 1000 BC, various indigenous cultures started producing stunning ceramic and gold work, as well as some monumental remains. These remains provide rich material evidence of their development. Nonetheless, there are significant gaps in the understanding of the history of these early peoples.

From around 700 BC, the area of San Agustín, near the origin of the Río Magdalena in southern Colombia, was settled by people who practiced agriculture and produced pottery. Starting in the 1st century AD, the people of San Agustín created hundreds of monumental stone statues set on large platforms, which comprise the largest pre-Columbian archaeological site extant between Mesoamerica and Peru. By AD 800, this society had disappeared.

In the northwestern plains of Colombia, south of present-day Cartagena, starting in the 1st century AD, the Sinú people constructed a large complex of mounds in the shape of fish bones. These mounds regulated flooding, allowing cultivation in both rainy and dry seasons. During rainy seasons, the water flooded the lower cavities, allowing for cultivation on the mounds; during dry season, cultivation took place in the cavities that had been enriched by the flood waters. These monumental formations are still visible from overhead. By the time of the Spanish conquest, these people no longer inhabited the area.

From AD 500 to 900, the area of Tierradentro, west of San Agustín, was settled by an agricultural society that dug magnificent decorated underground tombs, produced large stone statues, and built oval-shaped buildings on artificial terraces. As in the case of the San Agustín and the Sinú people, it is not known what happened to these people.

At the time of the conquest, present-day Colombia was populated by a large number of distinct agricultural societies that often maintained peaceful trading relations among themselves. The two largest groups were the Muisca people, who lived in the altiplano (highlands) of the Cordillera Oriental, and the Tayrona, who lived on the slopes of the Sierra Nevada de Santa Marta. Other groups included the Quimbaya, who settled the area of the present-day Coffee Region; the Calima, in present-day Valle del Cauca; and the Nariños, in the mountainous areas of southwest Colombia.

These indigenous societies were mostly organized at the village level with loose association with other villages. Only the Muisca and the Tayrona had a more developed political organization. Though these were all agricultural societies, they also engaged in hunting, fishing, and mining and produced sophisticated ceramics and goldwork. Each group specialized in what their environment had to offer and engaged in overland trade. For example, the Muiscas produced textiles and salt, which they traded for gold, cotton, tobacco, and shells from other groups.

The Muiscas, a Chibcha-speaking people, were the largest group, with an estimated 600,000 inhabitants at the time of the Spanish conquest. They settled the Cordillera Oriental in AD 300 and occupied a large territory that comprises most of the highland areas of the present-day departments of Cundinamarca and Boyacá. At the time of the conquest, they were organized into two large confederations: one in the south headed by the Zipa, whose capital was Bacatá near present-day Bogotá, and another headed by the Zaque, whose capital was at Hunza, the location of present-day Tunja. The Muiscas had a highly homogeneous culture, and were skilled in weaving, ceramics, and goldwork. Their cosmography placed significant importance on high Andean lakes, several of which were sacred, including Guatavita, Siecha, and Iguaque.

The Tayrona, who settled the slopes of the Sierra Nevada de Santa Marta, were also a Chibcha-speaking people. They had a more urban society, with towns that included temples and ceremonial plazas built on stone terraces, and practiced farming on terraces carved out of the mountains. There are an estimated 200 Tayrona sites, of which Ciudad Perdida (Lost City), built at 1,100 meters (3,600 feet) in the Sierra Nevada de Santa Marta, is the largest and best known. Many of these towns, including El Pueblito in the Parque Nacional Natural Tayrona, were occupied at the time of the Spanish conquest. The Kogis, Arhuacos, Kankuamos, and Wiwas, current inhabitants of the sierra, are their descendants and consider many places in the sierra sacred.

THE SPANISH CONQUEST (1499-1550)

As elsewhere in the New World, the arrival of Europeans was an unmitigated disaster for the Native American societies. Though there were pockets of resistance, on the whole the indigenous people were unable to push back the small number of armed Spanish conquistadores. Harsh conditions after the conquest and the spread of European diseases, such as measles and smallpox, to which the indigenous people had no immunity, killed off millions of natives. The Spanish conquest of present-day Colombia took about 50 years and was largely completed by the 1550s.

In 1499, the first European set foot on present-day Colombia in the northern Guajira Peninsula. In 1510, a first, unsuccessful colony was established in the Golfo de Urabá near the current border with Panama. In 1526, the Spanish established Santa Marta, their first permanent foothold, from where they tried, unsuccessfully, to subdue the Tayronas. In 1533, they established Cartagena, which was to become a major colonial port.

In 1536, Gonzalo Jiménez de Quesada set off south from Santa Marta to conquer the fabled lands of El Dorado in the Andean heartland. After a year of grueling travel up the swampy Río Magdalena valley, 200 surviving members of Jiménez de Quesada's 800 original troops arrived in the Muisca lands near present-day Bogotá. After a short interlude of courteous relations, the Spaniards' greed led them to obliterate the Muisca towns and temples. They found significant amounts of gold, especially in the town of Hunza, but they were, by and large, disappointed. In 1538, Jiménez de Quesada founded Santa Fe de Bogotá as the capital of this new territory, which he called Nueva Granada—New Granada—after his birthplace.

Sebastián de Belalcázar, a lieutenant of Francisco Pizarro, led a second major expedition that arrived in the Muisca lands from the south. Having conquered the Inca city of Quito, Belalcázar and his army traveled north, conquering a vast swath of land from present-day Ecuador to the *sábana* (high plateau) of Bogotá. Along the way, he founded several cities, including Popayán and Cali in 1536. He arrived shortly after Quesada had founded Bogotá. Incredibly, a third conquistador, the German Nikolaus Federmann, arrived in Bogotá at the same time, having traveled from Venezuela via the Llanos. Rather than fight for supremacy, the three conquistadores decided to take their rival claims to arbitration at the Spanish court. In an unexpected turn of events, none of the three obtained title to the Muisca lands: When Bogotá became the administrative capital of New Granada, they came under the sway of the Spanish crown. Other expeditions swept across the Caribbean coast, through current-day Antioquia and the Santanderes.

COLONIAL NUEVA GRANADA (1550-1810)

For most of its colonial history, Nueva Granada, as colonial Colombia was called, was an appendage of the Viceroyalty of Peru. In 1717, Spain decided to establish a viceroyalty in Nueva Granada but changed its mind six years later because the benefits did not justify the cost. In 1739, the viceroyalty was reestablished, with Santa Fe de Bogotá as its capital. It was an unwieldy territory, encompassing present-day Colombia, Venezuela, Ecuador, and Panama. To make it more manageable, Venezuela and Panama were ruled by captain-generals and Ecuador by a president. At the local level, the viceroyalty was divided into *provincias* (provinces), each with a local assembly called a *cabildo*.

Settlement in Nueva Granada occurred primarily in three areas: where there were significant indigenous populations to exploit, as in the case of Tunja in the former Muisca territory; where there were gold deposits, as in Cauca, Antioquia, and Santander; and along trade routes, for example at Honda and Mompox on the Río Magdalena. Cartagena was the main port of call for the biennial convoys of gold and silver sent to Spain. Bogotá lived off of the official bureaucracy and sustained a fair number of artisans. Present-day Antioquia and Santander supported small-scale farming to provide provisions to the gold mining camps. Nueva Granada was one of the least economically dynamic of Spain's New World possessions. The mountainous topography and high transportation costs meant that agricultural production was primarily for local consumption and gold was the only significant export.

Colonial society was composed of a small Spanish and Creole (descendants of Spanish settlers) elite class that governed a large mestizo (mixed indigenous-white) population. The Spanish had initially preserved indigenous communal lands known as *resguardos*, but the demographic collapse of the native population and intermarriage meant that, unlike in Peru or Mexico, there were relatively few people who were fully indigenous. There were also black slaves who were forced mostly to work in the mines and haciendas (plantations). Society was overwhelmingly Catholic and Spanish-speaking.

Culturally, Nueva Granada was also somewhat of a backwater. Though there was a modest flourishing of the arts, Bogotá could not compete with the magnificent architectural and artistic production of Quito, Lima, or Mexico City. The only truly notable event of learning that took place was the late 18th-century Expedición Botánica (Botanical Expedition), headed by Spanish naturalist José Celestino Mutis, the personal doctor to one of the viceroys. The aim of the expedition was to survey all the species of Nueva Granada—a rather tall order given that Colombia is home to 10 percent of the world's species. However, the expedition did some remarkable research and produced beautiful prints of the fauna and flora.

The late colonial period saw unrest in Nueva Granada. Starting in 1781, a revolt known as the Rebelión de los Comuneros took place in the province of Socorro (north of Bogotá) in present-day Santander as a result of an attempt by colonial authorities to levy higher taxes. It was not an antiroyalist movement, however, as its slogan indicates: *¡Viva el Rey, Muera el Mal Gobierno!* ("Long live the king, down with bad government!"). Rather it was a protest against unfair taxes, not much different from the Boston Tea Party. However, it gave the Spanish government a fright. A rebel army, led by José Antonio Galán, marched on Bogotá. Negotiations put an end to the assault, and later the authorities ruthlessly persecuted the leaders of the revolt.

STRUGGLE FOR INDEPENDENCE (1810-1821)

Though there was some ill feeling against the colonial government, as the Rebelión de los Comuneros attests, as well as rivalry between the Spanish- and American-born elites, it was an external event, the Napoleonic invasion of Spain, that set off the chain of events that led to independence of Nueva Granada and the rest of the Spanish dominion in the New World.

In 1808, Napoleon invaded Spain, took King Ferdinand VII prisoner, and tried to impose his own brother, Joseph, as king of Spain. The Spaniards revolted, establishing a Central Junta in Seville to govern during the king's temporary absence from power. Faced with the issue of whether to recognize the new Central Junta in Spain, the colonial elites decided to take matters in their own hands and establish juntas of their own. The first such junta in Nueva Granada was established in Caracas in April 1810. Cartagena followed suit in May and Bogotá on July 20, 1810. According to popular myth, the revolt in Bogotá was the result of the failure of a prominent Spaniard merchant to lend a flower vase to a pair of Creoles.

Though they pledged alliance to Ferdinand VII, once the local elites had tasted power, there was no going back. Spanish authorities were expelled, and in 1811, a government of sorts, under the loose mantle of the Provincias Unidas de Nueva Granada (United Provinces of New Granada), was established with its capital at Tunja. Bogotá and the adjoining province of Cundinamarca stayed aloof from the confederation, arguing that it was too weak to resist the Spanish. Subsequently, various provinces of Nueva Granada declared outright independence, starting with Venezuela and Cartagena in 1811 and Cundinamarca in 1813.

Several cities remained loyal to the crown, namely Santa Marta and deeply conservative Pasto in the south. From 1812 to 1814 there was a senseless civil war between the Provincias Unidas and Cundinamarca—that is why this period is called the Patria Boba, or Foolish Fatherland. Ultimately, the Provincias Unidas prevailed with the help of a young Venezuelan captain by the name of Simón Bolívar.

After the restoration of Ferdinand VII, Spain attempted to retake its wayward colonies, with a military expedition and reign of terror known as the Reconquista—the Reconquest. The Spanish forces took Cartagena by siege in 1815 and took control of Bogotá in May 1816. However, in 1819, a revolutionary army composed of Venezuelans, Nueva Granadans, and European mercenaries headed by Bolívar arrived across the Llanos from Venezuela and decisively defeated the Spanish army in the Batalla del Puente de Boyacá—the Battle of the Boyacá Bridge—on August 7, near Tunja. The rest of the country fell quickly to the revolutionary army. With support from Nueva Granada, Bolívar defeated the Spanish in Venezuela in 1821. Panama, which had remained under Spanish control, declared independence in 1821. Finally, Bolívar dispatched Antonio José de Sucre to take Quito in 1822, bringing an end to the Spanish rule of Nueva Granada.

GRAN COLOMBIA: A FLAWED UNION (1821-1830)

Shortly after the Battle of Boyacá, the Congress of Angostura, a city on the Río Orinoco in Venezuela, proclaimed the union of Nueva Granada, Venezuela, and Ecuador under the name of the República de Colombia. Historians refer to this entity as Gran Colombia. In 1821, while the fight for independence was still raging in parts of Venezuela and Ecuador, a constitutional congress met in Cúcuta. An ongoing debate about whether a centralist or federalist scheme was preferable resulted in a curious compromise: the República de Colombia assumed a highly centralist form, considered necessary to finish the battle for independence, but left the issue of federalism open to review after 10 years. The document was generally liberal, enshrining individual liberties and providing for the manumission of slaves, meaning that the children of slaves were born free.

Bolívar, who was born in Venezuela, was named president. Francisco de Paula Santander, who was born near Cúcuta in Nueva Granada, was named vice president. Santander had fought alongside Bolívar in the battles for independence of Nueva Granada and was seen as an able administrator. While Bolívar continued south to liberate Ecuador and Peru, Santander assumed the reins of power in Bogotá. He charted a generally liberal course, instituting public education and a curriculum that included avant-garde thinkers such as Jeremy Bentham. However, the highly centralist structure was unsavory to elites in Venezuela and Ecuador, who disliked rule from Bogotá. Shortly after the Congress of Cúcuta, revolt broke out in Venezuela and Ecuador. In 1826, Bolívar returned from Bolivia and Peru, hoping for the adoption in Gran Colombia of the Bolivian Constitution, an unusual document he drafted that called for a presidency for life.

There had been a growing distance between Bolívar and Santander: Bolívar saw Santander as an overzealous liberal reformer while Santander disliked Bolívar's authoritarian tendencies. In 1828, after a failed constitutional congress that met in Ocaña in eastern Colombia, Bolívar assumed dictatorial powers. He rolled back many of Santander's liberal reforms. In September 1828 there was an attempt on Bolívar's life in Bogotá. This was famously foiled by his companion, Manuela Sáenz. The last years of Gran Colombia were marked by revolts in various parts of the country and a war with Peru. In 1830, a further constitutional assembly was convened in Bogotá, but by that point Gran Colombia had ceased to exist: Venezuela and Ecuador had seceded. In March 1830, a physically ill Bolívar decided to leave for voluntary exile in Europe and died on his way in Santa Marta.

CIVIL WARS AND CONSTITUTIONS (1830-1902)

After the separation of Venezuela and Ecuador, what is now Colombia adopted the name República de Nueva Granada. In 1832, it adopted a new constitution that corrected many of the errors of the excessively centralist constitution of Gran Colombia. There was a semblance of stability with the orderly succession of elected presidents. The elimination of some monasteries in Pasto sparked a short civil conflict known as the Guerra de los Supremos, which lasted 1839-1842. During this war, Conservative and Liberal factions coalesced for the first time, establishing the foundation of Colombia's two-party system. Generally, the Conservative Party supported the Catholic Church, favored centralization, and followed the ideas of Bolívar. The Liberal Party supported federalism and free trade and identified with the ideas of Santander.

The country's rugged topography meant that Nueva Granada was not very integrated into the world economy. Gold, extracted mostly in Antioquia, was the main export. Most of the country eked out its subsistence from agriculture, with trade restricted within regions. This period saw some economic development, such as steam navigation on the Magdalena and Cauca Rivers, and a contract for the construction of the trans-isthmian railroad in Panama, which had yet to secede.

Midcentury saw the rise of a new class of leaders who had grown up wholly under Republican governments. They ushered in a period of liberal reform. In 1851, Congress abolished slavery. In 1853, a new constitution established universal male suffrage, religious tolerance, and direct election of provincial governors. The government reduced tariffs and Nueva Granada experienced a short export-oriented tobacco boom.

Conflicts between radical reformers within the Liberal Party, moderates, and Conservatives led to unrest in various provinces. In 1859, discontented Liberals under Tomás Cipriano de Mosquera revolted, leading to generalized civil war in which the Liberals were ultimately victorious. Once in power, they pushed radical reform. Mosquera expropriated all nonreligious church property, partly in vengeance for church support of the Conservatives in the previous civil war.

The 1863 constitution was one of the world's most audacious federalist experiments. The country was renamed the Estados Unidos de Colombia (United States of Colombia), comprising nine states. The president had a two-year term and was not immediately reelectable. All powers that were not explicitly assigned to the central government were the responsibility of the states. Many of the states engaged in true progressive policies, such as establishing public education and promoting the construction of railroads. This period coincided with agricultural booms in quinine, cotton, and indigo that, for the first time, brought limited prosperity. This period saw the establishment of the Universidad Nacional (National University) and the country's first bank.

In 1880 and then in 1884, a coalition of Conservatives and moderate Liberals, who were dissatisfied with radical policies, elected Rafael Núñez as president. Núñez tried to strengthen the power of the central government, sparking a Liberal revolt. The Conservatives were ultimately victorious and, in 1886, enacted a new centralist constitution that lasted through most of the 20th century. The country was rechristened República de Colombia, the name it has conserved since then. During the period from 1886 through 1904, known as the Regeneración, the Conservative Party held sway, rolling back many of the previous reforms, especially anticlerical measures and unrestricted male suffrage. The Liberal Party, excluded from power, revolted in 1899. The ensuing Guerra de los Mil Días (Thousand Days' War), which raged through 1902, was a terribly bloody conflict. It is not clear how many died in the war, but some historians put the figure as high as 100,000, or an incredible 2.5 percent of the country's population of four million at the time.

One year after the end of the war, Panama seceded. During the late 19th century, there had been resentment in Panama about the distribution of revenues from the transit trade that mostly were sent to Bogotá. However, in 1902 the local Panamanian elites had become alarmed at the lackadaisical attitude of the government in Bogotá regarding the construction of an interoceanic canal. After the failure of the French to build a canal, Colombia had entered into negotiations with the United States. In the closing days of the Guerra de los Mil Días, Colombia and the United States signed the Hay-Terran Treaty, which called for the construction of the canal, surrendering control over a strip of land on either side of the canal to the United States. The Americans threatened that if the treaty were not ratified, they would dig the canal in Nicaragua. Arguing that the treaty undermined Colombian sovereignty, the congress in Bogotá unanimously rejected it in August 1903. That was a big mistake: A few months later, Panama seceded with the support of the United States.

PEACE AND REFORM (1902-1946)

Under the leadership of moderate Conservative Rafael Reyes, who was president 1904-1909, Colombia entered a period of peace and stability. Reyes focused on creating a professional, nonpartisan army. He gave representation to Liberals in government, enacted a protective tariff to spur domestic industry, and pushed public works. During his administration, Bogotá was finally connected by railway to the Río Magdalena. He reestablished relations with the United States, signing a treaty that provided Colombia with an indemnity for the loss of Panama. During the 1920s and 1930s, Colombia was governed by a succession of Conservative Party presidents. Though there was often electoral fraud, constitutional reform that guaranteed minority representation ensured peace.

Expanding world demand for coffee spurred production across Colombia, especially in southern Antioquia and what is now known as the Coffee Region, creating a new class of independent farmers. Improved transportation, especially the completion of the railways from Cali to Buenaventura on the Pacific coast and from Medellín to the Río Magdalena, was key to the growth of coffee exports. In the Magdalena Medio region and in Norte de Santander, U.S. companies explored and started producing petroleum. Medellín became a center of textile manufacturing. With the country's broken geography, air transportation developed rapidly. The Sociedad Colombo Alemana de Transportes Aéreos (Colombian German Air Transportation Society) or SCADTA, the predecessor of Avianca, was founded in Barranquilla in 1919, and is reputedly the second-oldest commercial aviation company in the world (the oldest is KLM).

In 1930, a split Conservative ticket allowed the Liberals to win the elections. After being out of power for 50 years, the Liberal Party was happy to regain control of the state apparatus. This led to strife with Conservatives long accustomed to power—presaging the intense interparty violence that was to erupt 14 years later.

From 1932 to 1933, Colombia and Peru fought a brief war in the Amazon over the control of the port city of Leticia. The League of Nations brokered a truce, the first time that this body, which was a precursor to the United Nations, actively intervened in a dispute between two countries.

Starting in 1934, Liberal president Alfonso López Pumarejo undertook major social and labor reforms, with some similarities to Roosevelt's New Deal. His policies included agrarian reform, encouragement and protection of labor unions, and increased spending on education. He reduced the Catholic Church's sway over education and eliminated the literacy requirement for male voters. Many of these reforms simply returned the country to policies that had been enacted by Liberals in the 1850s, 80 years prior. In opposition to these policies, a new radical right, with a confrontational style and strains of fascism and anti-Semitism, arose under the leadership of Laureano Gómez.

During World War II, Colombia closely allied itself with the United States and eventually declared war on the Axis powers in retaliation for German attacks on Colombian merchant ships in the Caribbean Sea. The government concentrated those of German descent in a hotel in Fusagasugá near Bogotá and removed all German influence from SCADTA.

LA VIOLENCIA (1946-1953)

In the 1946 elections, the Liberal Party split its ticket between establishment-backed Gabriel Turbay and newcomer Jorge Eliécer Gaitán. Gaitán was a self-made man who had scaled the ladders of power within the Liberal Party despite the opposition of the traditional Liberal elite. He had a vaguely populist platform and much charisma. The moderate Conservative Mariano Ospina won a plurality of votes and was elected to the presidency. As in 1930, the transfer of power from Liberals to Conservatives and bureaucratic reaccommodation led to outbursts of violence.

On April 9, 1948, a deranged youth killed former presidential candidate Gaitán as he left his office in downtown Bogotá. His assassination sparked riots and bloodshed throughout the country, with severe destruction in the capital. The disturbance in Bogotá, known as El Bogotazo, occurred during the 9th Inter-American Conference, which had brought together leaders from all over the hemisphere. Young Fidel Castro happened to be in Bogotá that day, though he had no part in the upheaval.

The assassination of Gaitán further incited the violence that had started in 1946. Over the course of 10 years, an estimated 100,000-200,000 people died in what was laconically labeled La Violencia (The Violence). This conflict was comparable in destruction of human life with the Guerra de los Mil Días, the last civil war of the 19th century. The killing took place throughout the country, often in small towns and rural areas. Mostly it involved loyalists of the predominant party settling scores or intimidating members of the opposite party in order to extract land or secure economic gain. In some cases, the violence was sheer banditry. Numerous, horrific mass murders took place. The police often took sides with the Conservatives or simply turned a blind eye. In response, some Liberals resorted to armed resistance, giving birth to Colombia's first guerrilla armies. The Liberal Party boycotted the 1950 elections, and radical Conservative

Laureano Gómez was elected president. His government pursued authoritarian and highly partisan policies, further exacerbating the violence.

DICTATORSHIP (1953-1957)

In 1953, with the purported aim of bringing an end to fighting between Liberals and Conservatives, the Colombian army, under the command of General Gustavo Rojas Pinilla, staged a coup. Rojas was able to reduce, but not halt, the violence, by curtailing police support of the Conservatives and by negotiating an amnesty with Liberal guerrillas. In 1954, Rojas was elected for a four-term period by a handpicked assembly. Incidentally, it was this, nondemocratically elected assembly that finally got around to extending suffrage to women, making Colombia one of the last countries in Latin America to do so. Rojas tried to build a populist regime with the support of organized labor, modeled after Perón in Argentina. His daughter, María Eugenia Rojas, though no Evita, was put in charge of social welfare programs. Though a majority of Colombians supported Rojas at first, his repressive policies and press censorship ended up alienating the political elites.

THE NATIONAL FRONT (1957-1974)

In May 1957, under the leadership of a coalition of Liberals and Conservatives, the country went on an extended general strike to oppose the dictatorship. Remarkably, Rojas voluntarily surrendered power and went into exile in Spain. As a way to put an end to La Violencia, Liberal and Conservative Party leaders proposed alternating presidential power for four consecutive terms while divvying up the bureaucracy on a 50-50 basis. The proposal, labeled the National Front, was ratified by a nationwide referendum and was in effect 1958-1974.

The National Front dramatically reduced the level of violence. After years of fighting, both factions were ready to give up their arms. During this period, thanks to competent economic management, the economy prospered and incomes rose. The government adopted import substitution policies that gave rise to a number of new industries, including automobiles.

By institutionalizing the power of the two traditional parties, the National Front had the unintended consequence of squeezing out other political movements, especially from the left. As a result, during the 1960s a number of leftist guerrilla groups appeared. Some were simply the continuation, under a new name, of the guerrilla groups formed during La Violencia. The Fuerzas Armadas Revolucionarias de Colombia (FARC) was a rural, peasant-based group espousing Soviet Marxism. The Ejército de Liberación Nacional (ELN) was a smaller group inspired by the Cuban revolution. The even smaller Ejército Popular de Liberación (EPL) was a Maoist-inspired group. The Movimiento 19 de Abril (M-19) was a more urban group formed by middle-class intellectuals after alleged electoral fraud deprived the populist ANAPO Party (Alianza Nacional Popular; created by ex-dictator Rojas) of power. During the 1970s and 1980s, the M-19 staged flashy coups, such as stealing Bolívar's sword (and promising to return it once the revolution had been achieved) in 1974 and seizing control of the embassy of the Dominican Republic in Bogotá in 1980.

UNDER SIEGE (1974-1991)

The Drug Trade and the Rise of Illegal Armed Groups

Due to its relative proximity to the United States, treacherous geography, and weak government institutions, Colombia has been an ideal place for cultivation, production, and shipment of illegal drugs, primarily to the United States. During the 1970s, Colombia experienced a short-lived marijuana boom centered on the Sierra Nevada de Santa Marta. Eradication efforts by Colombian authorities and competition from homegrown marijuana produced in the United States quickly brought this boom to an end.

During the late 1970s, cocaine replaced marijuana as the main illegal drug. Though most of the coca cultivation at the time was in Peru and Bolivia, Colombian drug dealers based in Medellín started the business of picking up coca paste in Peru and Bolivia, processing it into cocaine in Colombia, and exporting the drug to the United States, where they even controlled some distribution at the local level. At its heyday in the mid-1980s, Pablo Escobar's Medellín Cartel controlled 80 percent of the world's cocaine trade. The rival Cali Cartel, controlled by the Rodríguez brothers, emerged in the 1980s and started to contest the supremacy of the Medellín Cartel, leading to a bloody feud.

During the 1980s and 1990s, coca cultivation shifted from Peru and Bolivia to Colombia, mainly to the Amazon regions of Putumayo, Caquetá, Meta, and Guaviare. Initially, leftist guerrillas such as the FARC protected the fields from the authorities in return for payment from the cartels. Eventually, they started processing and trafficking the drugs themselves. Though the guerrillas had other sources of income, such as kidnapping and extortion, especially of oil companies operating in the Llanos, the drug trade was a key factor in their growth. With these sources of income, they no longer needed popular support and morphed into criminal organizations. By the mid-1980s, the FARC had grown into a 4,000-person-strong army that controlled large portions of territory, especially in the south of the country.

During the 1980s and 1990s, the price of land was depressed as a result of the threat posed by the guerrillas. Using their vast wealth and power of intimidation, drug traffickers purchased vast swaths of land, mostly along the Caribbean coast of Colombia, at bargain prices. To defend their properties from extortion, they allied themselves with traditional landowners to create paramilitary groups. These groups often operated with the direct or tacit support of the army.

Colombian campesinos (small farmers), caught in the middle of the conflict between guerrillas and paramilitaries, suffered disproportionately. They were accused by both guerrillas and paramilitaries of sympathizing with the enemy, and the government was not there to protect them. The paramilitaries were particularly ruthless, often ordering entire villages to abandon their lands or massacring the population. The conflict between guerrillas and paramilitaries is at the source of the mass displacement of people in Colombia. According to the Office of the United Nations High Commissioner for Refugees, the number of displaced people in Colombia ranges 3.9-5.3 million, making it the country with the most internal refugees in the world.

Peace Negotiations with the FARC and M-19

In 1982, President Belisario Betancur was elected with the promise of negotiating peace with the guerrillas. The negotiations with the guerrillas got nowhere, but the FARC did establish a political party, the Unión Patriótica (UP), which successfully participated in the 1986 presidential elections and 1988 local elections, managing to win some mayoralties. The paramilitaries and local elites did not want the political arm of the FARC to wield local power. As a result, the UP was subjected to a brutal persecution by the paramilitaries, who killed more than 1,000 party members. In the midst of this violence, Colombia suffered one of its worst natural disasters: the eruption of the Nevado del Ruiz in November 1985, which produced a massive mudslide that engulfed the town of Armero, killing more than 20,000 people.

In 1985, the M-19 brazenly seized the Palacio de Justicia in Bogotá. The Colombian army responded with a heavy hand, and in the ensuing battle, half of Colombia's Supreme Court justices were killed. Many people, including many cafeteria employees, disappeared in the army takeover, and there is speculation that they were executed and buried in a mass grave in the south of Bogotá. Weakened by this fiasco, leaders of the M-19 took up President Virgilio Barco's offer to negotiate peace. The government set down clear rules, including a cease-fire on the part of the M-19, before talks could proceed. Unlike the FARC, the M-19 was still an ideological movement. The leaders of the M-19 saw that by participating in civil life they could probably gain more than by fighting. And they were right: In 2011 the people of Bogotá elected Gustavo Petro, a former M-19 guerrilla, as their mayor. On March 19, 1990, Barco and the M-19's young leader, Carlos Pizarro, signed a peace agreement, the only major successful peace agreement to date between the authorities and a major guerrilla group.

The Rise and Fall of the Medellín Cartel

Initially, the Colombian establishment turned a blind eye to the rise of the drug cartels and even took a favorable view of the paramilitaries, who were seen as an antidote to the scourge of the guerrillas. For a time, Escobar was active in politics and cultivated a Robin Hood image, funding public works such as parks and housing projects. Rather than stick to his business, as the Cali Cartel did, Escobar started to threaten any official who tried to check his power. In 1984, he had Rodrigo Lara Bonilla, the minister of justice, assassinated. When the government subsequently cracked down, Escobar declared outright war. He assassinated judges and political leaders, set off car bombs to intimidate public opinion, and paid a reward for every policeman that was murdered in Medellín—a total of 657. To take out an enemy, he planted a bomb in an Avianca flight from Bogotá to Cali, killing all passengers on board. The Medellín Cartel planted dozens of massive bombs in Bogotá and throughout the country, terrorizing the country's population. The cartel is allegedly responsible for the assassination of three presidential candidates in 1990: Luis Carlos Galán, the staunchly anti-mafia candidate of the Liberal Party; Carlos Pizarro, the candidate of the newly demobilized M-19; and Bernardo Jaramillo, candidate of the Unión Patriótica.

There was really only one thing that Escobar feared—extradition to the United States. Through bribery and intimidation, he managed to get extradition outlawed, and he negotiated a lopsided deal with the government of César Gaviria: In return for his surrender, he was allowed to control the jail where he was locked up. From the luxurious confines of La Catedral, as the prison was named, he continued to run his empire. In 1992 there was an outcry when it became known that he had interrogated and executed enemies within the jail. When he got wind that the government planned to transfer him to another prison, he fled. In December 1993, government intelligence intercepted a phone call he made to his family, located him in Medellín, and killed him on a rooftop as he attempted to flee. It is widely believed that the Cali Cartel actively aided the authorities in the manhunt.

A New Constitution

The 1990s started on a positive footing with the enactment of a new constitution in 1991. The Constitutional Assembly that drafted the charter was drawn from all segments of the political spectrum, including the recently demobilized M-19. The new constitution was very progressive, devolving considerable power to local communities and recognizing the rights of indigenous and Afro-Colombian communities to govern their communities and ancestral lands. The charter created a powerful new Constitutional Court, which has become a stalwart defender of basic rights, as well as an independent accusatory justice system, headed by a powerful attorney general, which was created to reduce impunity.

COLOMBIA ON THE BRINK (1992-2002)

New Cartels, Paramilitaries, and Guerrillas

Drug cultivation and production increased significantly during the 1990s. The overall land dedicated to coca cultivation rose from 60,000 hectares (148,300 acres) in 1992 to 165,000 hectares (407,700 acres) in 2002. As a result of the government's successful crackdown first on the Medellín Cartel and then on the Cali Cartel, drug production split into smaller, more nimble criminal organizations. During the 1990s, the paramilitaries became stand-alone organizations that engaged in drug trafficking, expanding to more than 30,000 men in 2002. They created a national structure called the Autodefensas Unidas de Colombia, or AUC, under the leadership of Carlos

Castaño. The AUC coordinated activities with local military commanders and committed atrocious crimes, often massacring scores of so-called sympathizers of guerrillas.

At the same time, the guerrillas expanded significantly during the 1990s. Strengthened by hefty revenues from kidnapping, extortion, and drug trafficking, they grew to more than 50,000 mostly peasant fighters in 2002. Their strategy was dictated primarily by military and economic considerations and they had little to no public support. At their heyday, the FARC covered the entire country, attacking military garrisons and even threatening major urban centers such as Cali. They performed increasingly large operations, such as attacking Mitú, the capital of the department of Vaupés, in 1998 or kidnapping 12 members of the Assembly of Valle del Cauca in Cali in 2002. The FARC commanders moved around the countryside unchecked. In the territories they controlled, they ruled over civilians, often committing heinous crimes. In 2002, they attacked a church in the town of Bojayá in Chocó, killing more than 100 unarmed civilians, including many children, who had sought refuge there.

Plan Colombia

The increasing growth of drug exports from Colombia to the United States in the 1990s became a source of concern for the U.S. government. From 1994 to 1998, the United States was reluctant to provide support to Colombia because the president at the time, Ernesto Samper, was tainted by accusations of having received campaign money from drug traffickers and because of evidence about human rights abuses by the Colombian army. When Andrés Pastrana was elected president in 1998, the Colombian and U.S. administrations designed a strategy to curb drug production and counteract the insurgency called Plan Colombia. This strategy had both military and social components, and was to be financed jointly by the United States and Colombia. Ultimately, the United States provided Colombia, which was becoming one of its strongest and most loyal allies in Latin America, with more than US$7 billion, heavily weighted toward military aid, especially for training and for providing aerial mobility to Colombian troops. While the impact of Plan Colombia was not immediately visible, over time it changed the balance of power in favor of the government, allowing the Colombian army to regain the upper hand in the following years.

Flawed Peace Negotiations with the FARC

President Pastrana embarked on what is now widely believed to have been an ill-conceived, hurried peace process with the FARC. He had met Manuel Marulanda, the head of the FARC, before his inauguration in 1998 and was convinced that he could bring about a quick peace. Without a clear framework, in November 1998 he acceded to the FARC's request to grant them a demilitarized zone the size of Switzerland in the eastern departments of Meta and Caquetá. In hindsight, it seems clear that the FARC had no interest or need to negotiate as they were at the peak of their military power. Rather, the FARC commanders saw the grant of the demilitarized zone as an opportunity to strengthen their organization.

From the beginning, it became clear that the FARC did not take the peace process seriously. Marulanda failed to show up at the inaugural ceremony of the peace process, leaving a forlorn Pastrana sitting alone on the stage next to a now famous *silla vacilla* (empty seat). They ran the demilitarized zone as a mini-state, nicknamed Farclandia, using it to smuggle arms, hold kidnapped prisoners, and process cocaine. During the peace negotiations, the FARC continued their attacks on the military and civilians. In February 2002, after the FARC kidnapped Eduardo Gechem, senator and president of the Senate Peace Commission, Pastrana declared the end of this ill-advised demilitarized zone and sent in the Colombian army.

A Failed State?

In 2002, the Colombian army was battling more than 50,000 guerrillas and 30,000 paramilitaries, with an estimated 6,000 child soldiers among those groups. The insurgents controlled approximately 75 percent of the country's territory. An estimated 100,000 antipersonnel mines covered 30 of 32 departments. More than 2.5 million people had been internally displaced between 1985 and 2003, with 300,000 people displaced in 2002 alone. Not surprisingly, prestigious publications such as *Foreign Policy* described Colombia at the time as failed state.

REGAINING ITS FOOTING (2002-PRESENT)

Álvaro Uribe's Assault on the Guerrillas

In the 2002 elections, fed-up Colombians overwhelmingly elected Álvaro Uribe, a former governor of Antioquia who promised to take the fight to the guerrillas. Uribe had a real grudge against the FARC, who had assassinated his father. The FARC were not fans of his, either. In a brazen show of defiance, during Uribe's inauguration ceremony in Bogotá on August 7, 2002, the guerrilla group fired various rockets aimed at the presidential palace during a post-swearing-in reception. Several rockets struck the exterior of the palace, causing minor damage (attendees were unaware of the attack), but many more fell on the humble dwellings in barrios nearby, killing 21.

During his first term, Uribe embarked on a policy of Seguridad Democrática, or Democratic Security, based on strengthening the army, eradicating illicit crops to deprive the guerrillas of revenues, and creating a controversial network of civilian collaborators who were paid for providing tips that led to successful operations against the insurgents. The government increased military expenditure and decreed taxes on the rich totaling US$4 billion to finance the cost of the war. Colombian military personnel grew from 300,000 in 2002 to 400,000 in 2007.

From 2002 to 2003, the army evicted the FARC from the central part of the country around Bogotá and Medellín, although that did not prevent them from causing terror in the cities. In February 2003, a car bomb attributed to the FARC exploded in the parking lot of the exclusive social club El Nogal, killing more than 30 people—mostly employees. From 2004 to 2006, the army pressed the FARC in its stronghold in the southern part of the country. Aerial spraying of coca crops brought down cultivated areas from 165,000 hectares (407,700 acres) in 2002 to 76,000 hectares (187,800 acres) in 2006.

In 2006, Uribe was reelected by a landslide, after Congress amended the constitution to allow for immediate presidential reelection. There is clear evidence that the government effectively bribed two congressmen whose votes were necessary for passage of the measure. Uribe interpreted the election results as a mandate to continue single-mindedly pursuing the guerrillas. The FARC came under severe stress, with thousands of guerrillas deserting, and for the first time, the FARC was subjected to effective strikes against top commanders. No longer safe in their traditional jungle strongholds in Colombia, many FARC operatives crossed the border into Venezuela and Ecuador, causing tension between Colombia and the governments of those countries.

In early 2008, the Colombian military bombed and killed leading FARC commander Raúl Reyes in a camp in Ecuador, causing a diplomatic crisis with that country. Later that year, the military executed Operación Jaque (Operation Checkmate), a dramatic rescue operation in which they duped the FARC into handing over their most important hostages. The hostages released included three U.S. defense contractors and Ingrid Betancur, a French Colombian independent presidential candidate who was kidnapped by the FARC during the 2002 presidential election as she proceeded by land, against the advice of the military, toward the capital of the former FARC demilitarized zone. In 2008, Manuel Marulanda, founder of the FARC, died a natural death. At that time, it was estimated that the FARC forces had plummeted to about 9,000 fighters, half of what they had been eight years before.

The Colombian army has been implicated in serious human rights abuses. Pressure from top brass to show results in the war against the guerrillas and the possibility of obtaining extended vacation time led several garrisons to execute civilians and present them as guerrillas killed in combat. In 2008, it was discovered that numerous young poor men from the city of Soacha, duped by false promises of work, had been taken to rural areas, assassinated by the army, and presented as guerrillas killed in anti-insurgency operations. This macabre episode—referred to as the scandal of *falsos positives* (false positives)—was done under the watch of Minister of Defense Juan Manuel Santos, who was later elected president of Colombia.

Peace Process with the AUC

From 2003 to 2008, the Uribe government pursued a controversial peace process with the right-wing paramilitaries, the Autodefensas Unidas de Colombia. As part of that process, an estimated 28,000 paramilitary fighters demobilized, including most of the high-level commanders. In 2005, the Colombian Congress passed the Justice and Peace Law to provide a legal framework for the process. Unlike previous peace laws that simply granted an amnesty to the insurgents, this law provided for reduced sentences for paramilitaries who had committed serious crimes in exchange for full confessions and reparation of victims. Domestic and international observers were extremely skeptical about the process, worrying that the paramilitaries would use their power to pressure for lenient terms. These misgivings were justified by evidence that they used their power of coercion to influence the results of the 2006 parliamentary elections, a scandal referred to as *parapolítica*. Many congresspersons, including a first cousin of Uribe, ended up in prison.

It soon became clear that the paramilitary commanders were not sincere in their commitment to peace. Many refused to confess crimes and transferred their assets to front men. Covertly, they continued their drug-trafficking operations. The government placed scant importance on the truth and reparation elements of the Justice and Peace Law, severely underfunding the effort to redress crimes committed against more than 150,000 victims who had signed up as part of the process. Through 2008, the paramilitaries had confessed to a mere 2,700 crimes, a fraction of the estimated total, and refused to hand over assets. Fed up with their lack of cooperation, in 2008 Uribe extradited 14 top-ranking paramilitary commanders to the United States, where they were likely to face long sentences. However, the extradition severely hampered the effort to obtain truth and reparation for the victims of their crimes.

The difficulty in redressing the crimes against victims has been further troubled by the growth of the dozens of small *bacrim (bandas criminals,* or illegal armed groups) who have taken territorial control of former paramilitary areas, intimidating victims who have returned to their rightful lands under the peace process. Many of these *bacrim* inherited the structures of the former AUC groups and employed former paramilitaries.

Social and Economic Transformation

During the past decade, Colombia has made some remarkable strides in improving social and economic conditions. Due to improved security conditions, investment, both domestic and international, has boomed, totaling almost US$80 billion from 2003 to 2012. Economic growth averaged 4.8 percent 2010-2014, a significant increase over the prior decades. The number of people below poverty, as measured by the ability to buy a wide basket of basic goods and services, has declined from 59.7 percent in 2002 to 27.8 percent in 2015. In Colombia's 13 largest cities, which represent 45 percent of the population, poverty has fallen to 18.9 percent. In terms of basic needs, most urban areas are well served in terms of education, health, electricity, water, and sewage. However, there is a wide gap between the cities and rural areas, where 30 percent of the country's population lives. As of 2013, rural poverty stood at 43 percent. Though income inequality has been slowly falling, Colombia still has one of the most unequal distributions of income in the world.

Peace with the FARC

In the 2010 elections, Uribe's former minister of defense, Juan Manuel Santos, was elected president by a large majority. Santos continued to pursue an aggressive strategy against the FARC. Army operations killed Alfonso Cano, the new leader of the FARC, as well as Víctor Julio Suárez Rojas, the guerrillas' military strategist. As evidenced in the diary of Dutch FARC member Tanya Nijmeijer, found by the Colombian army after an attack on a rebel camp, morale within the FARC had sunk to an all-time low.

At the same time, Santos recognized the need to address nonmilitary facets of the violence. In 2011, Congress passed the comprehensive Victims and Land Restitutions Law, meant to rectify Uribe's Justice and Peace Law. This law provides a framework to redress the crimes committed against all victims of violence since 1985.

After a year of secret negotiations, Santos announced the start of peace dialogues with the FARC in October 2012, first in Oslo, Norway, and then in Havana, Cuba. These have proceeded at a slow pace and have covered a large number of topics, including agrarian development and drug trafficking. Former president Uribe and his allies are against this initiative, claiming that a military defeat of the FARC is the best path forward.

In 2016, after four years of arduous negotiations, the government and the FARC agreed to comprehensive terms, which covered rural development, political participation, illegal drugs, justice for victims, and ending the armed conflict, among other topics. On September 26, 2016, the government and the FARC signed the agreement, only to have it rejected by a slim majority in a national vote. The government and the guerillas renegotiated the agreement, which was ratified on November 30, 2016, by Congress. Demobilization began in December 2016 and the guerillas are expected to hand over their weapons to the UN during the first half of 2017. President Juan Manuel Santos won the 2016 Nobel Peace Prize in honor of his efforts.

Government and Economy

Under the 1991 constitution, Colombia is organized as a republic, with three branches of power—the executive, the legislative, and the judicial. The country is divided into 32 *departamentos* (departments or provinces) and the Distrito Capital (Capital District), where Bogotá is located. The departments are in turn divided into *municipios* (municipalities). These *municipios* include towns and rural areas.

The president of the republic, who is both head of state and head of government, is elected for a four-year term. With the exception of the military dictatorship of Gen. Gustavo Rojas Pinilla from 1953 to 1957, presidents have been elected by the people since 1914. In 2005, then-president

Álvaro Uribe succeeded in changing the constitution to allow for one immediate presidential reelection. In 2009, he attempted to get the constitution changed once more to allow for a second reelection but was thwarted by the powerful Constitutional Court, which decreed that this change would break the necessary checks and balances of the constitutional framework.

Presidential elections are held every four years in May. If no candidate receives more than 50 percent of the votes, there will be a runoff election. Inauguration of the president takes place on August 7, the anniversary of the Batalla del Puente de Boyacá, which sealed Colombia's independence from Spain.

The legislative branch is made up of a bicameral legislature: the Senado (102 members) and the Cámara de Representantes (162 members). These representatives are elected every four years. Senators are voted for on a nationwide basis, while representatives are chosen for each department and the Distrito Capital. In addition, two seats in the Senate are reserved for indigenous representation. In the Cámara de Representantes, there are seats reserved for indigenous and Afro-Colombian communities as well as for Colombians who live abroad. As negotiated in 2016, the FARC will be assured 10 seats in Congress until 2022: 5 in the Senado and 5 in the Cámara de Representantes.

All Colombians over the age of 18—with the exception of active-duty military and police as well as those who are incarcerated—have the right to vote in all elections. Women only gained the right to vote in 1954.

POLITICAL PARTIES

Historically Colombia has had a two-party system: the Conservative Party and the Liberal Party. The Conservative Party has traditionally been aligned with the Catholic Church and has favored a more centralized government, and followed the ideas of Simón Bolívar. The Liberal Party favored a federal system of governing, has opposed church intervention in government affairs, and was aligned with the ideas of Gen. Francisco Paula Santander.

The hegemony of the two largest political parties came to a halt in the 2002 presidential election of rightist candidate Álvaro Uribe, who registered his own independent movement and then established a new party called El Partido de la Unidad. Since then, traditional parties have lost some influence. A third party, the Polo Democrático, became a relatively strong force in the early 2000s, capturing the mayorship of Bogotá, but has since faded, leaving no clear representative of the left.

Political parties today have become personality-oriented, and many candidates have been known to shop around for a party—or create their own—rather than adhere to the traditional parties. In 2014, President Juan Manuel Santos won a second term representing the Partido de la Unidad (known as La U), defeating a candidate allied with the founder of La U, former president Álvaro Uribe.

ECONOMY

Colombia has a thriving market economy based primarily on oil, mining, agriculture, and manufacturing. The country's GDP in 2015 was US$274 billion and per capita GDP was US$5,800, placing it as a middle-income country. Growth over the past decade has been a robust 3.29 percent. Inflation has averaged 3.8 percent in the past five years and unemployment has hovered around 10 percent.

During the colonial period and up until the early 20th century, small-scale gold mining and subsistence agriculture were the mainstays of Colombia's economy. Starting in the 1920s, coffee production spread throughout the country and rapidly became Colombia's major export good. Coffee production is of the mild arabica variety and is produced at elevations of 1,000 to 1,900 meters (roughly 3,000-6,000 feet), mostly by small farmers. During most of the 20th century, Colombia emphasized increasing the volume of production, using the Café de Colombia name and mythical coffee farmer Juan Valdez and his donkey Paquita to brand it. A severe global slump in coffee prices during the past decade has led to a reassessment of this strategy and an increasing focus on specialty coffees. Today, coffee represents only 3 percent of all Colombian exports.

Colombia's wide range of climates, from hot on the coast to temperate in the mountains, means that the country produces a wide range of products. Until recently, sugarcane production, fresh flowers, and bananas were the only major export-driven agribusiness. However, improvements in security in recent years have resulted in a boom in large-scale agricultural projects in palm oil, rubber, and soy. Cattle ranching occupies an estimated 25 percent of the country's land. Commercial forestry is relatively underdeveloped, though there is considerable illegal logging, especially on the Pacific coast.

In recent decades, oil production and mining have become major economic activities. The main center of oil production is the Llanos, the eastern plains of Colombia, with oil pipelines extending from there over the Cordillera Oriental to Caribbean ports. Oil currently represents roughly half of all Colombian exports. There are also significant natural gas deposits, mostly dedicated to residential use. Large-scale mining has been focused on coal and nickel, with large deposits in the Caribbean coastal region. With the improvement of security conditions in the past decade, many international firms, such as Anglogold Ashanti, have requested concessions for large-scale gold mining, often with opposition from the community. Illegal gold mining, often conducted with large machinery, is a severe threat to fragile ecosystems, especially in the Pacific coast rainforest.

During the postwar period, Colombia pursued an import substitution policy, fostering the growth of domestic industries such as automobiles, appliances, and petrochemical goods. Since the early 1990s, the government has been gradually opening the economy to foreign competition and tearing down tariffs. In recent years, the country has signed free-trade agreements with the United States and the European Union. Today, the country has a fairly diversified industrial sector. The country is self-sufficient in energy, with hydropower supplying the bulk of electricity needs.

Until recently, tourism was minimal because of widespread insecurity and a negative image. Things started to change in the mid-2000s, and the annual number of international visitors has increased from 600,000 in 2000 to 2.3 million in 2015. While Bogotá and Cartagena still receive the bulk of visitors, almost the entire country has opened up for tourism, though there are still pockets of no-go zones. This boom in tourism has fostered a growth of community and ecotourism options, often with the support from government. The network of *posadas nativas* (guesthouses owned and operated by locals) is one initiative to foment tourism at the community level, particularly among Afro-Colombians. In recent years, Parques Nacionales has transferred local operation of ecotourism facilities in the parks to community-based associations.

People and Culture

DEMOGRAPHY

Colombia was estimated to have had a population of a little over 48.7 million in 2016 and has the third-highest population in Latin America, behind Brazil and Mexico and slightly higher than Argentina. Around four million Colombians live outside of Colombia, mostly in the United States, Venezuela, Spain, and Ecuador. The population growth rate has fallen significantly in the past two decades and was estimated at 1.01 percent in 2016. The population of the country is relatively young, with a median age of 29.3 years. Average life expectancy is 75.5 years.

Sixty percent of the Colombian population lives in the highland Andean interior of the country, where the largest metropolitan areas are located: Bogotá (9.8 million), Medellín (3.9 million), and Cali (2.6 million). On the Caribbean coast, Barranquilla is the largest metropolitan area (2 million), followed by Cartagena (1.1 million).

It is increasingly an urban country, with around 76 percent of the population living in urban areas. This trend began during La Violencia and accelerated in the 1970s and 1980s. At least 3.9 million persons have been internally displaced due to the armed conflict in Colombia, leaving their homes in rural areas and seeking safety and economic opportunity in large cities.

Most of the population (over 84 percent) is either mestizo (having both Amerindian and white ancestry) or white. People of African (10.4 percent) and indigenous or Amerindian (over 3.4 percent) origin make up the rest of the Colombian population. There is a tiny Romani or Roma population of well under 1 percent of the population, but nonetheless they are a protected group according to the constitution.

There are more than 80 indigenous groups, with some of the largest

Happy Monday!

Colombians enjoy a long list of holidays (over 20). With a few exceptions, such as the independence celebrations on July 20 and August 7, Christmas, and New Year's Day, holidays are celebrated on the following Monday, creating a *puente* (literally bridge, or three-day weekend).

During Semana Santa and between Christmas Day and New Year's, interior cities such as Bogotá and Medellín become ghost towns as locals head to the nearest beach or to the countryside. Conversely, beach resorts, natural reserves and parks, and pueblos fill up. Along with that, room rates and airfare can increase substantially.

The following is a list of Colombian holidays, but be sure to check a Colombian calendar for precise dates. Holidays marked with an asterisk are always celebrated on the Monday following the date of the holiday.

- Año Nuevo (New Year's Day): January 1
- Día de los Reyes Magos (Epiphany)*: January 6
- Día de San José (Saint Joseph's Day)*: March 19
- Jueves Santo (Maundy Thursday): Thursday before Easter Sunday
- Viernes Santo (Good Friday): Friday before Easter Sunday
- Día de Trabajo (International Workers' Day): May 1
- Ascensión (Ascension)*: Six weeks and one day after Easter Sunday
- Corpus Christi*: Nine weeks and one day after Easter Sunday
- Sagrado Corazón (Sacred Heart)*: Ten weeks and one day after Easter Sunday
- San Pedro y San Pablo (Saint Peter and Saint Paul)*: June 29
- Día de la Independencia (Independence Day): July 20
- Batalla de Boyacá (Battle of Boyacá): August 7
- La Asunción (Assumption of Mary)*: August 15
- Día de la Raza (equivalent of Columbus Day)*: October 12
- Todos Los Santos (All Saint's Day)*: November 1
- Día de la Independencia de Cartagena (Cartagena Independence Day)*: November 11
- La Inmaculada Concepción (Immaculate Conception): December 8
- Navidad (Christmas): December 25

Gay Rights in Colombia

In a country still struggling with armed conflict and basic human rights, it might come as a surprise that gay and lesbian rights have not been pushed aside. Colombia has some of the most progressive laws regarding the rights of LGBT people in the western hemisphere. Since 2007, same-sex partners have enjoyed full civil union rights with a wide range of benefits, such as immigration, inheritance, and social security rights.

However, when it comes to marriage, it's a little more complicated. In 2016, the top judicial body, the Colombian Constitutional Court, legalized marriage and adoption by same-sex couples. These rulings created a backlash with conservative politicians, who have vowed to hold a referendum to block the marriage and adoption rights.

being the Wayúu, who make up the majority in La Guajira department; the Nasa, from Cauca; the Emberá, who live in the isolated jungles of the Chocó department, and the Pastos, in Nariño. Departments in the Amazon region have the highest percentages of indigenous residents. In Vaupés, for example, 66 percent of the population is of indigenous background. Many indigenous people live on *resguardos*, areas that are collectively owned and administered by the communities.

Afro-Colombians, descendants of slaves who arrived primarily via Spanish slave trade centers in the Caribbean, mostly live along both Pacific and Caribbean coasts and in the San Andrés Archipelago. Chocó has the highest percentage of Afro-Colombians (83 percent), followed by San Andrés and Providencia (57 percent), Bolívar (28 percent), Valle del Cauca (22 percent), and Cauca (22 percent). Cali, Cartagena, and Buenaventura have particularly large Afro-Colombian populations. In the Americas, Colombia has the third-highest number of citizens of African origin, behind Brazil and the United States.

While Colombia has not attracted large numbers of immigrants, there have been periods in which the country opened its doors to newcomers. In the early 20th century, immigrants from the Middle East—specifically from Lebanon, Syria, and Palestine—arrived, settling mostly along the Caribbean coast, especially in the cities of Barranquilla, Santa Marta, Cartagena, and Maicao in La Guajira. From 1920 to 1950, a sizable number of Sephardic and Ashkenazi Jews immigrated. Colombia has not had a large immigration from Asia, although in the early 20th century there was a small immigration of Japanese to the Cali area.

RELIGION

Over 90 percent of Colombians identify as Roman Catholics, and it has been the dominant religion since the arrival of the Spaniards. The numbers of evangelical Christians, called simply *cristianos*, continue to grow, and there are other Christian congregations, including Mormons and Jehovah's

Witnesses, but their numbers are small. In San Andrés and Providencia, the native Raizal population—of African descent—is mostly Baptist.

The Jewish community—estimated at around 5,000 families—is concentrated in the large cities, such as Bogotá, Medellín, Cali, and Barranquilla. There are significant Muslim communities, especially along the Caribbean coast, and there are mosques in Barranquilla, Santa Marta, Valledupar, Maicao (La Guajira), San Andrés, and Bogotá.

Semana Santa—Holy or Easter Week—is the most important religious festival in the country, and Catholics in every village, town, and city commemorate the week with a series of processions and masses. The colonial cities of Popayán, Mompox, Tunja, and Pamplona are known for their elaborate Semana Santa processions. Popayán and Mompox in particular attract pilgrims and tourists from Colombia and beyond. In cities such as Bogotá, Cali, and Cartagena, there are multitudinous processions to mountaintop religious sites, such as Monserrate, the Cerro de la Cruz, and El Monasterio de la Popa, respectively.

LANGUAGE

Spanish is the official language in Colombia. In the San Andrés Archipelago, English is still spoken by native islanders who arrived from former English colonies after the abolition of slavery, but Spanish has gained prominence.

According to the Ministry of Culture, there are at least 68 native languages, which are spoken by around 850,000 people. These include 65 indigenous languages, two Afro-Colombian languages, and Romani, which is spoken by the small Roma population.

Three indigenous languages have over 50,000 speakers: Wayúu, primarily spoken in La Guajira; Páez, primarily spoken in Cauca; and Emberá, primarily spoken in Chocó.

Essentials

Getting There

AIR

Most visitors to Colombia arrive by air at the **Aeropuerto Internacional El Dorado** in Bogotá, with some carrying on from there to other destinations in the country. There are also nonstop international flights to the **Aeropuerto Internacional José María Córdova** in Medellín and to the airports in Cali, Cartagena, Barranquilla, and Armenia.

From North America

Avianca (www.avianca.com) has nonstop flights between Bogotá and Miami, Fort Lauderdale, Orlando, Washington, Los Angeles, and New York-JFK. From Miami there are also nonstops to Medellín, Cali, Barranquilla, and Cartagena.

American (www.american.com) flies between Miami and Dallas and Bogotá; Miami and Medellín; and Cali and Medellín. **Delta** (www.delta.com) flies from Atlanta and New York-JFK to Bogotá; they also fly between Atlanta and Cartagena. **United** (www.united.com) has flights from Newark and Houston to Bogotá.

JetBlue (www.jetblue.com) has nonstop service to Bogotá from Orlando and Fort Lauderdale; to Cartagena from New York and Fort Lauderdale; and to Medellín from Fort Lauderdale. **Spirit** (www.spirit.com) has flights from Fort Lauderdale to Bogotá, Medellín, Cartagena, and Armenia.

Air Canada (www.aircanada.com) operates nonstop flights from Toronto to Bogotá. **Air Transat** (www.airtransat.com) provides seasonal service to Cartagena and San Andrés from Montreal.

From Europe

Avianca (www.avianca.com) has service to Bogotá and Medellín from Madrid and Barcelona, and between Bogotá and London. **Air France** (www.airfrance.com) flies from Paris to Bogotá. **Iberia** (www.iberia.com) serves Bogotá from Madrid, as does **Air Europa** (www.aireuropa.com). **Lufthansa** (www.lufthansa.com) offers service between Bogotá and Frankfurt. **Turkish Airlines** (www.turkishairlines.com) flies between Bogotá and Istanbul. **KLM** (www.klm.com) serves Amsterdam from Bogotá with a stopover in Cali.

From Latin America

Avianca (www.avianca.com) flies to Bogotá from many capitals in Latin America, including Buenos Aires, São Paulo, Rio de Janeiro, Valencia, Caracas, Lima, Santiago, and La Paz in South America; Cancún, Guatemala

Previous: country road; TransMilenio buses.

City, Mexico City, San José, San Juan, San Salvador, and Panama City in Central America; and Havana, Santo Domingo, Punta Cana, Aruba, and Curaçao in the Caribbean. Aerolíneas Argentinas, AeroGal, Aeromexico, Air Insel, Conviasa, Copa, Cubana, LATAM, Gol, TACA, and Tiara Air Aruba also have connections to Colombia.

CAR OR MOTORCYCLE

A growing number of travelers drive into Colombia in their own car or with a rented vehicle. The most common point of entry is at the city of Ipiales on the Pan-American Highway, the site of the Rumichaca border crossing with Ecuador at Ipiales (Tulcán on the Ecuador side). This entry point is open 5am-10pm daily.

On the Venezuelan side, the border at Cúcuta and San Antonio del Táchira is open 24 hours a day. Although there are other border crossings with Venezuela, this is the recommended overland point of entry.

For those taking the Pan-American Highway southbound, note that you will run out of pavement in Panama. In the Darién Gap, the road is interrupted by the Darién mountain range. The road picks up again in the town of Turbo on the Golfo de Urabá. Many travelers ship their vehicle from Panama City to Cartagena, which is not difficult to arrange, and will set you back about $1,000 USD. It takes about 10 days to be able to retrieve your vehicle in Cartagena.

BUS

Frequent buses depart Quito bound for Cali (20 hours) or Bogotá (30 hours). You can also take a taxi from the town of Tulcán to the border at Ipiales and from there take an onward bus to Pasto, Popayán, Cali, or beyond. In Quito contact **Líneas de los Andes** (www.lineasdelosandes.com.co).

BOAT

It is possible to enter the country from Panama, usually via the San Blas Islands. **Blue Sailing** (U.S. tel. 203/660-8654, www.bluesailing.net) offers sailboat trips between various points in Panama to Cartagena. The trip usually takes about 45 hours and costs around US$500. Sometimes, particularly during the windy season between November and March, boats stop in Sapzurro, Colombia, near the border. **San Blas Adventures** (www.sanblasadventures.com, contact@sanblasadventures.com) offers multi-day sailboat tours to the San Blas Islands that usually depart from Cartí and end up in the Panamanian border village of La Miel. From there you can walk over the border to Sapzurro and take a *lancha* (boat) from there to Capurganá. There are regular morning boats from Capurganá to both Acandí and Turbo. During the windy season, especially between December and February, this trip can be quite rough.

It is also possible to hitch a ride on a cargo boat from Ecuador to Tumaco or Buenaventura; however, service is irregular.

Getting Around

AIR

Air travel is an excellent, quick, and, thanks to discount airlines such as VivaColombia, economical way to travel within Colombia. Flying is the best option for those looking to avoid spending double-digit hours in a bus or for those with a short amount of time—and sometimes it's cheaper than taking a bus, as well. Airlines have excellent track records and maintain modern fleets.

Bogotá is the major hub in the country, with the majority of domestic **Avianca** (tel. 1/401-3434, www.avianca.com) flights departing from the Puente Aéreo terminal (not the main terminal of the adjacent international airport). Other domestic carriers **LATAM Airlines** (Colombian toll-free tel. 01/800-094-9490, www.latam.com), **VivaColombia** (tel. 1/489-7989, www.vivacolombia.co), **EasyFly** (tel. 1/414-8111, www.easyfly.com.co), **Satena** (Colombian toll-free tel. 01/800-091-2034, www.satena.com), and **Copa** (Colombian toll-free tel. 01/800-011-0808, www.copaair.com) fly out of the new domestic wing of the international airport.

For Leticia in the Amazon, the Pacific coast destinations of Bahía Solano and Nuquí, La Macarena (Caño Cristales) in Los Llanos, and San Andrés and Providencia in the Caribbean, the only viable way to get there is by air.

If you plan to fly to Caribbean destinations such as Cartagena, San Andrés, Providencia, and Santa Marta during high tourist season, be sure to purchase your ticket well in advance, as seats quickly sell out and prices go through the roof. If your destination is Cartagena or Santa Marta, be sure to check fares to Barranquilla. These may be less expensive, and that city is only about an hour away. Similarly, if you plan to go to the Carnaval de Barranquilla in February, check fares to both Cartagena and Santa Marta. If you are flying to the Coffee Region, inquire about flights to Pereira, Armenia, and Manizales, as the distances between these cities are short. The Manizales airport, however, is often closed due to inclement weather.

Medellín has two airports: **Aeropuerto Internacional José María Córdova** (in Rionegro) and **Aeropuerto Olaya Herrera.** All international flights and most large airplane flights depart from Rionegro, a town about an hour away from Medellín. The airport is simply referred to as "Rionegro." **Satena** (Colombian toll-free tel. 01/800-091-2034, www.satena.com) and **Aerolíneas de Antioquia-ADA** (Colombian toll-free tel. 01/800-051-4232, www.ada-aero.com) use the Olaya Herrera airport, which is conveniently located in town. This is a hub for flights to remote communities in the western and Pacific region, including Acandí and Capurganá near the Panamanian border.

There are strict weight restrictions for flights to Providencia from San Andrés, which are generally on small planes such as those used by the military-owned Satena airline. These island flights sell out fast.

LONG-DISTANCE BUS

Travel by bus is the money-saving choice and often the only option for getting to smaller communities. There are different types of buses, from large coaches for long-distance travel to *colectivos* for shorter distances. *Colectivos* (minivans) are often much quicker, although you won't have much legroom. There are also shared taxis that run between towns, a cramped but quick option. During major holidays, purchase bus tickets in advance if you can, as buses can quickly fill up.

When you arrive at a bus station with guidebook in hand and backpack on, you will be swarmed by touts barking out city names to you, desperately seeking your business on their bus. You can go with the flow and follow them, or, if you prefer a little more control and calm, you can instead walk past them to the ticket booths. Forge ahead and shake your head while saying *gracias*. You can try to negotiate better fares at the ticket booths, as there are often various options for traveling the same route. Find out what time the bus is leaving, if the vehicle is a big bus, a *buseta*, or minivan, and where your seat is located (try not to get stuck in the last row).

Be alert and aware of your surroundings and of your possessions when you arrive at bus stations, are waiting in the bus terminal, and are on board buses. Try to avoid flashing around expensive gadgets and cameras while on board. If you check luggage, request a receipt. During pit stops along the way, be sure to keep your valuables with you at all times.

During most bus rides of more than a few hours' length, you will be subjected to loud and/or violent films. Earplugs, eye masks, and even sleeping pills available at most pharmacies for those long journeys may come in handy, but make sure your possessions are well guarded. Expect the air-conditioning to be cranked to full blast, so have a layer or two at the ready. Pick up some provisions like apples or nuts before departing, because food options are generally unhealthy.

Bus drivers like to drive as fast as possible, and generally have few qualms about overtaking cars even on hairpin curves. Large buses tend to be safer than smaller ones, if only because they can't go as fast.

Buses may be stopped by police, and you may be required to show or temporarily hand over your passport (keep it handy). Sometimes passengers may be asked to disembark from the bus so that the police can search it for illegal drugs or other contraband. Young males may be given a pat-down. Even if it annoys you, it is always best to keep cool and remain courteous with police officers who are just doing their job.

PUBLIC TRANSPORTATION

Bogotá has a useful public transportation network. SITP buses are clean, safe, and only pick up passengers at designated stops. You will need to purchase an electronic refillable bus card. These can be purchased at *papelerías* (stationery shops), which are often close to bus stops and stations.

The free app **Moovit** provides route information for public transportation options in many Colombian cities.

CAR, MOTORCYCLE, OR BICYCLE

Although conditions are improving, driving in Colombia is generally a poor idea for international tourists. Roads are often in a poor state and are almost always just two lanes, speed limits and basic driving norms are not respected, driving through large towns and cities can be supremely stressful, signage is poor, sudden mudslides can close roads for hours on end during rainy seasons, and roads can be unsafe at night. One exception is in Boyacá, where the countryside is beautiful and traffic is manageable.

There are car rental offices in all the major airports in the country. **Hertz** (tel. 1/756-0600, www.rentacarcolombia.co) and the national **Colombia Car Rental** (U.S. tel. 913/368-0091, www.colombiacarsrental.com) are two with various offices nationwide.

Touring Colombia on motorcycle is an increasingly popular option. One of the best motorcycle travel agencies in the country is **Motolombia** (tel. 2/665-9548, www.motolombia.com). A growing number of travelers are motoring the Pan-American Highway, shipping their bikes from Panama or the United States to Cartagena, or vice versa.

Bicyclists will not get much respect on Colombian roads, and there are rarely any bike lanes of significance. In Santander and in Boyacá the scenery is absolutely spectacular; but, especially in Santander, it is often quite mountainous. **Colombia en Bicicleta** (www.colombiaenbicicleta.com) caters to bike enthusiasts living in Bogotá.

Every Sunday in Bogotá thousands of cyclists (joggers, skaters, and dog walkers, too) head to the city streets for some fresh air and exercise. This is the **Ciclovía,** an initiative in which city streets are closed to traffic. The city also has an extensive *cicloruta* (bike path) network. Again, cyclists don't get much respect from motorists, so be careful!

Visas and Officialdom

PASSPORTS AND VISAS

U.S. and Canadian citizens do not need a visa for visits to Colombia of less than 90 days. You may be asked to show a return ticket.

There is an exit tax (Tasa Aeroportuaría Internacional) of around US$37 (COP$122,000). This is often automatically tacked onto your ticket price, but the airline agents will let you know upon check-in. If you are visiting for under 60 days, you are exempt. Prior to check-in, inquire with the airline if you qualify for an exemption. You may be directed to the Aeronáutica Civil booth across from the airline check-in counter, where you'll show your passport to get an exemption stamp.

To renew a tourist visa, you must go to an office of **Migración Colombia** (www.migracioncolombia.gov.co) to request an extension of another 90 days.

CUSTOMS

Upon arrival in Colombia, bags will be spot-checked by customs authorities. Duty-free items up to a value of US$1,500 can be brought in to Colombia. Firearms are not allowed into the country, and many animal and vegetable products are not allowed. If you are carrying over US$10,000 in cash you must declare it.

Departing Colombia, expect a pat-down by police (looking for illegal drugs?) at the airport. In addition, luggage may be screened for drugs, art, and exotic animals.

EMBASSIES AND CONSULATES

The **United States Embassy** (Cl. 24 Bis No. 48-50, tel. 1/275-2000, http://bogota.usembassy.gov) is in Bogotá, near the airport. In case of an emergency, during business hours contact the **U.S. Citizen Services Hotline** (business hours tel. 1/275-2000, after-hours and weekends tel. 1/275-4021). Non-emergency calls are answered at the American Citizen Services Section from Monday through Thursday 2pm-4pm. To be informed of security developments or emergencies during your visit, you can enroll in the Smart Traveler Enrollment Program (STEP) on the U.S. Embassy website. In Barranquilla, there is a **Consular Agency Office** (Cl. 77B No. 57-141, Suite 511, tel. 5/353-2001 or tel. 5/353-2182), but its hours and services are limited.

The **Canadian Embassy** (Cra. 7 No. 114-33, Piso 14, tel. 1/657-9800, www.canadainternational.gc.ca) is in Bogotá. There is a **Canadian Consular Office** (Bocagrande Edificio Centro Ejecutivo Oficina 1103, Cra. 3, No. 8-129, tel. 5/665-5838) in Cartagena. For emergencies, Canadian citizens can call the **emergency hotline** (Can. tel. 613/996-8885) in Canada collect.

Accommodations and Food

Most hotels include free wireless Internet and breakfast (although the food quality will vary). While all the fancy hotels and backpacker places have English-speaking staff—at least at the front desk—smaller hotels may not. Room rates usually depend on the number of occupants, not the size of the room. Except for some international chains and upper-end hotels, most hotels will not have heating or air-conditioning in their rooms.

Note that *moteles* are always, *residencias* are usually, and *hospedajes* are sometimes Colombian love hotels.

VALUE-ADDED TAX EXEMPTION

Non-Colombian visitors are exempt from IVA, a sales tax, which is around 16 percent. To qualify for the exemption, you must make your hotel reservation by email or phone from abroad, there must be at least two services included (such as the room fee and an included breakfast), and you must show proof of being in Colombia for less than six months.

HOTELS

Midrange hotels are often harder to find and their quality can be unpredictable. Beds can be uncomfortable, rooms may be small, views might be unappealing, and service hit-or-miss. Spanish is the most prevalent language spoken at these types of accommodations.

High-end hotels, including international brands, are in all large cities. In tourist centers such as Cartagena and Santa Marta, boutique hotels are good options for those seeking charm. Expect courteous service and comfort. The only place to expect international television channels and access for travelers with disabilities are at high-end international hotels.

HOSTELS

Hostels catering to backpackers are a relatively new phenomenon, and more are offering private rooms for those not interested in sharing a dorm room with strangers. Young people are drawn to hostels, but an increasing number of older travelers opt for hostels, as these, in addition to offering budget accommodations, are also the best places for information on activities. Most hostel staff speak English. **Hostel Trail** (www.hosteltrail.com) is a good resource for information on Colombian hostels. Hostels generally maintain updated information on their Facebook pages.

FOOD AND DRINK

In Bogotá, Colombian foodie culture is alive and well, and visitors will have a wealth of excellent dining options—if they don't mind the occasional Manhattan prices. In the major cities, a 10 percent tip is usually included in the price of a meal, but it is a requirement for the server to ask to include it. You can say no, but that would be considered harsh. If you are truly impressed with the service, you can always leave a little additional on the table.

While seafood, especially *pescado frito* (fried fish), is de rigueur on the coasts, in the interior beef and chicken rule. In Bogotá, the dish for cool evenings is *ajiaco*, a chicken and potato soup. In rural areas, the typical lunchtime meal will include soup and a main dish (*seco*) such as *arroz con pollo* (chicken with rice). Eat what you can, but foreigners are forgiven if they can't finish a plate.

Vegetarians have decent options available to them, especially in tourist centers. A can of lentils can be a helpful travel companion in rural areas.

Be sure to try the many unusual fruits and juices in Colombia. Juice is either served in water or in milk, and sometimes has a lot of sugar. The same goes for freshly squeezed lemonade.

Tinto (percolated coffee), can be downright dismal in rural areas, where it is served very sweet. For a good cup of coffee, head to a national brand like Juan Valdez or Oma. Non-coffee drinkers will enjoy *aromatica,* herbal tea that is typically served after dinner.

Colombia is a major chocolate producer and has some award-winning local brands, such as Cacao Hunter's Chocolate, which works with small farmers in different regions including the Sierra Nevada and near Tumaco.

Breakfast almost universally consists of eggs, bread or arepas, juice, and coffee. Fresh fruit is not that common at breakfast. Arepas are important in Colombia: Every region has its own take on these starchy corn cakes, which may be cheese-filled.

Travel Tips

ACCESS FOR TRAVELERS WITH DISABILITIES

Only international and some national hotel chains offer rooms (usually just one or two) that are wheelchair-accessible. Hostels and small hotels in secondary cities or towns will not. Airport and airline staff will usually bend over backwards to help those with disabilities, if you ask.

Getting around cities and towns is complicated, as good sidewalks and ramps are the exception, not the rule. Motorists may not stop—or even slow down—for pedestrians.

WOMEN TRAVELING ALONE

Women traveling alone should expect to be on the receiving end of flirting and various friendly offers by men and curiosity by everyone. Women should be extra cautious in taxis and buses. Always order taxis by phone and avoid taking them alone at night. While incidents are unlikely, it is not a fantastic idea to go out for a jog on your own. Don't reveal personal information, where you are staying, or where you are going to inquisitive strangers.

GAY AND LESBIAN TRAVELERS

Colombia has some of the western hemisphere's most progressive laws regarding the rights of LGBT people. The Constitutional Court legalized same-sex marriage and adoption in 2016 after a torturous, decades-long struggle marked by court victories, legislative defeats, and much debate.

Bogotá is one of the most gay-friendly cities on the continent, with a large gay nightlife scene and city-supported LGBT community centers. In many neighborhoods, passersby don't blink an eye when they see a gay couple holding hands on the sidewalk. The online guide **Guia GAY Colombia** (www.guiagaycolombia.com) has a listing of meeting places for LGBT people throughout the country.

Discrimination, especially against transgender people and even more so against trans sex workers, continues to be a problem in many cities and towns. The award-winning nonprofit group **Colombia Diversa** (www.colombiadiversa.org) is the main advocate for LGBT rights in the country.

Gay men in particular should be cautious using dating apps, keep an eye on drinks at nightclubs, and avoid cabs off the street when departing clubs.

Same-sex couples should not hesitate to insist on *matrimonial* (double) beds at hotels. At guesthouses, hostels, and at some midsized hotels, front desk staff may charge if you invite a guest to the room. At large international hotels and at apartments for rent, this is never the case.

CONDUCT AND CUSTOMS

Colombians are generally friendly to visitors and are often inquisitive about where you are from and how you like Colombia so far. This is most often the case in rural areas. Colombians are also quite proud of their country, after emerging from decades of armed conflict.

With acquaintances and strangers alike, it is customary to ask how someone is doing before moving on to other business. You're even expected to issue a blanket *buenos días* ("Good morning") in the elevator. When greeting an acquaintance, it's customary to shake hands (between men) or give an air kiss on the cheek (for women), although this is mostly the case in urban areas, especially with the upper crust.

Colombians are comfortable with noise—expect the TV to always be on and music blasting almost everywhere. Many Colombians you meet will ask about your family. Family ties are very important to Colombians. Sundays often mean lunch in the countryside with nuclear and extended family members.

While tourists get a pass on appearance, it's preferred that men avoid wearing shorts, especially at restaurants, except on the Caribbean coast. Dress up, like the locals do, when going out on the town.

Indigenous cultures are much more conservative, and women are expected to refrain from showing much skin.

Health and Safety

VACCINATIONS

There are no vaccination requirements for travel to Colombia. At present, proof of vaccination is no longer required in the national parks (namely Parque Nacional Natural Tayrona). However, having proof of vaccination may make life easier, especially if you plan on traveling onward to Brazil or other countries.

The Centers for Disease Control (CDC) recommends that travelers to Colombia get up-to-date on the following vaccines: measles-mumps-rubella (MMR), diphtheria-tetanus-pertussis, varicella (chicken pox), polio, and the yearly flu shot.

DISEASES AND ILLNESSES

Malaria, Zika, Chikungunya, and Dengue Fever

In low-lying tropical areas of Colombia, mosquito-borne illnesses such as malaria, dengue fever, chikungunya, and Zika are common. It is best to assume that there is a risk, albeit quite small, in all areas of the country.

Malaria is a concern in the entire Amazon region and in the lowland departments of Antioquia, Chocó, Córdoba, Nariño, and Bolívar. There is low to no malarial risk in Cartagena and in areas above 1,600 meters (5,000 feet). The Colombian Ministry of Health estimates that there are around 63,000 annual cases of malaria in the country, 20 of which result in death. Most at risk are children under the age of 15. Malaria symptoms include fever, headache, chills, vomiting, fatigue, and difficulty breathing. Treatment involves the administration of various antimalarial drugs. If you plan on spending a lot of time outdoors in lowland tropical areas, consider taking an antimalarial chemoprophylaxis.

The number of cases of **dengue fever** in Colombia has grown from 5.2 cases per 100,000 residents in the 1990s to around 18.1 cases per 100,000 in the 2000s. It is another mosquito-borne illness. The most common symptoms of dengue fever are fever; headaches; muscle, bone, and joint pain; and pain behind the eyes. It is fatal in less than 1 percent of the cases. Treatment usually involves rest and hydration and the administration of pain relievers for headache and muscle pain. **Chikungunya virus** has similar symptoms to dengue, and an infection, involving painful aches, can last for several months. It is spread, like dengue, by the *Aedes aegypti* mosquito, often during daytime.

Zika virus is the latest scare to grip South America, and is a concern to pregnant women, as there is a link between the virus and birth defects. Pregnant women should avoid traveling to low-lying areas (under 2,000 meters/6,000 feet), where Zika is present. This includes much of Colombia. Symptoms include fever, rash, joint pains, and conjunctivitis.

The Centers for Disease Control (www.cdc.gov) remains the best resource on health concerns for worldwide travel.

PREVENTION

Use mosquito nets over beds when visiting tropical areas of Colombia. Examine them well before using, and if you notice large holes in the nets request replacements. Mosquitoes tend to be at their worst at dawn, dusk, and in the evenings. Wear lightweight, long-sleeved, and light-colored shirts, long pants, and socks, and keep some insect repellent handy.

DEET is considered effective in preventing mosquito bites, but there are other, less-toxic alternatives, most available from online retailers.

If you go to the Amazon region, especially during rainy seasons, take an antimalarial prophylaxis starting 15 days before arrival, and continuing 15 days after departing the region. According to the CDC, the recommended chemoprophylaxis for visitors to malarial regions of Colombia is atovaquone-proguanil, doxycycline, or mefloquine. These drugs are available at most pharmacies in Colombia with no prescription necessary.

Altitude Sickness

The high altitudes of the Andes, including in Bogotá (2,625 meters/8,612 feet), can be a problem for some. After arriving in Bogotá, take it easy and avoid drinking alcohol for the first couple of days. You can also take the drug acetazolamide to help speed up your acclimatization. Drinking coca tea or chewing on coca leaves may help prevent *soroche*, as altitude sickness is called in Colombia.

Traveler's Diarrhea

Stomach flu or traveler's diarrhea is a common malady when traveling through Colombia. These are usually caused by food contamination resulting from the presence of *E. coli* bacteria. Street foods, including undercooked meat, raw vegetables, dairy products, and ice, are some of the main culprits. If you get a case of traveler's diarrhea, be sure to drink lots of clear liquids, avoid caffeine, and take an oral rehydration solution of salt, sugar, and water.

Tap Water

Tap water is fine to drink in Colombia's major cities. As an alternative to buying plastic bottles, look for *bolsitas* (bags) of water. They come in a variety of sizes and use less plastic.

MEDICAL SERVICES

Over 20 hospitals in Colombia (in Bogotá, Medellín, Bucaramanga, and Cali) have been listed in the *América Economía* magazine listing of the top 40 hospitals of Latin America, including the **Fundación Cardioinfantil** (www.cardioinfantil.org) in Bogotá. For sexual and reproductive health issues, **Profamilia** (www.profamilia.org.co) has a large network of clinics that provide walk-in and low-cost services throughout the country.

Travel insurance is a good idea to purchase before arriving in Colombia, especially if you plan on doing a lot of outdoor adventures. One recommended provider of travel insurance is **Assist Card** (www.assist-card.com). Before taking a paragliding ride or white-water rafting trip inquire to see whether insurance is included in the price of the trip—it should be.

CRIME

Colombia is safe to visit, and the majority of visitors have a wonderful experience in the country. For international travelers, there is little to worry about when it comes to illegal armed groups today. The threat of kidnapping of civilians and visitors has been almost completely eliminated.

Even in the worst of times, Bogotá has always been less affected by violence from the armed conflict plaguing the rest of the country. Now, with implementation of a peace deal between FARC guerrillas and the Colombian government, the outlook is brighter than ever. However, uncertainty remains and smaller groups of former paramilitaries (*bacrim*) and guerrillas operate in some cities and towns, while drug lords and dangerous gangs rule marginalized urban areas. For updated travel advisories, check the website of the **U.S. Embassy** (http://bogota.usembassy.gov/) in Bogotá. The embassy always errs on the side of caution.

Street Crime

Cell phone theft continues to plague much of the country. Keep wallets in front pockets, be aware of your surroundings, and keep shopping bags and backpacks near you at all times. Muggings in major cities are not unheard of, but are quite rare. Be alert to your surroundings late at night.

Always order cabs instead of hailing them off the street. Fortunately, taxi crimes have diminished greatly in recent years, in no small part due to the advent of apps like Uber and Easy Taxi.

Police

Police can be reached by dialing 123 on any phone. Otherwise, many parks are home to neighborhood police stations, called CAI (Centros de Atención Inmediata). Authorities may not be able to do much about petty theft, however.

Recreational Drugs

In Colombia, the legal status of the use, transport, and possession of recreational drugs can be best described as murky. A 1994 high court decision legalized a "personal dose" of recreational drugs for adults. The sale of drugs is prohibited. An attempt by President Uribe to criminalize recreational drugs failed in 2005. In practice, police may harass those caught with drugs, in addition to confiscating drugs, and may solicit bribes.

Medical use of marijuana was legalized in 2015.

Information and Services

MONEY

Currency

Colombia's official currency is the peso, which is abbreviated as COP. Prices in Colombia are marked with a dollar sign, but remember that you're seeing the price in Colombian pesos. COP$1,000,000 isn't enough to buy a house in Colombia, but it will usually cover a few nights in a nice hotel!

Bills in Colombia are in denominations of $1,000, $2,000, $5,000, $10,000, $20,000, $50,000, and $100,000. Some of the bills got a makeover in 2016, so you may see two different versions of the same amount. Coins in Colombia are in denominations of $50, $100, $200, $500, and $1,000. The equivalent of cents is *centavos* in Colombian Spanish.

Due to dropping oil prices, the Colombian peso has devalued to record levels, making the country a bargain for international visitors. In 2016, one US dollar was the equivalent of COP$3,000.

Most banks in Colombia do not exchange money. For that, you'll have to go to an exchange bank, located in all major cities. There are money changers on the streets of Cartagena, but the street is not the best place for safe and honest transactions.

Travelers checks are not worth the hassle, as they are hard to cash. Dollars are sometimes accepted in Cartagena and other major tourist destinations. To have cash wired to you from abroad, look for a Western Union office. These are located only in major cities.

Counterfeit bills are a problem in Colombia, and unsuspecting international visitors are often the recipients. Bar staff, taxi drivers, and street vendors are the most common culprits. It's good to always have a stash of small bills to avoid getting large bills back as change. Tattered and torn bills will also be passed off to you, which could pose a problem. Try not to accept those.

Consignaciones

Consignaciones (bank transfers) are a common way to pay for hotel reservations (especially in areas such as Providencia and remote resorts), tour packages or guides, or entry to national parks. It's often a pain to make these deposits in person, as the world of banking can be confusing for non-Colombians. On the plus side, making a deposit directly into the hotel's bank account provides some peace of mind because it will diminish the need to carry large amounts of cash. To make a *consignación* you will need to know the recipient's bank account and whether that is a *corriente* (checking) or *ahorros* (savings) account, and you will need to show some identification and probably have to provide a fingerprint. Be sure to hold onto the receipt to notify the recipient of your deposit.

ATMs

The best way to get cash is to use your bank ATM card. These are almost universally accepted at *cajeros automáticos* (ATMs) in the country. *Cajeros* are almost everywhere except in the smallest of towns or in remote areas. Withdrawal fees are relatively expensive, although they vary. You can usually take out up to around COP$300,000-500,000 (the equivalent of around US$150-250) per transaction. Many banks place limits on how much one can withdraw in a day (COP$1,000,000).

Credit and Debit Cards

Credit and debit card use is becoming more prevalent in Colombia; however, online credit card transactions are still not so common except for the major airlines and some of the event ticket companies, such as www.tuboleta.com or www.colboletos.com. When you use your plastic, you will be asked if it's *credito* (credit) or *debito* (debit). If using a *tarjeta de credito* (credit card) in restaurants and stores, you will be asked something like, "*¿Cuantas cuotas?*" or "*¿Numero de cuotas?*" ("How many installments?"). Most visitors prefer one *cuota* ("*Una, por favor*"). But you can have even your dinner bill paid in up to 24 installments! If using a *tarjeta de debito,* you'll be asked if it is a *corriente* (checking) or *ahorros* (savings) account.

Tipping

In most sit-down restaurants in cities, a 10 percent service charge is automatically included in the bill. Waitstaff are required to ask you, "*¿Desea incluir el servicio?*" ("Would you like to include the service in the bill?"). Many times restaurant staff neglect to ask international tourists about the service inclusion. If you find the service to be exceptional, you can leave a little extra in cash. Although tipping is not expected in bars or cafés, tip jars are becoming more common. International visitors are often expected to tip more than Colombians. In small-town restaurants throughout the country, tipping is not the norm.

It is not customary to tip taxi drivers. But if you feel the driver was a good one who drove safely and was honest, or if he or she made an additional stop for you, waited for you, or was just pleasant, you can always round up the bill (instead of COP$6,200 give the driver COP$7,000 and say "*Quédese con las vueltas por favor*" ("Keep the change"). Note that sometimes a "tip" is already included in the fare for non-Colombian visitors!

In hotels, usually a tip of COP$5,000 will suffice for porters who help with luggage, unless you have lots of stuff. Tips are not expected, but are certainly welcome, for housekeeping staff.

Value-Added Tax

Non-Colombian visitors are entitled to a refund of value-added taxes for purchases on clothing, jewelry, and other items if their purchases total more than COP$300,000. Save all credit card receipts and fill out Form 1344 (available online at www.dian.gov.co). Submit this to the **DIAN office** (tel. 1/607-9999) at the airport before departure. You may have several hoops to go through to achieve success. Go to the DIAN office before checking your luggage, as you will have to present the items you purchased.

INTERNET AND TELEPHONES

Being connected makes travel throughout Colombia so much easier. Free Wi-Fi is available at most hotels, restaurants, and cafés in major cities. An important Spanish phrase to learn is "*Como es la contraseña para el wifi*?" ("What's the password for the Wi-Fi?")

Obtaining a SIM card for your cell phone will ensure connectivity in all but the most remote locations. Sometimes low-tech phones work better than smartphones in very rural or remote locations like Providencia. SIM cards (*datos de prepago*) are available at mobile-phone carriers in all major towns and cities. Three main cell phone companies are Claro, Movistar, and Tigo.

Facebook and Whatsapp are often the best bets for contacting hotels, restaurants, and shops.

The telephone country code for Colombia is 57. Cell phone numbers are 10 digits long, beginning with a 3. To call a Colombian cell phone from abroad, you must use the country code followed by that 10-digit number. Landline numbers in Colombia are seven digits long. An area code is necessary when calling from a different region. To call a landline from a cell phone, dial 03 + area code + 7-digit number. To reach a cell phone from a landline, dial 03 + 10-digit number.

Resources

Spanish Phrasebook

Knowing some Spanish is essential to visit Colombia, as relatively few people outside the major cities speak English. Colombian Spanish is said to be one of the clearest in Latin America. However, there are many regional differences.

Spanish commonly uses 30 letters—the familiar English 26, plus four straightforward additions: ch, ll, ñ, and rr, which are explained in "Consonants," below.

PRONUNCIATION

Once you learn them, Spanish pronunciation rules—in contrast to English—don't change. Spanish vowels generally sound softer than in English. (*Note:* The capitalized syllables below receive stronger accents.)

Vowels

a like ah, as in "hah": *agua* AH-gooah (water), *pan* PAHN (bread), and *casa* CAH-sah (house)

e like ay, as in "may:" *mesa* MAY-sah (table), *tela* TAY-lah (cloth), and *de* DAY (of, from)

i like ee, as in "need": *diez* dee-AYZ (ten), *comida* ko-MEE-dah (meal), and *fin* FEEN (end)

o like oh, as in "go": *peso* PAY-soh (weight), *ocho* OH-choh (eight), and *poco* POH-koh (a bit)

u like oo, as in "cool": *uno* OO-noh (one), *cuarto* KOOAHR-toh (room), and *usted* oos-TAYD (you); when it follows a "q" the **u** is silent; when it follows an "h" or has an umlaut, it's pronounced like "w"

Consonants

b, d, f, k, l, m, n, p, q, s, t, v, w, x, y, z, and ch pronounced almost as in English; **h** occurs, but is silent—not pronounced at all

c like k as in "keep": *cuarto* KOOAR-toh (room), casa KAH-sah (house); when it precedes "e" or "i," pronounce **c** like s, as in "sit": *cerveza* sayr-VAY-sah (beer), *encima* ayn-SEE-mah (atop)

g like g as in "gift" when it precedes "a," "o," "u," or a consonant: *gato* GAH-toh (cat), *hago* AH-goh (I do, make); otherwise, pronounce **g** like h as in "hat": *giro* HEE-roh (money order), *gente* HAYN-tay (people)

j like h, as in "has": *Jueves* HOOAY-vays (Thursday), *mejor* may-HOR (better)

ll like y, as in "yes": *toalla* toh-AH-yah (towel), *ellos* AY-yohs (they, them)

ñ like ny, as in "canyon": *año* AH-nyo (year), *señor* SAY-nyor (Mr., sir)

r is lightly trilled, with tongue at the roof of your mouth like a very light English d, as in "ready": *pero* PAY-roh (but), *tres* TRAYS (three), *cuatro* KOOAH-troh (four)

rr like a Spanish r, but with much more emphasis and trill. Let your tongue flap. Practice with *burro* (donkey), *carretera* (highway), and Carrillo (proper name), then really let go with *ferrocarril* (railroad)

Note: The single small but common exception to all of the above is the pronunciation of Spanish **y** when it's being used as the Spanish word for "and," as in "Ron y Kathy." In such case, pronounce it like the English ee, as in "keep": Ron "ee" Kathy (Ron and Kathy).

Accent

The rule for accents, the relative stress given to syllables within a given word, is straightforward. If a word ends in a vowel, an n, or an s, accent the next-to-last syllable; if not, accent the last syllable.

Pronounce *gracias* GRAH-seeahs (thank you), *orden* OHR-dayn (order), and *carretera* kah-ray-TAY-rah (highway) with stress on the next-to-last syllable.

Otherwise, accent the last syllable: *venir* vay-NEER (to come), *ferrocarril* fay-roh-cah-REEL (railroad), and *edad* ay-DAHD (age).

Exceptions to the accent rule are always marked with an accent sign: (á, é, í, ó, or ú), such as *teléfono* tay-LAY-foh-noh (telephone), *jabón* hah-BON (soap), and *rápido* RAH-pee-doh (rapid).

BASIC AND COURTEOUS EXPRESSIONS

Colombians use many courteous formalities. Whenever approaching anyone for information or some other reason, do not forget the appropriate salutation—good morning, good evening, etc. Standing alone, the greeting *hola* (hello) can sound brusque.

Hello. *Hola.*

Good morning. *Buenos días.*

Good afternoon. *Buenas tardes.*

Good evening. *Buenas noches.*

How are you? Colombians have many ways of saying this: *¿Cómo estás/como está? ¿Qué hubo/Qu'hubo? ¿Cómo va/vas? ¿Que tal?*

Very well, thank you. *Muy bien, gracias.*

Okay; good. *Bien.*

Not okay; bad. *Mal.*

So-so. *Más o menos.*

And you? *¿Y Usted?*

Thank you. *Gracias.*

Thank you very much. *Muchas gracias.*

You're very kind. *Muy amable.*

You're welcome. *De nada.*

Goodbye. *Adiós.*

See you later. *Hasta luego. Chao.*

please *por favor;* (slang) *por fa*
yes *sí*
no *no*
I don't know. *No sé.*
Just a moment, please. *Un momento, por favor.*
Excuse me, please (when you're trying to get attention). *Disculpe.*
Excuse me (when you've made a mistake). *Perdón. Que pena.*
I'm sorry. *Lo siento.*
Pleased to meet you. *Mucho gusto.*
How do you say . . . in Spanish? *¿Cómo se dice . . . en español?*
What is your name? *¿Cómo se llama (Usted)? ¿Cómo te llamas?*
Do you speak English? *¿Habla (Usted) inglés? ¿Hablas inglés?*
Does anyone here speak English? *¿Hay alguien que hable inglés?*
I don't speak Spanish well. *No hablo bien el español.*
Please speak more slowly. *Por favor hable más despacio.*
I don't understand. *No entiendo.*
Please write it down. *Por favor escríbalo.*
My name is . . . *Me llamo . . . Mi nombre es . . .*
I would like . . . *Quisiera . . . Quiero . . .*
Let's go to . . . *Vamos a . . .*
That's fine. *Está bien.*
All right. *Listo.*
cool, awesome *chévere, rico, super*
Oh my god! *¡Dios mío!*
That's crazy! *¡Qué locura!*
You're crazy! *¡Estás loca/o!*

TERMS OF ADDRESS

When in doubt, use the formal *Usted* (you) as a form of address.

I *yo*
you (formal) *Usted*
you (familiar) *tú*
he/him *él*
she/her *ella*
we/us *nosotros*
you (plural) *Ustedes*
they/them *ellas* (all females); *ellos* (all males or mixed gender)
Mr., sir *señor*
Mrs., madam *señora*
miss, young lady *señorita*
wife *esposa*
husband *esposo*
friend *amigo/a*
girlfriend/boyfriend *novia* (female); *novio* (male)
partner *pareja*
daughter; son *hija; hijo*

brother; sister *hermano; hermana*
mother; father *madre; padre*
grandfather; grandmother *abuelo; abuela*

TRANSPORTATION

Where is . . . ? *¿Dónde está . . . ?*
How far is it to . . . ? *¿A cuánto queda . . . ?*
from . . . to . . . *de . . . a . . .*
How many blocks? *¿Cuántas cuadras?*
Where (Which) is the way to . . . ? *¿Cuál es el camino a . . . ? ¿Por dónde es . . . ?*
bus station *la terminal de buses/terminal de transporte*
bus stop *la parada*
Where is this bus going? *¿A dónde va este bús?*
boat *el barco, la lancha*
dock *el muelle*
airport *el aeropuerto*
I'd like a ticket to . . . *Quisiera un pasaje a . . .*
roundtrip *ida y vuelta*
reservation *reserva*
baggage *equipaje*
next flight *el próximo vuelo*
Stop here, please. *Pare aquí, por favor.*
the entrance *la entrada*
the exit *la salida*
(very) near; far *(muy) cerca; lejos*
to; toward *a*
by; through *por*
from *de*
right *la derecha*
left *la izquierda*
straight ahead *derecho*
in front *en frente*
beside *al lado*
behind *atrás*
corner *la esquina*
stoplight *la semáforo*
turn *una vuelta*
here *aquí*
somewhere around here *por aquí*
there *allí*
somewhere around there *por allá*
road *camino*
street *calle, carrera*
avenue *avenida*
block *la cuadra*

highway *carretera*
kilometer *kilómetro*
bridge; toll *puente; peaje*
address *dirección*
north; south *norte; sur*
east; west *oriente (este); occidente (oeste)*

ACCOMMODATIONS

hotel *hotel*
Is there a room available? *¿Hay un cuarto disponible?*
May I (may we) see it? *¿Puedo (podemos) verlo?*
How much is it? *¿Cuánto cuesta?*
Is there something cheaper? *¿Hay algo más económico?*
single room *un cuarto sencillo*
double room *un cuarto doble*
double bed *cama matrimonial*
single bed *cama sencilla*
with private bath *con baño propio*
television *televisor*
window *ventana*
view *vista*
hot water *agua caliente*
shower *ducha*
towels *toallas*
soap *jabón*
toilet paper *papel higiénico*
pillow *almohada*
blanket *cobija*
sheets *sábanas*
air-conditioned *aire acondicionado*
fan *ventilador*
swimming pool *piscina*
gym *gimnasio*
bike *bicicleta*
key *llave*
suitcase *maleta*
backpack *mochila*
lock *candado*
safe *caja de seguridad*
manager *gerente*
maid *empleada*
clean *limpio*
dirty *sucio*
broken *roto*
(not) included *(no) incluido*

FOOD

I'm hungry. *Tengo hambre.*
I'm thirsty. *Tengo sed.*
Table for two, please. *Una mesa para dos, por favor.*
menu *carta*
order *orden*
glass *vaso*
glass of water *vaso con agua*
fork *tenedor*
knife *cuchillo*
spoon *cuchara*
napkin *servilleta*
soft drink *gaseosa*
coffee *café, tinto*
tea *té*
drinking water *agua potable*
bottled carbonated water *agua con gas*
bottled uncarbonated water *agua sin gas*
beer *cerveza*
wine *vino*
glass of wine *copa de vino*
red wine *vino tinto*
white wine *vino blanco*
milk *leche*
juice *jugo*
cream *crema*
sugar *azúcar*
cheese *queso*
breakfast *desayuno*
lunch *almuerzo*
daily lunch special *menú del día*
dinner *comida*
the check *la cuenta*
eggs *huevos*
bread *pan*
salad *ensalada*
lettuce *lechuga*
tomato *tomate*
onion *cebolla*
garlic *ajo*
hot sauce *ají*
fruit *fruta*
mango *mango*
watermelon *patilla*
papaya *papaya*
banana *banano*

apple *manzana*
orange *naranja*
lime *limón*
passionfruit *maracuyá*
guava *guayaba*
grape *uva*
fish *pescado*
shellfish *mariscos*
shrimp *camarones*
(without) meat *(sin) carne*
chicken *pollo*
pork *cerdo*
beef *carne de res*
bacon; ham *tocino; jamón*
fried *frito*
roasted *asado*
Do you have vegetarian options? *¿Tienen opciones vegetarianas?*
I'm vegetarian. *Soy vegetarian(o).*
I don't eat . . . *No como . . .*
to share *para compartir*
Check, please. *La cuenta, por favor.*
Is the service included? *¿Está incluido el servicio?*
tip *propina*
large *grande*
small *pequeño*

SHOPPING

cash *efectivo*
money *dinero*
credit card *tarjeta de crédito*
debit card *tarjeta de débito*
money exchange office *casa de cambio*
What is the exchange rate? *¿Cuál es la tasa de cambio?*
How much is the commission? *¿Cuánto es la comisión?*
Do you accept credit cards? *¿Aceptan tarjetas de crédito?*
credit card installments *cuotas*
money order *giro*
How much does it cost? *¿Cuánto cuesta?*
expensive *caro*
cheap *barato; económico*
more *más*
less *menos*
a little *un poco*
too much *demasiado*
value added tax *IVA*
discount *descuento*

HEALTH

Help me please. *Ayúdeme por favor.*
I am ill. *Estoy enferma/o.*
Call a doctor. *Llame un doctor.*
Take me to . . . *Lléveme a . . .*
hospital *hospital, clínica*
drugstore *farmacia*
pain *dolor*
fever *fiebre*
headache *dolor de cabeza*
stomach ache *dolor de estómago*
burn *quemadura*
cramp *calambre*
nausea *náusea*
vomiting *vomitar*
medicine *medicina*
antibiotic *antibiótico*
pill *pastilla, pepa*
aspirin *aspirina*
ointment; cream *ungüento; crema*
bandage (big) *venda*
bandage (small) *cura*
cotton *algodón*
sanitary napkin *toalla sanitaria*
birth control pills *pastillas anticonceptivas*
condoms *condones*
toothbrush *cepillo de dientes*
dental floss *hilo dental*
toothpaste *crema dental*
dentist *dentista*
toothache *dolor de muelas*
vaccination *vacuna*

COMMUNICATIONS

Wi-fi *wifi*
cell phone *celular*
username *usuario*
password *contraseña*
laptop computer *portátil*
prepaid cellphone *celular prepago*
post office *4-72*
phone call *llamada*
letter *carta*
stamp *estampilla*
postcard *postal*
package; box *paquete; caja*

AT THE BORDER

border *frontera*
customs *aduana*
immigration *migración*
inspection *inspección*
ID card *cédula*
passport *pasaporte*
profession *profesión*
vacation *vacaciones*
I'm a tourist. *Soy turista.*
student *estudiante*
marital status *estado civil*
single *soltero*
married; divorced *casado; divorciado*
widowed *viudado*
insurance *seguro*
title *título*
driver's license *pase de conducir*

AT THE GAS STATION

gas station *estación de gasolina*
gasoline *gasolina*
full, please *lleno, por favor*
tire *llanta*
air *aire*
water *agua*
oil (change) *(cambio de) aceite*
My . . . doesn't work. *Mi . . . no funciona.*
battery *batería*
tow truck *grúa*
repair shop *taller*

VERBS

Verbs are the key to getting along in Spanish. They employ mostly predictable forms and come in three classes, which end in *ar*, *er*, and *ir*, respectively:

to buy *comprar*
I buy, you (he, she, it) buys *compro, compra*
we buy, you (they) buy *compramos, compran*

to eat *comer*
I eat, you (he, she, it) eats *como, come*
we eat, you (they) eat *comemos, comen*

to climb *subir*
I climb, you (he, she, it) climbs *subo, sube*
we climb, you (they) climb *subimos, suben*

Here are more (with irregularities indicated):

to do or make *hacer* (regular except for *hago,* I do or make)
to go *ir* (very irregular: *voy, va, vamos, van*)
to walk *caminar*
to wait *esperar*
to love *amar*
to work *trabajar*
to want *querer* (irregular: *quiero, quiere, queremos, quieren*)
to need *necesitar*
to read *leer*
to write *escribir*
to send *enviar*
to repair *reparar*
to wash *lavar*
to stop *parar*
to get off (the bus) *bajar*
to arrive *llegar*
to stay (remain) *quedar*
to stay (lodge) *hospedar*
to rent alquilar
to leave *salir* (regular except for *salgo,* I leave)
to look at *mirar*
to look for *buscar*
to give *dar* (regular except for *doy,* I give)
to give (as a present or to order something) *regalar*
to carry *llevar*
to have *tener* (irregular: *tengo, tiene, tenemos, tienen*)
to come *venir* (irregular: *vengo, viene, venimos, vienen*)

Spanish has two forms of "to be":

to be *estar* (regular except for *estoy,* I am)
to be *ser* (very irregular: *soy, es, somos, son*)

Use *estar* when speaking of location or a temporary state of being: "I am at home." *"Estoy en casa."* "I'm happy." *"Estoy contenta/o."* Use *ser* for a permanent state of being: "I am a lawyer." *"Soy abogada/o."*

NUMBERS

zero *cero*
one *uno*
two *dos*
three *tres*
four *cuatro*
five *cinco*
six *seis*
seven *siete*
eight *ocho*
nine *nueve*
10 *diez*
11 *once*
12 *doce*
13 *trece*
14 *catorce*
15 *quince*
16 *dieciseis*
17 *diecisiete*
18 *dieciocho*
19 *diecinueve*
20 *veinte*
21 *veinte y uno* or *veintiuno*
30 *treinta*
40 *cuarenta*
50 *cincuenta*
60 *sesenta*
70 *setenta*
80 *ochenta*
90 *noventa*
100 *cien*
101 *ciento y uno*
200 *doscientos*
500 *quinientos*
1,000 *mil*
10,000 *diez mil*
100,000 *cien mil*
1,000,000 *millón*
one half *medio*
one third *un tercio*
one fourth *un cuarto*

TIME

What time is it? *¿Qué hora es?*

It's one o'clock. *Es la una.*

It's three in the afternoon. *Son las tres de la tarde.*

It's 4 a.m. *Son las cuatro de la mañana.*

six-thirty *seis y media*

quarter till eleven *un cuarto para las once*

quarter past five *las cinco y cuarto*

hour *una hora*

late *tarde*

DAYS AND MONTHS

Monday *lunes*

Tuesday *martes*

Wednesday *miércoles*

Thursday *jueves*

Friday *viernes*

Saturday *sábado*

Sunday *domingo*

today *hoy*

tomorrow *mañana*

yesterday *ayer*

day before yesterday *antier*

January *enero*

February *febrero*

March *marzo*

April *abril*

May *mayo*

June *junio*

July *julio*

August *agosto*

September *septiembre*

October *octubre*

November *noviembre*

December *diciembre*

week *una semana*

month *un mes*

after *después*

before *antes*

holiday *festivo*

long weekend *puente*

Suggested Reading

HISTORY

Bushnell, David. *The Making of Modern Colombia: A Nation in Spite of Itself.* Berkeley, CA: University of California Press, 1993. Mandatory reading for students of Colombian history. Bushnell, an American, is considered the "Father of the Colombianists".

Hemming, John. *The Search for El Dorado.* London: Joseph, 1978. Written by a former director of the Royal Geographical Society, this book explores the Spanish gold obsession in the New World. It's a great companion to any visit to the Gold Museum in Bogotá.

Lynch, John. *Simón Bolívar: A Life.* New Haven, CT: Yale University Press, 2007. This biography of the Liberator is considered one of the best ever written in English, and is the result of a lifetime of research by renowned English historian John Lynch.

Palacios, Marco. *Between Legitimacy and Violence: A History of Colombia, 1875-2002.* Durham, NC: Duke University Press Books, 2006. Written by a Bogotano academic who was a former head of the Universidad Nacional, this book covers Colombia's economic, political, cultural, and social history from the late 19th century to the complexities of the late 20th century, and drug-related violence.

THE DRUG WAR AND ARMED CONFLICTS

Bowden, Mark. *Killing Pablo: The Hunt for the World's Greatest Outlaw.* New York: Grove Press, 2001. This account of U.S. and Colombian efforts to halt drug trafficking and terrorism committed by drug lord Pablo Escobar was originally reported in a 31-part series in *The Philadelphia Inquirer.*

Dudley, Steven. *Walking Ghosts: Murder and Guerrilla Politics in Colombia.* New York: Routledge Press, 2004. Essential reading for anyone interested in understanding the modern Colombian conflict, this book is written by an expert on investigating organized crime in the Americas.

Gonsalves, Marc, Tom Howes, Keith Stansell, and Gary Brozek. *Out of Captivity: Surviving 1,967 Days in the Colombian Jungle.* New York: Harper Collins, 2009. Accounts of three American military contractors who were held, along with former presidential candidate Ingrid Betancourt, by FARC guerrillas for over five years in the Colombian jungle.

Leech, Garry. *Beyond Bogotá: Diary of a Drug War Journalist in Colombia.* Boston: Beacon Press, 2009. The basis for this book is the author's 11 hours spent as a hostage of the FARC.

Otis, John. *Law of the Jungle: The Hunt for Colombian Guerrillas, American Hostages, and Buried Treasure.* New York: Harper, 2010. This is a thrilling account of the operation to rescue Ingrid Betancourt and American government contractors held by the FARC. It's been called a flip-side to *Out of Captivity.*

NATURAL HISTORY

Hilty, Steven L., William L. Brown, and Guy Tudor. *A Guide to the Birds of Colombia.* Princeton, NJ: Princeton University Press, 1986. This massive 996-page field guide to bird-rich Colombia is a must for any serious bird-watcher.

McMullan, Miles, Thomas M. Donegan, and Alonso Quevedo. *Field Guide to the Birds of Colombia.* Bogotá: Fundación ProAves, 2010. This pocket-sized field guide published by ProAves, a respected bird conservation society, is a more manageable alternative to Hilty's guide.

ETHNOGRAPHY

Davis, Wade. *One River: Explorations and Discoveries in the Amazon Rain Forest.* New York: Simon & Schuster, 1997. From the author of *The Serpent and the Rainbow*, this is a rich description of the peoples of the Amazonian rain forest, and the result of Davis' time in the country alongside famed explorer Richard Evan Schultes.

Reichel-Dolmatoff, Gerardo. *Colombia: Ancient Peoples & Places.* London: Thames and Hudson, 1965. A thorough anthropological investigation of the indigenous cultures across Colombia by an Austrian-born anthropologist who emigrated to Colombia during World War II.

——. *The Shaman and the Jaguar: A Study of Narcotic Drugs Among the Indians of Colombia.* Philadelphia: Temple University Press, 1975. An examination of shamanic drug culture in Colombia, particularly among indigenous tribes from the Amazon jungle region.

ARCHITECTURE

Escovar, Alberto, Diego Obregón, and Rodolfo Segovia. *Guías Elarqa de Arquitectura.* Bogotá: Ediciones Gamma, 2005. Useful guides for anyone wishing to learn more about the architecture of Bogotá, Cartagena, and Medellín.

TRAVEL

Lamus, María Cristina. *333 Sitios de Colombia Que Ver Antes de Morir.* Bogotá: Editorial Planeta Colombiana, 2010. Colombian version of *1,000 Places to See Before You Die* (only available in Spanish).

Mann, Mark. *The Gringo Trail.* West Sussex: Summersdale Publishers, 2010. A darkly comic tale of backpacking around South America.

Nicholl, Charles. *The Fruit Palace.* New York: St. Martin's Press, 1994. A wild romp that follows the seedy cocaine trail from Bogotá bars to Medellín to the Sierra Nevada and a fruit stand called the Fruit Palace during the wild 1980s. The English author was jailed in Colombia for drug smuggling as he conducted research for the book.

Internet and Digital Resources

ACCOMMODATIONS

Hostel Trail
www.hosteltrail.com
Run by a Scottish couple living in Popayán, this is an excellent resource on hostels throughout South America.

Posadas Turísticas de Colombia
www.posadasturisticasdecolombia.gov.co
Find information on interesting accommodations alternatives, like home stays.

ECO-TOURISM

Parques Nacionales Naturales de Colombia
www.parquesnacionales.gov.co
Colombia's national parks website has information on all of the natural parks and protected areas in the country.

Aviatur Ecoturismo
www.aviaturecoturismo.com
Package tours of the Amazon, PNN Tayrona, PNN Isla Gorgona, and more are available from one of Colombia's most respected travel agencies.

EMBASSIES AND VISAS

U.S. Embassy in Colombia
http://bogota.usembassy.gov
The Citizen Services page often has security information for visitors, and is where you can register your visit in case of an emergency.

Colombian Ministry of Foreign Relations

www.cancilleria.gov.co

Offers information on visas and other travel information.

ENTERTAINMENT, CULTURE, AND EVENTS

Vive In

www.vive.in

Updated information on restaurants, entertainment, and cultural events in Bogotá.

Plan B

www.planb.com.co

Competitor of Vive In, Plan B offers information on what's going on in Bogotá.

Tu Boleta

www.tuboleta.com

The top event ticket distributor in the country, Tu Boleta is a good way to learn about concerts, theater, parties, and sporting events throughout Colombia.

Banco de la República

www.banrepcultural.org

Information on upcoming cultural activities sponsored by the Banco de la República.

HISTORY AND HUMAN RIGHTS ISSUES

CIA World Factbook Colombia

www.cia.gov

Background information on Colombia from those in the know.

Centro de Memoria Histórica

www.centrodememoriahistorica.gov.co

Excellent website on the human toll of the Colombian conflict.

International Crisis Group

www.crisisgroup.org

In-depth analysis of the human rights situation in Colombia.

Colombia Diversa

www.colombiadiversa.org

Covers LGBT rights in Colombia.

LANGUAGE COURSES

Spanish in Colombia
www.spanishincolombia.gov.co
Official government website on places to study Spanish in Colombia.

NEWS AND MEDIA

El Tiempo
www.eltiempo.com
El Tiempo is the country's leading newspaper.

El Espectador
www.elespectador.com.co
This is Colombia's second national newspaper.

Revista Semana
www.semana.com
Semana is the top news magazine in Colombia.

La Silla Vacia
www.sillavacia.com
Political insiders dish about current events.

Colombia Reports
http://colombiareports.co
Colombian news in English.

The City Paper Bogotá
www.thecitypaperbogota.com
Website of the capital city´s English-language monthly.

Colombia Calling
www.richardmccoll.com/colombia-calling
Weekly online radio program on all things Colombia from an expat perspective.

TRANSPORTATION

Moovit
This app will help you figure out public transportation in Bogotá.

Tappsi
To order a safe taxi, first upload this excellent app.

SITP
www.sitp.gov.co
This is the official website of the ever-improving (yet confusing) public bus transportation system in Bogotá.

TRAVEL INFORMATION

Colombia Travel

www.colombia.travel

This is the official travel information website of Proexport, Colombia's tourism and investment promotion agency.

VOLUNTEERING

Conexión Colombia

www.conexioncolombia.com

This website is one-stop shopping for the nonprofit sector in Colombia.

Index

DE

F

G

HI

JKL

M

NOP

QR

S

T

UVWXYZ

List of Maps

Photo Credits

All photos © Andrew Dier except title page photo: © Jkraft5/Dreamstime.com; page 3 © Sevenkingdom/Dreamstime.com; page 4 © Patriciahoyos1971/Dreamstime.com; page 5 © Jesse Kraft /123rf.com; page 7 © Amanogawa/Dreamstime.com; page 52 © Andrés Carne de Res; page 74 © Sophie Traen/123rf.com; page 124 © Jkraft5/Dreamstime.com

Also Available

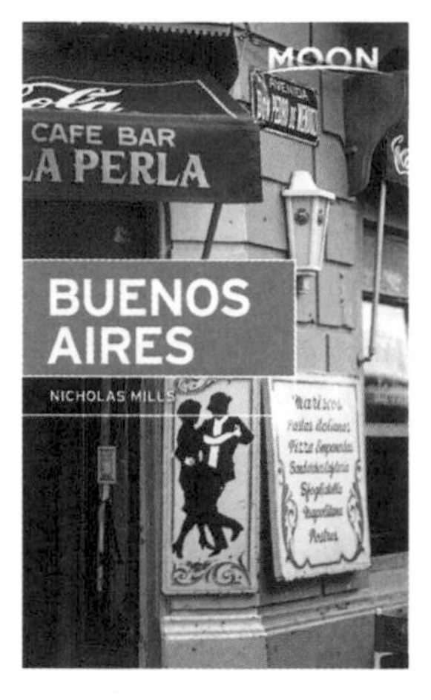

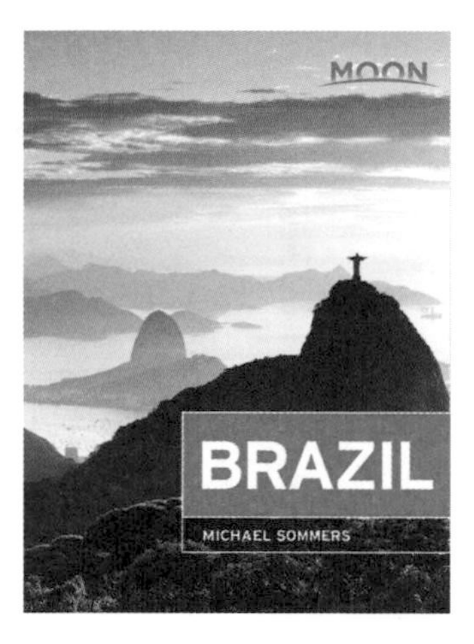

MAP SYMBOLS

Expressway
Primary Road
Secondary Road
Unpaved Road
Trail
Ferry
Railroad
Pedestrian Walkway
Stairs

Highlight
City/Town
State Capital
National Capital
Point of Interest
Accommodation
Restaurant/Bar
Other Location
Campground

Airfield
Airport
Mountain
Unique Natural Feature
Waterfall
Park
Trailhead
Skiing Area

Golf Course
Parking Area
Archaeological Site
Church
Gas Station
Glacier
Mangrove
Reef
Swamp

CONVERSION TABLES

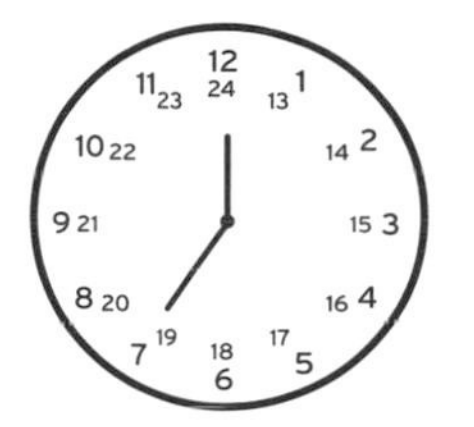

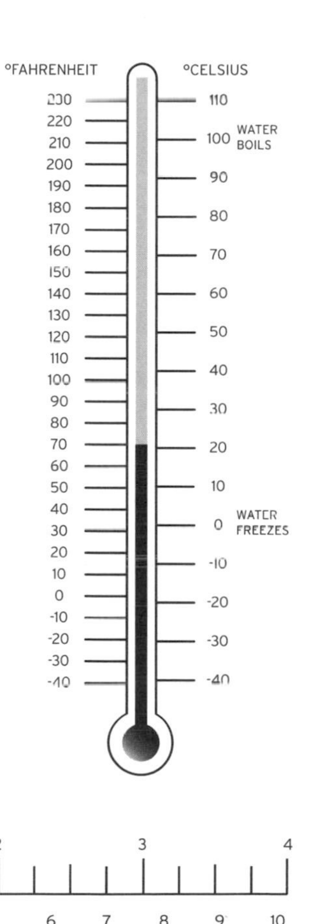

°C = (°F - 32) / 1.8
°F = (°C x 1.8) + 32
1 inch = 2.54 centimeters (cm)
1 foot = 0.304 meters (m)
1 yard = 0.914 meters
1 mile = 1.6093 kilometers (km)
1 km = 0.6214 miles
1 fathom = 1.8288 m
1 chain = 20.1168 m
1 furlong = 201.168 m
1 acre = 0.4047 hectares
1 sq km = 100 hectares
1 sq mile = 2.59 square km
1 ounce = 28.35 grams
1 pound = 0.4536 kilograms
1 short ton = 0.90718 metric ton
1 short ton = 2,000 pounds
1 long ton = 1.016 metric tons
1 long ton = 2,240 pounds
1 metric ton = 1,000 kilograms
1 quart = 0.94635 liters
1 US gallon = 3.7854 liters
1 Imperial gallon = 4.5459 liters
1 nautical mile = 1.852 km

INCH 0 1 2 3 4

CM 0 1 2 3 4 5 6 7 8 9 10

MOON BOGOTÁ
Avalon Travel
a member of the Perseus Books Group
1700 Fourth Street
Berkeley, CA 94710, USA
www.moon.com

Editor: Leah Gordon
Series Manager: Kathryn Ettinger
Copy Editor: Brett Keener
Graphics Coordinator: Rue Flaherty
Production Coordinator: Rue Flaherty
Cover Design: Faceout Studios, Charles B
Moon Logo: Tim McGrath
Map Editor: Mike Morgenfeld
Cartographers: Brian Shotwell, Austin El
Proofreader: Deana Shields
Indexer: Greg Jewett

ISBN-13: 978-1-63121-588-9

Printing History
1st Edition — July 2017
5 4 3 2 1

Front cover photo: Transmilenio bus stop at the intersections of Avendia Jimenez and Carrera Septima, Bogotá © John Coletti/Getty Images.
Back cover photo: La Candelaria neighborhood, Bogotá © Jesse Kraft | Dreamstime.com

Printed in Canada by Friesens

All recommendations, including those for sights, activities, hotels, restaurants, and shops, are based on each author's individual judgment. We do not accept payment for inclusion in our travel guides, and our authors don't accept free goods or services in exchange for positive coverage.